THE CHALLENGE OF PLURALISM
EDUCATION, POLITICS AND VALUES

THE CHALLENGE OF PLURALISM
EDUCATION, POLITICS AND VALUES

edited by

F. Clark Power
and
Daniel K. Lapsley

UNIVERSITY OF NOTRE DAME PRESS

NOTRE DAME   LONDON

Library of Congress Cataloging-in-Publication Data

The Challenge of pluralism : education, politics, and
    values / F. Clark Power and Daniel K. Lapsley, editors.
        p.   cm.
    Developed from a symposium held at the University
of Notre Dame.
    Includes bibliographical references.
    ISBN 0-268-00787-X
    1. Moral education—United States—Congresses.   2.
Moral education—United States—History—Congresses.
3. Pluralism (Social Sciences)—United States—
Congresses.   4. Intercultural education—United
States—Congresses.   I. Power, F. Clark.   II. Lapsley,
Daniel K.
LC311.C45   1992
370.11′4′0973—dc20   91-50571
                                                CIP

ACKNOWLEDGMENT

This volume developed out of the symposium, "Moral Education in a Pluralist Society," sponsored by the Institute for Scholarship in the College of Arts and Letters, the University of Notre Dame, through an AT&T visiting Scholars Grant. The editors wish to thank AT&T and the Institute for their support.

CONTENTS

INTRODUCTION

MORAL EDUCATION AND PLURALISM

F. Clark Power

> By the year 2000, one out of every three elementary
> and secondary school students in the United States
> will be from an ethnic minority family. In Califor-
> nia and many other states, minority youngsters will
> make up the majority of the student population.[1]

As these opening lines from an Executive Committee Report of the National Education Association reveal, pluralism
has arrived in America's public schools. While public school
educators from Horace Mann to the present have grappled
with pluralism, the challenge of meeting the diverse needs of
so-called minority populations has never been greater. That
challenge brings with it the thorniest of ethical problems. Discussions of tuition credits for private schools, bi-lingual education, bussing, ethnic studies, and affirmative action bring
to the surface deep-seated concerns about cultural diversity,
discrimination, and prejudice.

We expect that on some level our schools will reflect our
ideals of pluralistic harmony and prepare the young for participation in a pluralistic society. Pluralism, as Dwight Boyd
notes (chapter 6), has become a taken-for-granted prescription for tolerance, sensitivity, and fair treatment.[2] Pluralism
is thus, in Walter Nicgorski's words (chapter 1), not only a
condition but a generally accepted (however vaguely articulated) goal for moral education. In spite of a commitment
to teach the values that would sustain pluralism, Americans
have been ambivalent about explicit moral education programs. On the one hand, as Philip Gleason notes, the American identity, going back to the founding, has been based on
the abstract, universalist moral ideals of liberty, equality, and

1

democracy, rather than on a particular ethnic heritage.[3] On the other hand, many policymakers have feared that state-sponsored moral education might lead to an oppressive indoctrination.[4] Today while there is substantial public support for teaching morality in the schools, serious disagreements arise about the content and methods to be used. In order to avoid controversy, many teachers and administrators opt to keep moral education out of the curriculum. But educational sociologists from Emile Durkheim to Philip Jackson have shown us that values are inescapably taught in the hidden curriculum of school organization, governance, and discipline.

As members of democratic society, we must undertake an open and sustained analysis of the kind of moral education necessary for a responsible engagement with pluralism. In considering approaches to moral education, we must determine how to respect cultural diversity, avoid relativism, and overcome prejudice and alienation. Because the task raises profound historical, philosophical, political, sociological, and religious considerations, this volume brings together leading scholars from across the disciplines. Although approaching the topic from very different perspectives, they agree that beneath the surface celebration of cultural pluralism lie troubling questions about pluralism's implications for a democratic society.

Webster defines pluralism as "the quality or condition of existing in more than one part or form."[5] Pluralism implies both unity and diversity; the one nation existing in multiple forms or parts. In political terms, the "multiple forms or parts" may refer to groupings based on such characteristics as race, religion, heritage, ethnicity, ideology, social class, and gender. The authors in this volume vary in describing pluralism from Nicgorski's references to special interest "factions" to Boyd's and Michael Olneck's focus on ethnic groups. If these descriptions have anything in common, it is an engagement with a pluralism of value systems distinguishable from mere diversity in customs, language, foods, etc.

Liberal Moral Theory

Liberal moral theory, as embodied in the Constitution of the United States and in the moral philosophical tradition from Kant to Rawls, has provided an attractive and, arguably, effective way of maintaining a cohesive society in spite of significant value differences. Key to liberal theory is a distinction between the right and the good. Liberals insist upon a unified notion of justice, while allowing multiple conceptions of the good life embodied within ethnic groups, religions, ideologies, etc. In this scheme, justice is a public matter, subject to state regulation and teachable in public schools, while good life issues are for private groups (e.g., the family, church, synagogue, etc.). Critics of liberal moral theory, like Alasdair MacIntyre (whose views are discussed by Daniel Lapsley in chapter 7), charge that divorcing the right from the good has robbed morality of its motive and substance. Others more sympathetic with liberal theory, like Michael Himes (chapter 5) and James Fowler (chapter 9), object that liberalism has avoided serious pluralistic dialogue through treating religion as an exclusively private affair.

Pluralism and Developmental Education

Lapsley acknowledges that the developmental approach to moral psychology and education still reigns as the dominant paradigm in the field; and the chapters by Nicgorski, Ronnie and Charles Blakeney and Fowler attest to the extraordinary influence that the developmental tradition, beginning with John Dewey and culminating with Lawrence Kohlberg, has had. The major contributors to moral development theory, Dewey, Jean Piaget and Kohlberg, saw pluralism not as a threat to moral education but as an indispensable resource. Dewey wrote, "Only diversity makes change and progress."[6] In his view, pluralism is a necessary but not sufficient condition for personal and social development. Pluralism can challenge and provoke; in a genuine democracy, it prevents a society from becoming routinized and static.

Dewey offered two criteria for assessing the adequacy of a group's social life, two criteria that formed his definition of democracy: (1) "how numerous and varied are the interests that are consciously shared? and (2) how full and free is the interplay with other forms of association?"[7] For Dewey, pluralism is effective only within a broad communicative context marked by free and reciprocal exchange. In such a context, pluralism stimulates and enlarges dialogue, promoting the development of the individual and the group.

Piaget and Kohlberg followed Dewey in their attempts to demonstrate that development depends upon interactions that challenge primitive ways of problem solving.[8] Using notions such as disequilibrium and cognitive conflict, they showed how experiences of incongruity can encourage individuals to reconstruct more adequate means of problem solving. All of their accounts assume that the developed person can draw from the diverse treasures of particular cultures without being caught in the web of any one culture's traditional authority and blind conformity. Kohlberg's theory, for example, describes a sequence of six stages that culminates in autonomy and moral universalism. At the first two stages (the preconventional level), moral decisions are based on authority and anticipated punishments and rewards. At the middle stages (the conventional level), moral judgments are based on a concern to meet the formal and informal expectations of primary and secondary groups. At the final stages (the postconventional level), moral judgments are based on self-chosen principles and procedures that transcend particular social arrangements. Those reasoning at the post-conventional stages have the capacity to reflect upon and criticize cultural norms and values.

Dewey, Piaget, and Kohlberg thus favored a vigorous pluralism as means of societal progress and individual development. In various ways, they upheld the liberal view that morality is based on a procedure for decision making rather than on a set of enculturated virtues or moral rules.[9] Moral education, they believed, must therefore be rooted in democratic methods involving discussion and cooperative problem solving.

Weak and Strong Pluralism

At a minimum, pluralism implies what Ann Diller calls an ethic of peaceful co-existence (chapter 8), that is, a toleration of differences and an overcoming of the tendency to regard the unfamiliar other with suspicion and fear. Behind pluralism is, therefore, a morality of justice, of treating others with respect. But by "others" do we (and should we) mean individuals, groups or both? As Michael Olneck so trenchantly observes (chapter 10), multicultural education, however benign its purposes, almost invariably reduces the problem of pluralism to overcoming individual differences and the solution to promoting prosocial attitudes, such as empathy and understanding. This process, Olneck claims, results in assimilationism, the washing out of group identities. But would a thoroughgoing multicultural approach, based on respect for cultural groups as groups, protect and strengthen group identification and interests at the expense of individual liberties and societal cohesion?

Nathan Glazer envisions two polar types of pluralism: weak and strong.[10] He epitomizes weak pluralism in the American interculturalism of the 1940s, which arose in reaction to Hitler. Its centerpiece was the multiethnic festival, and its goal was to foster toleration for individual differences. This toleration was strategic, he notes; it was a means to assimilation. In contrast, he exemplifies strong pluralism in the separatist movements proposed, for example, by the black power advocates of the late 1960s and 1970s. Glazer's analysis suggests that at its extremes, pluralism loses its identity, reducing either to an encompassing unity or to an independent multiplicity. Pluralism exists somewhere between the poles, holding the many together without eradicating their distinctiveness.

Pluralism: The Social Challenge

The first three chapters of this volume provide an overview of the context in which pluralism must be addressed. In the first chapter, "American Pluralism: A Condition or a

Goal?" Walter Nicgorski undercuts simplistic views of pluralism as an unambiguous asset or threat to a democratic society. Drawing on philosophers and political scientists from Socrates to Calvin Schrag, he describes various attempts to address the tensions that invariably arise between majoritarian rule and the freedom of expression. Turning to *The Federalist*, paper No. 10 as the "foundational text" for American pluralism, Nicgorski cites Madison's prescription for dealing with the tension of factions: contain its effects by multiplying factions, but do not remove its causes by curtailing liberty. Madison proposes a kind of invisible hand process in which differences of interest will cancel each other out, leaving only a shared concern for justice and the common good. Unsatisfied with Madison's failure to give education a significant role in the cultivation of a civic morality, Nicgorski turns to Dewey's vision of democratic education.

Nicgorski views pluralism within the political dynamics of liberty and unity. Michael Apple takes a complementary but different perspective, seeing pluralism within a struggle for power and equality (chapter 2). Although Apple would certainly agree with the Madisonian view, cited by Nicgorski, that economic differences are the most "common and durable" causes of factionalism, Apple gives economic inequality a more decisive role in the interplay between culture and politics. Apple suggests that our current political and educational differences reflect the perennial conflict between property rights and personal rights. In the 1960s and 1970s, he claims, proponents of personal rights made advances in such areas as civil rights, welfare, environmental and consumer protection, and democratic control of the workplace, the school, and the home. In the 1970s, however, the defenders of property, aligned with conservative evangelicals to form the New Right, began to react; as we open the 1990s, this coalition has seized control of social policy initiative and now frames the terms of political and educational debate. Whether the pendulum of social change will shift again to the personal rights agenda of the Left remains to be seen. Apple hints that it may and suggests a role for schooling in bringing about that shift.

The struggle of certain minority groups to secure personal rights has often been impeded by fierce prejudices, which can be and often are exploited by the politics of resentment. Grasping the moral challenge of pluralism demands understanding the dynamics of the relationship between the perpetrators and victims of prejudice. Charles and Ronnie Blakeney provide a fresh psychological perspective to a well-worn research topic by examining attitudes of the minority toward the majority (chapter 3). On the surface at least, the negative appraisal of the majority by members of the minority appears to fit the concept of prejudice; the psychological research, however, calls this into question. From Davidson's seminal moral development study of Boston school children in the midst of the Boston school desegregation crisis to more recent studies by the Blakeneys and others, a consistent pattern has emerged showing that racial prejudice among whites is negatively correlated with moral reasoning development and interracial exposure but that racial prejudice among blacks is positively correlated with these factors or non-existent.[11]

Positing that the "prejudice" of the minority towards the majority is not the moral equivalent of its opposite, the Blakeneys call the former "discordance." Discordance, they theorize, differs from prejudice most fundamentally by being a judgment constructed after reflection upon perceived injustices. Prejudice, on the other hand, appears to be a spontaneous product of psycho-dynamic and socio-cultural forces. Persons at higher stages of moral reasoning are, the Blakeneys posited, more likely to dismiss prejudice as irrational and accept discordance as rational. Administering Kohlberg's moral dilemmas to a cross-sectional age sample of blacks and Jews, the Blakeneys did not confirm the hypothesis that discordance will increase with moral stage. Instead, they found stages of discordance corresponding to the moral stages. They discuss these stages of discordance, which illuminate different ways of suffering injustice and coping with the frustration, bewilderment, and rage that follow.

Pluralism and Religion

Nicgorski and Apple's chapters allude to the decisive role that religious groups have played and continue to play in shaping our moral and political responses to pluralism. Intractable religious conflict gave birth to liberal moral and political theory and led to the constitutional separation of church and state. While the American founders envisioned a purely secular state, they accorded religion the significant role of the moral education of the common citizen. As William Reese shows in the fourth chapter, moral education from the colonial period until the beginning of the twentieth century was steeped in the evangelical Christian tradition. Even when schools became public, their unofficial moral education policy was based in a "consensual" Protestantism that emphasized Bible reading (King James Version) and prayer in addition to the religiously neutral practices of example and instruction. Failing to find common ground with Catholics, Jews, atheists, and agnostics and facing internal division as the mainstream of Protestantism liberalized in the beginning of the twentieth century, evangelicals lost their grip on public education. The Supreme Court decisions banning prayer and Bible reading in the 1960s officially terminated their hegemony.

Conservative evangelicals, smarting over their loss of influence, have retaliated by mounting a powerful attack on moral education in the public schools. Claiming that non-religious approaches to moral education, such as values clarification and Lawrence Kohlberg's moral discussion approach, enshrine a pseudo-religious secular humanism, evangelicals have evoked the church-state separation clause to ban moral and values education from the public schools. In alliance with conservative political groups (see also Apple's chapter 2), evangelicals press to restore Christian values in the public schools even as they campaign for tuition tax credits in support of private Christian schools.

The polarization between conservative evangelicals and secular humanists is not a necessary outgrowth from Christian belief according to Michael Himes in chapter 5. Writing from a Catholic theological standpoint, Himes argues that the Christian understanding of Jesus as human and divine

leads to a profound humanism. Himes counters the pessimism
about human nature found in the traditional beliefs about
original sin and in Madison's understanding of the causes
of factionalism. Reinterpreting the creation and fall myths
in Genesis, Himes suggests that Adam and Eve sinned by
denying the goodness of their humanity, thereby rejecting
God's judgment that they, created in God's image and likeness, were "very good." He sees this notion of the goodness
of humanity radically intensified in the doctrine of the incarnation. In Jesus, he notes, humanity and divinity do not
compete; rather the divine finds its most complete expression
in the human.

An acceptance of pluralism, Himes holds, follows from
the idea that neither divinity, which is transcendent, or humanity, which is open to transcendence, can be understood
in any definitive way. Religious traditions can at best provide partial and provisional insights into God and humanity; dogmatic absolutism is idolatrous. Himes's embrace of
humanism and pluralism is remarkable when one recalls
that the Catholic church did not officially recognize the principle of religious liberty until the Second Vatican Council
(1962–1966). Clearly a liberalization within Catholicism has
occurred with parallels to the earlier liberalization of American Protestantism, described by Reese. It would be a mistake,
however, to understand that liberalization as an acquiescence
in the privatization of religion. Himes is no less adamant
than the conservative evangelicals that religious concerns not
be edged out of public moral debate. He parts company with
the evangelicals, however, in his confidence that rational discourse can resolve human conflicts.

Liberal Theory Reconsidered

In the next two chapters, Boyd and Lapsley shift the
focus from the concerns of religious groups within a pluralistic framework to the liberal moral theory that informs the
framework itself. Drawing upon Canadian multi-cultural experience, Boyd employs Habermas's theory of communicative
action to describe the non-relativistic moral stance necessary
to sustain what he calls the multicultural mosaic of pluralism.

Boyd avoids espousing a particular liberal moral theory, for example Kant's, because in pluralistic societies there are culturally based disagreements on fundamental principles. Furthermore, Boyd does not exclude claims about the good from public discussion.

Moving beyond some of the strictures of liberal theory, Boyd argues for moral dialogue from within "the performative attitude." Taking up the performative attitude requires participation as an equal in an open-ended exchange of viewpoints. The performative attitude contrasts with the objectivating attitude of making judgments from a privileged position beyond criticism. From within the performative attitude, no one can appeal to an *a priori* set of norms or moral prescriptions; rather, norms, prescriptions, and their justification are to be constructed through rational dialogue. Education, Boyd contends, demands that teachers initiate such an ongoing moral dialogue with their students over the kind of persons and society they are to become.

In the following chapter, Daniel Lapsley challenges the liberal philosophy still evident in Boyd's chapter but more fully embodied in Kohlberg's approach to moral psychology and education. Lapsley joins a growing number of virtue theorists and feminists who attack liberal moral theory for the very limitations and generality that allow it to mediate among different cultures and belief systems. He takes up MacIntyre's position in charging that the liberal formalism of Kohlberg's moral development theory is ultimately self-defeating. Lapsley focuses on Kohlberg's stage six, arguing that however formulated (whether according to Kant's categorical imperative, Rawls's original position, justice as reversibility, or Habermas's ideal communication ethic), it cannot but fall prey to the very relativism it seeks to overcome. Urging that moral psychology pay more attention to the virtues and to the self, Lapsley heralds a new post-Kohlbergian era in psychology and education. His proposal juxtaposes a "thick" conception of the moral life against Kohlberg's "thin" approach, centered on justice. In acquiring greater specificity, however, can the virtue approach avoid becoming "culture bound" and thus fail to provide the moral glue for the multi-cultural mosaic or the critical edge for the liberation of the oppressed?

Nevertheless, a communicative ethic boldly presupposes, perhaps too optimistically, that individuals can transcend their own cultural embeddedness in order to listen to and understand others on those others' own terms and coordinate the positions of self and others in an effort to reach a rationally based consensus. But is such communication possible, as Boyd and Himes seem to believe, or are humans far more limited, as Lapsley, Nicgorski, and Reese suggest? The question might be settled empirically, if Kohlberg's post-conventional stages could be seen as an index of dialogical competence, a move that Boyd might endorse but Lapsley would question. Lapsley, himself, argues that achievement of a certain character or moral self may be more important than such a competence for successful participation in pluralistic dialogue.

Educational Applications

Although all of the chapters in this book make reference to educational applications, the last three focus explicitly on approaches to moral and multicultural education. Synthesizing the contributions of Annette Baier, Carol Gilligan, Nel Noddings, and other feminists, Diller outlines the main features of an ethics of care. She contrasts this ethic, which aims at enhancing relationships through its method of attentiveness, with approaches that aim at independence. At first blush, it would appear that an ethics of care would lead to separatism, as the maintenance of existing family and friendship ties dominates the moral agenda. Indeed, in presenting a typology of pluralistic relationships, Diller begins with a pluralism of co-existence, which is based on an ethic of non-interference and mutual toleration. But Diller believes that constructive engagements across cultural boundaries are both possible and desirable. Yet what would lead an individual to move beyond her circle of established relationships to relate to those from another culture? Diller responds by developing three additional forms of pluralism, cooperation, co-exploring, and co-enjoyment, unfolding the educational implications of each. The centerpiece of Diller's educational recommendations is a method of co-exploring, which facilitates self-revelation and honest communication. Diller believes that it is possible to replace contentious moral argumentation over *the* right answer with a shared pursuit of mutually satisfying relations.

The following chapter by Fowler develops the kind of character education approach suggested by Lapsley. Fowler critiques the formalism of progressive education and the privatization of the human good and religion brought about by liberal theory and practice. Rejecting the values clarification approach and cautiously appropriating elements of Kohlberg's cognitive developmentalism, Fowler offers a five-component model of character education, which adds narrative, virtue, information, and attitudinal content to the structural features of the developmental approach. This comprehensive model is attractive especially in contrast to more narrowly defined approaches, such as Kohlberg's. Fowler speaks to the silences of Kohlberg's theory, addressing conscience, the emotions, cultural content, the virtues, and the good life. Fowler's expansiveness, however, presents new problems in a pluralistic context. For example, if stories are to be a central feature of character education, then whose stories are to be told and to what end? Making matters even more concrete, Glazer asks whether the stories we impart to elementary and secondary school children should evoke loyalty or disdain for the dominant culture.[12] Should our stories advise children to remain within their ethnic groups, venture into the dominant culture, or decide as individuals what to do? Fowler does not avoid such hard questions although in the confines of a single chapter he can provide only hints of his response.

In the concluding chapter, Olneck contends that, like it or not, American public schools are not and will not be pluralistic (at least in the foreseeable future). Olneck's thesis rests on his view that genuine pluralism requires a "strong pluralism" bordering on separatism. According to Olneck, pluralism must acknowledge the identities, desires (especially for boundary maintenance), rights, and responsibilities of "groups as groups." Multicultural education as generally practiced is assimilationist rather than pluralistic because,

Olneck explains, multiculturalists proceed from an individualistic moral and psychological perspective in a setting that isolates students from their particular cultural groups.

Olneck also takes aim at the tendency of some multiculturalists to equate diversity with pluralism. This leads to what may be thought of as a modified values clarification pedagogy in which children are encouraged to become more self-aware, tolerant of differences, and "appreciative" of the "contributions" of other cultures. Although such a pedagogy may have a place within a more comprehensive multi-cultural program, taken alone, it tends to trivialize cross-cultural encounters (Nicgorski), mask the realities of oppression, injustice, and prejudice (Apple and the Blakeneys), and promote assimilation to the dominant culture. Boyd and Lapsley would no doubt also fault such a practice for failing to come to terms with moral relativism.

The alternative to the unconscious assimilationism promoted by the status quo and even well-intentioned multicultural programs would seem to involve separating culturally defined groups of students into either different schools or subunits within the same school. As Olneck points out, such a policy raises troubling questions about the kinds of groupings that would be used. Although many Afro and Hispanic Americans identify with distinctive cultural groups, many Euro-Americans do not. A more meaningful way to deal with those of European descent would be to leave them in a single group or divide them according to their religion. But even that classification scheme would not work well for many individuals, who would find such categories highly artificial and constraining. If the problem of classification could be resolved, would separatist educational communities have the moral resources necessary to protect individual rights and the integrity of all groups? The research cited by the Blakeneys suggests that separatist communities would breed prejudice and intolerance. Is not some level of integration necessary to safeguard pluralism?

Pluralism challenges moral educators to find a pedagogy that respects value differences without dissolving into relativism, that forms character and virtue without hardening into absolutism, that assures cohesiveness without encouraging conformity, and that promotes justice without becoming uncaring. The task is daunting but nonetheless urgent, as our society becomes all the more diverse. We hope that this volume will contribute to the effort.

Notes

1. *Report of the National Educational Association Executive Study Groups on Ethnic Minority Concerns* (Washington, D.C.: Human and Civil Rights, NEA, 1987).

2. See also Nicholas Appleton, *Cultural Pluralism in Education: Theoretical Foundations* (New York: Longman, 1983).

3. Philip Gleason, "American Identity and Americanization," *Harvard Encyclopedia of American Ethnic Groups*, ed. S. Ternstrom (Cambridge, Mass.: Harvard University Press, 1980), 31–58.

4. Irving Lewis Horowitz articulates some of the dangers of state-sponsored moral education in "Moral Development, Authoritarian Distemper, and Democratic Persuasion," *Moral Development and Politics*, ed. Richard W. Wilson, Gordon J. Schochet (New York; Praeger, 1980), 5–21. A case can be made that Constitutional Law now supports public school moral education understood as teaching the habits of open-mindedness and critical inquiry. See John Robinson, "Why Schooling Is So Controversial in America Today," *Notre Dame Journal of Law Ethics and Public Policy* 3, no. 4 (1988): 519–533.

5. *Webster's New Twentieth-Century Dictionary of the English Language, Unabridged, Second Edition* (New York: Simon and Schuster, 1983): 1385.

6. John Dewey, *Democracy and Education* (New York: Macmillan, 1916/1966), 90.

7. Ibid., 83.

8. See Jean Piaget, *The Moral Judgment of the Child* (Glencoe, Ill.: Free Press, 1932/1965) and F. Clark Power, Ann Higgins, and Lawrence Kohlberg, *Lawrence Kohlberg's Approach to Moral Education* (New York: Columbia University Press, 1989).

9. Kohlberg argued that moral development is a universal phenomenon. Cross-cultural research supports his claim but only through the first four stages. See John Snarey, "Cross-cultural Universality of Social-Moral Development: A Critical View of Kohlbergian Research," *Psychological Bulletin* 97 (1985): 202–232.

10. Nathan Glazer, "Cultural Pluralism: The Social Aspect," *Pluralism in a Democratic Society*, ed. M. M. Tumin and W. Plotch (New York: Praeger, 1977), 3–24.

11. References to Davidson's study and the research on prejudice are provided in chapter 3.

12. Glazer, "Cultural Pluralism: The Social Aspect," 21–23.

AMERICAN PLURALISM:
A CONDITION OR A GOAL?

Walter Nicgorski

That pluralism is a feature of American society and a critical facet of American politics remains a common observation. There is less agreement—but not much less—in the assessment of this American feature. Quite overwhelmingly of late and throughout the last quarter century, pluralism is seen as a good and enriching dimension of American life. We believe ourselves better for our pluralism, and we celebrate it and seek to reinforce it. Our efforts range from events such as black or Native American awareness weeks and programs on cultural diversity to the delights of ethnic food festivals. We are drawn to represent our diversity in our organizations and political assemblies; thus political parties and their conventions, local police departments, presidential cabinets and university faculties are among the groups we expect to reflect, in at least some ways, the many splendored mosaic that American society is thought to be. Pluralism is clearly no longer simply a fact of American history and thus a condition of our social and political life; pluralism, now much examined and reflected upon, is also consciously embraced. It is widely hailed as an important, if not great, discovery of modernity.[1] The very loss of confidence in our ability to know critical standards and potentially unifying principles, a loss much in evidence and much noted in post–World War II America, appears to nourish pluralism.[2] Closely related to this condition is the present pervasive postmodernism of intellectual and university circles, a current that the philosopher Calvin Schrag sees as marked by a "celebration of pluralism."[3]

15

Though this general picture of pluralism seems to fit with what is seen and heard around us, some qualifications and caveats are necessary for a more accurate portrayal of the state of American pluralism. First of all, the celebration of pluralism and efforts to foster it may not reflect so much its healthy state as its threatened state. The forces of homogenization are powerful indeed; the great geographical extent of territory on which key founding fathers relied to maintain and nourish diversity in the American Republic appears to have become less significant by dint of the technology that provides national media and communications and a tighter and faster web of national transportation. The nationalization, not to speak of the internationalization, of the economy and American business not only tie much of America more closely together but also uproot and disperse families and neighborhoods with a startling frequency, making locales and roots less important in accentuating and maintaining diversity. Is there anyone who is still surprised to find that a McDonald's or Burger King has appeared in the place of a once frequented local diner, or that the last locally owned and somewhat distinctive drugstore has now been purchased by a national chain? A case then can be made that the "melting pot," with its imagery of varied and distinctive elements being forged together, has turned out to be a sterile "melt down."

A second caveat relates to how to interpret efforts to celebrate and to strengthen pluralism. These efforts may not always be motivated by a valuing and delighting in differences. This becomes evident when one considers the push for informal or formal quotas, as in the form of affirmative action efforts in political assemblies, organizations, and businesses. The intent in these cases is often to achieve fairness and justice in decisions and policies of such assemblies and organizations; the outcomes sought are uniform and universal. Representation of diversity is in such cases but a tactic, a form of leverage under certain historical conditions, to achieve a quite standardized goal. Even in the case of the efforts to represent one or another group in the business world and professions, the intent is usually to strengthen group visibility, group confidence through role-models, and to achieve financial and social clout for the group. All of these, however, may be intermediate goals, sought for the sake of achieving parity and justice for the group as a whole or, in language commonly heard, for a share in the American Dream.

There is an ambivalence about this phrase, "sharing in the American Dream," that comes into a little more clarity when we notice how often it is simply understood as a "fair share of the pie." The American Dream then, while it could be primarily understood as full acceptance under certain principles of a common way of life, seems to be primarily understood as a certain perceived level of common prosperity and even luxury. In either case, pluralism in the form of diversity and group consciousness and group effort is embraced as a tactical good or device; diversity is accentuated and utilized as a means to a kind of uniformity. Is it too cynical to notice that beneath the exhortations to and celebrations of pluralism is a significant, steady movement, perhaps more desired than now realized for some groups, into what is called "the mainstream"? Consider not only the much heralded (and much celebrated on television) black upper middle class that seems so fully assimilated, but also that there is good reason to see in that recent experience a well-worn and generally welcomed route into the mainstream. Ethnic-Americans who have "made it" past the handicaps of their "funny" name, Jews who want for one reason or another to escape the shackles of the past in this dynamic society, and Catholics, in name only, must be seen as part of the picture of who we Americans are and aspire to be.

The picture we are apt to draw of a healthy and vigorous state of American pluralism must also acknowledge the direct and open efforts to limit it and resist it.[4] There is steady opposition to publicly supported bilingual education and strong opposition to representing, in the form of informal or formal quotas, American social variety whether the issue is constituting a panel of judges or court, admitting a class to medical school, or the letting of contracts from the public purse. American oneness and unity is at issue in the minds of some. There are thought to be limits to our diversity. Specifically in the resistance to quotas, part of American unity is understood to be a living by a principle of competence or merit. The paradox thus arises that there is considerable diversity in

America over questions of the degree and nature of the unity which this society should maintain. What do the moral foundations and other requisites of the American republic (e.g., capacity for common discourse) entail as the necessary core of our unity? What is the uncompromisable American way? The answers vary from some forms of fundamentalism whose flag-draped platforms match a rhetoric that nearly merges Americanism with a specific religious denomination and style to groups like the People for the American Way who find that "Way" in the freedom for all ways extending, it seems, even to that of the pornographer.

Significant Pluralism

This kind of resistance, in the name of some essential core of American unity, to an unlimited pluralism or pluralism as an end and good in itself brings into focus pluralism in its most significant form. This significant pluralism is found, insofar as it is present, beneath the level of racial awareness weeks, the rage for ethnic foods, and other efforts to represent and even delight in the colorful mosaic of peoples and traditions that is America.[5] This pluralism is significant precisely because it is at once both the most threatening to essential societal unity and the most damaging for a society to be without.

Just as pluralism has so far in this essay been used in the ordinary sense of diversity or the esteeming of diversity, so this significant pluralism is diversity of ways of life, of values; it might properly be called moral pluralism or moral diversity, though it is important to understand moral as encompassing the principles of public as well as private life.[6] In fact, the possibility of or the precise point of a division between private and public life becomes itself a matter for contention among different perspectives. This pluralism of different outlooks is rooted in individual differences, but like other differences and probably even more so, these express themselves through associations or groups wherein perspectives on important matters are shared. In fact, such associations may be especially important in the case of moral pluralism where the internal life of the association can intensify and/or develop the perspectives that brought the group together. This moral pluralism, by encompassing ways of life, includes not simply differences on ultimate ends or primary imperatives but also differences on means, secondary imperatives and applications among those who may agree on the ultimate or primary level. All such differences are not, of course, articulated by most people in the language of moral and political philosophy that has intruded here, but it does appear that under Socratic-like questioning, the spirited and important differences among people would fall themselves into such classifications.

The significance of moral pluralism as an invigorating and essential presence in a healthy society and simultaneously as a threat to the health of any society is an inescapable theme in the history of moral and political philosophy. Socrates' example seems to make both points; his was a challenge to the way of life of most Athenians, and though Socrates' view and that of others who followed him was that his probing presence was just what Athens needed, a fatal majority thought otherwise and saw in him a destructive threat to their way of life. Even if one argues that this majority was wrong and that what Socrates represented was indeed good for Athens, one could not comfortably conclude that significant dissent in the form of moral pluralism is not really a threat to good societies. This truth is evident in Socrates' own persistent critique of the sophists; he appears to have thought that under the guise of sophistic relativism certain moral perspectives (e.g., personal power as a supreme good) that threatened the just society he sought would find shelter and encouragement. The fear of significant pluralism is sometimes expressed as a fear of the diversity, factionalism, and even chaos that are associated with the liberty of democratic institutions. Threatened by such diversity, Thomas Hobbes, perhaps more than any other political thinker, sought a decisive consolidation of all power in the hands of the state and pushed the consolidation, in the name of maximum security, to resting all state power in the hands of a monarch. However, two of the most notable and influential defenses of moral pluralism, that of Alexis De Tocqueville in *Democracy In America* and John Stuart Mill in *On Liberty*, are directed not at the homogenizing and stultifying power of a monarchical sovereign but rather at what was perceived as more dangerous, the emergent power of the democratic sovereign, namely the majority.

Tocqueville saw in the United States of the early nineteenth century with its fledgling democracy and thorough democratic social commitment an instructive laboratory for the world, most immediately the Western European world, about to be swept up by the democratic idea. Among Tocqueville's European readers was John Stuart Mill who then took up his own pen to join Tocqueville in the effort to educate democratic majorities of the future on the value of significant diversity and the danger of an egalitarian homogenization. It is interesting to notice that the dominant perspective from abroad on America, as represented in Tocqueville and Mill, has been to express concern for vital diversity, for meaningful pluralism in the United States. At the same time, the dominant perspective from within American society, at least for most of our history until the recent celebration of pluralism, has been a concern with our unity, with our capacity to assimilate and to become one out of many.

Though that motto of the United States, *e pluribus unum*, which articulates the aspiration to become one from many originates in the challenge of thirteen separate political jurisdictions endeavoring after the Revolution to become one political state, latent in the motto from the beginning is the challenge of cultural diversity in this new nation. What is latent then comes to the fore in the nineteenth and early twentieth century, as the United States more consciously recognizes itself as a land of immigrants and struggles to assimilate wave after wave of new arrivals. Over this time *e pluribus unum* comes above all to be associated in the American mind with this ongoing effort to make a single nation from the diverse and "huddled masses" regularly drawn to the torch of liberty.

In the *pluribus* of that motto, there is engraved on the cornerstone of the American nation what could be taken as a "prophetic" indicator that pluralism was to be an important dimension of the nation's conscious experiment in popular government. Thus as the struggle for unity took the form of assimilating the immigrant waves, that struggle itself and the apparent successes in it were seen ever more as a part of a distinctive American destiny and achievement. Whether the terms used to describe the American experience are those of the Puritan aspiration to build here "a city on a hill" for all the world to see, or those of the *au courant* formulation that describes the United States as a "lead society," the American experiment in free democratic government has come to be bound up with the effort, successful yet ongoing, to become one out of many. Pluralism then and the harnessing of it into unity is an integral part of what the United States holds before the world as an example.

The pride in our pluralism and in our taming of it can obscure the ways in which the experience of the United States is like that of other nations. Perhaps pluralism in this nation has been and is greater than that of most nations. Perhaps this nation's effort to assimilate, to become one rather than to lock in a static pluralism, has been among the more extensive and successful in human experience. Such conclusions arise easily within the American self-understanding, but even they warrant and admit of more careful, and of course comparative, empirical examination. In one respect, however, the vaunted American effort to bring oneness out of many is but one instance of an experience every nation must necessarily have. Since it is significant or moral pluralism that is under discussion here, the taming or harnessing of that pluralism turns out to be a way of talking about socialization.

Socialization, Moral Education, and Pluralism

Socialization can be understood as the process of "passage into participation in some community by coming to share its convictions and ways of acting."[7] Education, inclusive of but not restricted to formal schooling, has always been seen as a society's major instrument of socialization. Since all communities have some convictions and ways of acting which go more to the heart of the community than others, which are central and primary, which concern, in other words, the morals or ethics of the community, moral education "is the most important part, the very substance, of socialization." Socialization or moral education is then everywhere a process of limiting and overcoming, at least in some degree, pluralism.

Socialization most often suggests acculturation across generations, the passing on of a moral tradition, and in this, which might be called vertical socialization, there is a pluralism of different ages and generations that poses the challenge of differentiation to the socializing process. Socialization is also inevitably horizontal, and in this respect it confronts significant differences not necessarily age-related and often expressed in the organized form of associations and groups which the concept of pluralism usually brings to mind. Without pluralism there would be no need for moral education; without moral education in some form there could be no society in a meaningful and enduring sense. Pluralism is implicated in the very ideas of moral education and society. Moral education cannot then avoid encountering moral pluralism if it is to be moral education in any real sense of the terms.

There are front lines in the necessary encounter of moral education with pluralism, and there are also enclaves of hesitation and retreat as well as Olympian overviews. An illustration of these locales can now also serve the purpose of redirecting attention to American pluralism. Olympian overviews are, of course, what we have already seen much of in this essay: generalizations, often proud ones, about this nation's proven capacity to assimilate its diversity, celebrations of its pluralism, concerns over its loss of diversity, speculations on the superficiality of its current pluralism, and even some current manifestations of a long-standing concern for its unity. Such overviews are heard from social commentators, cultural historians, and even American political leaders. Valuable as such perspectives might be in trying to understand this dimension of the American experience, they are well removed from the process of socialization, from moral education's encounter with pluralism. They are devoid not just of the "blood, sweat and tears" of the front lines but also of practical suggestions for the encounter with pluralism.

Hesitation and retreat have their place in many a well-executed encounter or battle plan, but when are they cowardly and ultimately harmful to the community rather than prudent and useful appears to be a question difficult to answer with assurance without the specifics of a concrete context for choice. In the case of American pluralism, hesitation and retreat is exemplified in national political parties when their conventions and platforms seek to represent diversity and to avoid or minimize any kind of encounter or choice between divergent perspectives on important questions. To notice this is not necessarily to claim that it should be otherwise for national parties or that every dimension of social and public life must provide an occasion to encounter pluralism and to try to work through the significant differences in society. This established tendency of the parties, however, clearly displays what is found to be an attractive and recurrent strategy to which other organizations and agencies in the society turn in the face of significant pluralism. This strategy entails an effort to represent pluralism and to balance different views, while avoiding encounters (often seen simply as "confrontations") and maintaining official neutrality. The strategy is captured in the folk wisdom that one would best avoid discussing religion or politics in gatherings of family and friends. On a larger scale it is reflected in that understandable but cynical estimate of democracy, that "government by discussion works best when there is nothing fundamentally important to discuss."[8] The strategy of hesitation and retreat is without question often motivated by the desire for peace, harmony, survival of the relevant group and the effectiveness of the group at attaining purposes other than those touched by its internal pluralism. These motives may be masked, and this strategy may be openly defended with claims about the need to respect and preserve pluralism.

If it were possible to attain a society that carried out this strategy in a pervasive way, what kind of society would it be? Imagine one whose media, whose churches, and whose schools were driven by a passion for neutrality, and for representing and not confronting significant differences. At the most, the result would be a static pluralism for that is what the strategy appears to intend. There is good reason, however, to suspect that beneath the surface of this pluralism, of an apparently dead society, there would be interaction and movement. The interaction might be in the form of the quiet assertion of dominance by powerful groups and their perspectives; and the movement could well be in the direction of one or another form of ever greater homogenization. Whatever may be happening beneath the placid and colorful surface of diversity, there arises the question whether such a society could be humanly satisfying.

Although this imagined society is not entirely capable of realization, the powerful pull in its direction felt by national political parties trying to put together a winning coalition is also evident in such agencies of societal moral education as the media, the churches, and the schools. The imagined society is not possible because significant moral and political questions cannot be buried or dodged as long as a people is free. The moral sphere is unavoidable, and those who most regularly face this truth are the very agencies and organizations primarily responsible for socialization and expected to be in close touch with significant human choices and with the development of the understanding and horizons that affect such choices. These are the front lines of the encounter with moral pluralism.

In this encounter, the agencies and organizations on the front lines face tough practical questions on a day-to-day basis. These are questions like how much effort should go into representing diversity? how much to cultivating pluralism? how much to avoiding real interaction between divergent perspectives? and how much to stimulating interaction in the interest of resolving (or practicing the resolution of) differences? It is not difficult to see that these practical front line questions of the classroom and newsroom entail important questions about American pluralism. How does pluralism relate to the American way? What is the core of our unity? Is pluralism a blessing or a curse? a condition or a goal? Clearly those on the front lines are caught with having to work out in practice the long-standing problem in democratic theory about the appropriate mix of unity and diversity for a healthy society.[9]

Pluralism and Democracy

Having looked at the current status and history of American pluralism and focused on the challenges of the encounter with moral pluralism by the agencies of socialization, this essay turns in its final section not to offering direct practical guidance to those on the front lines but to an effort to think out pluralism's role in a democracy. Kant's observation that nothing is so practical as a good theory is a general reminder, however, that clarifying and refining how we think about pluralism is likely to be immensely practical. The search for a good theory of pluralism in what follows is done through explication of and in dialogue with two American efforts to understand the proper role of pluralism in democracy. That of James Madison in *The Federalist*, primarily in paper No. 10, receives the most attention, though at the end some consideration is given to the thought of John Dewey as reflected in *The Public and Its Problems* and *Democracy and Education*.

If there is a foundational text for American pluralism, a *classicus locus*, it is Madison's paper No. 10. This paper is the starting point for much of this century's discussion of pluralism's role in American society and politics. Its powerful analysis includes an exploration of the basis of pluralism in human nature and freedom, a linking of pluralism with enlarged geographic size of a political society, and an argument that claims both of these, pluralism and enlarged size, as necessary conditions of healthy popular government. The term "pluralism" does not appear in the paper, but the idea of diversity and specifically significant diversity expressing itself in organized groups is integral to the paper's argument. In fact, the paper's explicit topic is the contention that the proposed union of thirteen states—hence enlarged size—under the United States Constitution will have the "tendency" to control the harmful results of "faction." "Faction" is Madison's word, and a fairly common word in the political discourse of the time, for a harmful concert or group of citizens. The danger of faction was seen by Madison and others as the great threat, evident from history and the experience of their lives, to stable and successful popular government. Early in paper No. 10, faction is defined as

> a number of citizens, whether amounting to a majority or minority of the whole, who are united and actuated by some common impulse of passion, or of interest, adverse to the rights of other citizens, or to the permanent and aggregate interests of the community.[10]

The first major step in the argument of the paper is a demonstration that faction must be controlled by containing its effects rather than by "removing its causes." To remove its causes would entail (1) a denial of liberty or (2) a futile effort to homogenize the citizenry by leading them all to "the same opinions, the same passions, and the same interests." When Madison probes the basis for his rejection of the methods of removing the causes, we are treated to a revealing exploration not merely of the causes of faction but also of the causes of pluralism.

Elemental as it may seem to notice that faction—and hence pluralism—are entailed in liberty, it is critical to thinking through pluralism that this foundational step be clearly understood and appreciated. Thus Madison's own powerful metaphor, utilized by him to illustrate that the remedy of denying liberty is worse than the disease of faction, should be savored:

> Liberty is to faction, what air is to fire, an aliment without which it instantly expires. But it could not be less folly to abolish liberty, which is essential to political life, because it nourishes faction, than it would be to wish the annihilation of air, which is essential to animal life, because it imparts to fire its destructive agency.

Madison thus makes clear that liberty is such a high communal goal that one cannot consider removing it in the interest of avoiding the disruptive effects of faction or presumably the difficulties of diversity and concomitant contention in society. Madison here writes of liberty as "essential to political life"; this commitment to liberty, in the light of other parts of paper No. 10 and *The Federalist*, is to be understood as a commitment to what we would call democratic government and to widespread freedom of expression and action. Madison explicitly insists that the remedy for the disease of faction had to be consistent with governance by the will of the majority, with republican government which was his phrase for popular government or democratic government through elected representatives.[11]

However, for Madison, faction (and hence pluralism) is not merely to be understood as an offspring of a commitment to liberty; rather, it is liberty combined with the kind of beings we are, with, in other words, our nature or our human condition, that makes faction and pluralism inevitable. He specifically argues that humans are factious and diverse because they are fallible and self-centered and possess different natural capacities and abilities.

> As long as the reason of man continues fallible, and he is at liberty to exercise it, different opinions will be formed. As long as the connection subsists between his reason and his self-love, his opinions and his passions will have a reciprocal influence on each other, and the former will be objects to which the latter will attach themselves. The diversity in the faculties of men from which the rights of property originate, is not less an insuperable obstacle to a uniformity of interests.

Since "the latent causes of faction are thus sown in the nature of man," Madison concludes that as long as humans are free one could not, presumably through forms of education and persuasion, bring about uniformity of opinions, passions, and interests.

What then does Madison propose to do about the danger of faction? What specifically would he do to control the effects of this unavoidable danger to free and popular government? Before this part of his argument is pursued to learn how a free people might live well with its inherent pluralism, it is important to clarify some significant but frequently misunderstood passages that occur in the early pages of paper No. 10. Those causes of faction rooted in human nature are seen by Madison to be everywhere "brought into different degrees of activity, according to the different circumstances of civil society." Madison adds,

> A zeal for different opinions concerning religion, concerning Government and many other points, as well of speculation as of practice; an attachment to different leaders ambitiously contending for pre-eminence and power; or to persons of other descriptions whose fortunes have been interesting to the human passions, have in turn divided mankind into parties, inflamed them with mutual animosity, and rendered them much more disposed to vex and oppress each other, than to co-operate for their common good.

Thus a free society for Madison will inevitably be marked by much diversity, some of it "frivolous and fanciful," and it will be marked by the contention between diverse groups. Economic diversity, which Madison calls "the various and unequal distribution of property," is "the most common and durable source of factions," and therefore "the regulation of these various and interfering interests forms the principal task of modern Legislation, and involves the spirit of party and faction in the necessary and ordinary operations of Government." It is important to notice that in elevating economic diversity to a special position Madison does not claim that it is the source of all other differences; nor does he claim that the only significant form of economic diversity is that of the possessed and the dispossessed, namely the "unequal distribution of property." Rather, he sees economic diversity and thus economic factions as one very important manifestation of human diversity which is rooted in human nature, and he observes that economic diversity takes various forms including different and contending interests within the class possessing significant property. Economic diversity is singled out for special attention and elevated in importance by Madison because, being the most constant source of faction in human experience, it intrudes itself into the business of government, and regulating "the various and interfering interests" becomes the principal task of legislation in modern, civilized nations. That government must be much concerned with economic contention, that, in other words, regulating such contention forms the principal work of its legislation is not to say that it is the end or goal of government any more than it would be right to conclude that the coach or teacher who said most of his effort had to go into discipline and maintaining order would be asserting that the goal in coaching or teaching is simply the maintenance of order.

Furthermore, regulation of economic pluralism itself raises the question of regulation in terms of what standard, of what goal? It is too easy to slip to a conclusion that since the regulation of economic contention is the primary work of government the way that work is done is through some kind of brokering among economic interests in which those interests are simply maintained. Madison, however, did not seem to envision regulation, or in fact an entire political process, that seeks the maintenance of the existing pluralism. In the paragraph that immediately follows his statement that "the regulation of these various and interfering interests forms the principal task of modern Legislation," he observes at one point that "justice ought to hold the balance" between contending economic interests and at another point that regulation is to be done "with a sole regard to justice and the public good." Later, in *The Federalist* paper No. 51 where he returns to consider the diversity and factionalism of a free society, Madison quite eloquently insists that "justice is the end of government. It is the end of civil society. It ever has been, and ever will be pursued, until it be obtained, or until liberty be lost in the pursuit." Thus for Madison some conception of justice and the public good is to be the standard in regulation as well as the very end of society and government.

At this point in unfolding his argument, it is useful to notice that Madison's envisioning the possible loss of liberty in the pursuit of justice implies that there is a goal beyond liberty itself, and given the great and high importance of liberty as already noted, it is reasonable to conclude that for Madison that goal beyond liberty could be expressed as the rightful or just exercise of liberty. Out of the pluralism that liberty allows, justice is sought. There is also, back in paper No. 10, another useful indicator, relevant to the topic of pluralism, of how Madison understood justice. Recall that he had pointed to "diversity in the faculties of men from which the rights of property originate" as one of the causes of faction latent in human nature. Immediately following that observation, Madison adds the simple sentence, "The protection of these faculties is the first object of Government." Thus at least a part of justice, which he has called the end of government, is the protection of the natural diversity in human faculties. Justice itself, so understood, entails ensuring at least a certain kind of pluralism in society by protecting one of pluralism's chief sources.

After this clarification of the predominance Madison assigns to economic diversity, of the nature of that diversity and of justice as an end of government that is something other than mere maintenance of the existing pluralism, it is possible to return to the main line of paper No. 10's argument with the prospect of greater understanding. If the causes of faction cannot be touched, how then are the effects to be controlled? How, in other words, are we to live well with our inevitable pluralism? At this point Madison focuses the question on majority faction, noting that under popular government minority factions can simply be voted down and the danger from them checked in that way. So the problem, in Madison's eyes, comes down to majority faction. Expressed more fully, the problem is how to control the effects of majority faction in a system committed to majority rule. Madison will seek to affect the way a majority is formed.

Madison's response to the problem constitutes what seems to be the most remembered and cited aspect of his argument in paper No. 10. This aspect of his argument especially tends to give rise to or lend support to confusion in the way we think about pluralism. Madison's response or "solution" to the problem is to increase pluralism, to multiply factions, by enlarging the extent or geographic territory of the republic. Majority faction then will be considerably less a threat in the large republic proposed for the United States than in the popularly ruled city-states of much of the past.[12] In turning to an enlargement of the territory and a multiplication of faction as the "solution," Madison explicitly rejected reliance on "moral and religious motives . . . as an adequate control" on a majority or, in fact, on an individual. Such motives, he claims, are ineffective at curtailing "the injustice and violence of individuals, and lose their efficacy in proportion to the number combined together; that is, in proportion as their efficacy becomes needful."

This powerful Madisonian solution leads easily to the conclusion that security and decency among a free people are not attained by moral or religious education but by the maintenance of pluralism and the extension of it. At the least pluralism comes to be taken, as it widely is in the writings on democracy in this century, as a necessary condition of this security and decency; from that critical position, it may become an end in itself especially when agreement on other ends or goals as justice and truth seems elusive. Thus Madison himself in the matter of religion, where he seemed little if at all personally interested in working out the differences among sects and striving for the truth, emphatically draws attention to the value of pluralism. Ralph Ketcham's biography of Madison recalls his argument in the Virginia Ratification Convention of 1788 that a bill of rights would be a poor protection for religious freedom and that "this freedom arises from the multiplicity of sects, which pervades America, and which is the best and only security for religious liberty in any society." Ketcham added a report that Madison approved and often quoted Voltaire's observation that "if one religion only were allowed in England, the government would possibly be arbitrary; if there were but two, the people would cut each other's throats; but, as there are such a multitude they all live happy and in peace."[13] Thus religious pluralism, though still formally described by Madison as an instrumental good, nearly becomes a good in itself.[14]

With respect to politics, however, Madison clearly and explicitly points to a goal beyond liberty and therefore a goal for the pluralism that helps to support liberty. He would multiply factions and the pluralism of the nation in the interest of wiser and juster public policies. Thus when he explains the expected impact of an enlarged territory with its increased pluralism, he writes,

> Extend the sphere, and you take in a greater variety of parties and interests; you make it less probable that a majority of the whole will have a common motive to invade the rights of other citizens; or if such a common motive exists, it will be more difficult for all who feel it to discover their own strength, and to act in unison with each other.

Increased pluralism entailed for Madison the decreased likelihood that a majority faction or ill-intentioned majority can be formed and can act effectively. His intent appears to be to so stalemate or complicate the formation and effectiveness of a majority faction that the door opens more widely for the possibility of a deliberative and responsible majority.[15] Madison's major collaborator in authoring *The Federalist*, Alexander Hamilton, described the inner operations of the legislature in a way consistent with Madison's expectations for the overall political process. In paper No. 70, Hamilton observes that "the differences of opinion, and the jarrings of parties in that department of government, though they may sometimes obstruct salutary plans, yet often promote deliberation and circumspection...."[16] In summary, it can be said that the primary concern for Madison was not that the majority will rule—that was assumed in the American system—his concern was with the kind of majority that will rule.[17]

Madison's argument on pluralism concerns the political process as a whole; he was interested in effecting how the majority is formed in the interest of getting a certain kind of majority. That kind of majority was to be responsive to justice and the public good which concepts entailed liberty but also went beyond it. Paradoxically Madison proposed, as so many have after him in one form or another, to increase pluralism as a means to overcome pluralism in a responsible or principled way. The engagement of pluralism, which earlier was said to be inherent to socialization and moral education, is treated by Madison as occurring in the political process. The question arises whether certain kinds of leaders and of citizens are not required or assumed by Madison for the intended political dynamics to take place, a dynamics of a responsible majority forming while factious elements are stalemated. Would there not have to be at least for a substantial number of the citizens, a prior socialization, a prior working through of pluralism if the outcome of the political process was to be as Madison intended? Would there not have to be, in other words, significant moral and religious education in the underlying society and thus more acceptance of the critical role the development of "moral and religious motives" will play in a stable and successful democratic political process? *The Federalist* in particular and the American Founders in general, save for Jefferson, gave little to no attention to education and its place in the political experiment in freedom on which they launched this nation.[18] This topic is, however, a central concern in the work of John Dewey.

Though Dewey went beyond Madison in his concern with education and its social and political role, there are indications that he shared much of Madison's understanding of pluralism and how it relates to the political life of a free people. Near the very end of *The Public and Its Problems*, Dewey takes stock of prevalent criticisms of democracy and concedes that they are justified if democracy is understood simply as majority rule; he then approvingly cites Samuel Tilden's observation that "the means by which a majority comes to be a majority is the more important thing." In the very next paragraph Dewey observes, "The essential need, in other words, is the improvement of the methods and conditions of debate, discussion and persuasion."[19] Not only does this comment signal a certain clear expectation of Dewey for schooling in a democratic society, but it also relates to the fact that Dewey expected the school to be heavily involved in assimilating and integrating the inherent diversity of a free society.[20]

Dewey acknowledged and appreciated pluralism, but there is an ambivalence about it in his work quite comparable to that of Madison. Dewey recognized that some of the multifarious associations and societies that people form would have ill effects on the society as a whole and be constraining on their own members. He thought the state and the public beneath the state had to assert control over pluralism and "the negative struggle" that can occur among groups.[21] The lever of this control would be that proper mode of majority rule. Dewey sought what might be called a dynamic rather than a static pluralism, a pluralism that would, in other words, ever recur in new forms as individuals and the public developed through inquiry and discussion.[22]

How then should we think about pluralism? Where have Madison and Dewey left us or pointed us? Pluralism seems one of the blessings of liberty. It is not an unmixed blessing. It is rooted not only in freedom but also in human fallibility, self-centeredness, and natural diversity. It is implied in being free and human and thus a condition of a free society, not its goal. The task of a free people is, in one sense, ever trying to overcome pluralism through the finding of shared principles and the application of them to their common way of life. This is a task that cannot be left to the political process alone; it must be begun and experienced in the course of education. This task is, in other terms, the striving of a free people for truth and justice, but if it is a justice in freedom or through freedom that is sought, then it is likely that pluralism will continually be reasserting itself in some forms even as it is overcome in others. Such a blessing is pluralism that, even though it is not the goal, at times it is to be cultivated and encouraged for pedagogical and political reasons. It does at times work to protect the liberty which spawns it, and it can enrich perspectives and thereby contribute to reaching those goals of truth and justice.

Notes

1. Robert Dahl, a leading political theorist of the last generation, describes this century and specifically the post–World War II period as a time which saw "the gradual acceptance of pluralism as an inherent, inescapable, and even desirable aspect of democracy. . ." (*Democracy, Liberty and Equality* [Oslo: Norwegian University Press, 1986], 235). Reinhold Niebuhr and Paul Sigmund, using the "rise of pluralistic liberal democracy in Europe and the United States" as an instructive experience for the world, argue that one of the conditions of successful democracy is the presence of "a pluralism of interests which is enforced by an equilibrium of economic, social, and political power" (*The Democratic Experience: Past and Prospects* [New York: Praeger, 1969], 125, 173, *passim*).

2. The loss of confidence and its impact have been highlighted in works ranging from Walter Lippmann's *The Public Philosophy* (New York: New American Library, 1955) to Alasdair MacIntyre's *After Virtue* (Notre Dame, Ind.: University of Notre Dame Press, 1981).

3. Calvin O. Schrag, "Liberal Learning in the Postmodern World," *Key Reporter* 54, no. 1 (Autumn 1988): 2. Writing in the same year, Huston Smith finds a "drive towards pluralism" part of the "crisis" in twentieth-century philosophy, a crisis which finds "philosophers in appreciable numbers. . . moving towards closing down their discipline" ("Philosophy, Theology, and the Primordial Claim," *Cross Currents* 38, no. 3 [Fall 1988]: 278–280).

4. Less direct and open than these efforts but nonetheless evident in American society is the residual fear of Catholics as not wholly assimilable and fears with respect to the Asiatic immigration and presence and to the followers of Islam.

5. To draw attention to another level beneath surface differences is not to deny that there is probably a positive relationship between welcoming acceptance and tolerance of surface diversity and a comparable acceptance and tolerance of significant pluralism. What is claimed is that there is no necessary relationship. It seems that one can dabble in the delightful variety of different customs while being insistently uniform regarding life-forming personal and communal values.

6. Dahl treats the contemporary usage of the term "pluralism," which he calls "something of a neologism in political science," against the background of earlier ecclesiastical and philosophical usages. While

acknowledging the common use of "pluralism" as a synonym for "diversity," he chooses to use "pluralism" primarily to describe enduring cleavages in a society which take an organizational form. See p. 233 ff of his *Democracy, Liberty, and Equality*.

7. This understanding and some of what follows on socialization and moral education was first worked out in Walter Nicgorski, "Environment: The Social Dimension of Moral Education," in *Act and Agent*, ed. G. McLean, F. Ellrod, D. Schindler, and J. Mann (Lanham, Md.: University Press of America, 1986), 308–309.

8. This observation is known to me via an oral tradition; it has been attributed to the intellectual historian Carl Becker. Frank Knight did write about his own doubts concerning the capacity of human beings to settle issues by discussion: "Reflection on what actually happens in the simplest cases—say the discussion of presumably scientific problems by two social scientists—is hardly conducive to faith in the possibilities when larger groups and more tangible differences are involved." Later he adds, "In the field of morals and politics—to say nothing of religion—it is questionable whether the net result [of discussion] has been progress toward consensus or the multiplication of controversy" ("Economic Theory and Nationalism," *The Ethics of Competition and Other Essays* [New York: Augustus Kelly, 1935], 304, 353).

9. From the perspective of the front lines, one educator warns of a conception of pluralism "robbed of its ethical connotations" and "wielded as a sledge-hammer to smash any notion of a shared morality, any form of consensus. Divisiveness is all that 'pluralism' is seen to connote." Earlier the author, Madhu Suri Prakash, had commented that the idea of governmental neutrality in matters of morality "translated into curriculum for the schools" produces "a hollow, anesthetized 'education' progressively empty of moral content and an increasing threat to the formation of community-minded individuals" ("Partners in Moral Education: Communities and Their Public Schools," in *Character Development in Schools and Beyond*, ed. K. Ryan and G. McLean [New York: Praeger, 1987], 137, 135).

10. This and all subsequent quotations from *The Federalist* are taken from the Jacob E. Cooke edition (Cleveland: World, 1961).

11. See especially the last paragraphs of papers No. 10 and 51.

12. Popular government over a large territory implied for Madison the rule of the people through representatives rather than their direct rule, republican rather than democratic government. In paper No. 10, Madison not only argues that republican government is entailed in the "principal" solution of an enlarged territory but also that this indirect rule of the people contributes itself to reducing the likelihood of majority faction. Madison offers no solution to the problem of majority faction in direct democracies.

13. Ralph Ketcham, *James Madison: A Biography* (New York: Macmillan, 1971), 166. Relevant to Madison's overall view on pluralism, Ketcham noted that "Madison's experience in finding that religious diversity confounded those inclined to seek privilege or to oppress dissent, helped importantly in forming his more general theory that freedom was safest in

the presence of a multitude of counterbalancing forces, which acted to check the tyrannical impulses of any one of them." Ketcham also, throughout the biography, provided the basis for the inference above about Madison's lack of interest in religious inquiry.

14. Note the contrasting thrust of the thought of John Courtney Murray, S.J., on religious pluralism. He describes religious pluralism as "lamentable" and "against the will of God," but he adds that "it is the human condition; it is written into the script of history." He then counsels that one cherish "only modest expectations with regard to the solution of the problem of religious pluralism and civic unity." The problem is to be met, though with the modest expectations noted, by dissolving "the structure of war that underlies the pluralistic society" and erecting "the more civilized structure of the dialogue" (*We Hold These Truths* [New York: Sheed and Ward, 1960], 74, 23–24).

15. In his closing comments in paper No. 51 Madison is even more sanguine on the effect of increased pluralism: "In the extended republic of the United States, and among the great variety of interests, parties and sects which it embraces, a coalition of a majority of the whole society could seldom take place on any other principles than those of justice and the general good . . . ."

16. Benjamin Franklin in what has been described as "an undated but late sociological musing" reveals that at least at this point he shared the perspective of *The Federalist* which connected liberty and pluralism and sought the procedures to bring light and the public good from them. Franklin writes,

> It is true that in some of our States there are Parties and Discords; but let us look back and ask if we were ever without them? Such will exist wherever there is Liberty; and perhaps they help to preserve it. By the Collision of different Sentiments, Sparks of Truth are struck out, and political Light is obtained. The different Factions, which at present divide us, aim all at the Publick Good; the Differences are only about the various Modes of promoting it. Things, Actions, Measures and Objects of all kinds, present themselves to the Minds of Men in such a Variety of Lights, that it is not possible we should all think alike at the same time on every Subject, when hardly the same Man retains at all times the same Ideas of it. Parties are therefore the common Lot of Humanity . . . .

Franklin does not share the negative denotation of "faction" found in *The Federalist* (Clinton Rossiter, *Six Characters in Search of a Republic* [New York: Harcourt, Brace & World, 1964], 255).

17. Notice how this dimension of Madison and the Federalists is taken by the historian Gordon Wood to make them something less than real pluralists. Wood remarks in a recent essay that "in 1787–1788 it was not the Federalists but the Antifederalists who were the real pluralists and the real prophets of the future of American politics. They not only foresaw but endorsed a government of jarring individuals and interests. Unlike

the Federalists, however, they offered no disinterested umpires, no mechanisms at all for reconciling and harmonizing these clashing selfish interests" ("Interests and Disinterestedness in the Making of the Constitution," in *Beyond Confederation*, ed. R. Beeman, S. Botein, and E. Carter, [Chapel Hill, N.C.: University of North Carolina Press, 1987], 102).

18. This is not to say that they were unaware of the importance of moral virtue and strong religious foundations for the citizenry.

19. John Dewey, *The Public and Its Problems* (New York: Henry Holt, 1927), 207–208.

20. See especially *Democracy and Education* (New York: Macmillan, 1924), 24–27.

21. *Democracy and Education*, 94–95; *The Public and Its Problems*, 70–73, 137.

22. See especially *Democracy and Education*, 99.

IDEOLOGY, EQUALITY,
AND THE NEW RIGHT

Michael W. Apple

We live in a period in which our educational system has become increasingly politicized. The curriculum and the values that underpin it, and that are included and excluded from it, are now being placed under intense ideological scrutiny. The Spencerian question, "What knowledge is of most worth?" has now been replaced with an even more pointed question, "Whose knowledge is of most worth?" That this later question has become so powerful highlights the profoundly political nature of educational policy and practice. This is not simply an abstract issue. It is made strikingly clear in the fact that the curriculum of many school districts throughout the country has been turned into what can best be described as a political football. Conservative groups in particular have attacked the school and, in the process, have had a major impact on educational debate not only in the United States but in other nations as well.

As is evident all around us, there has been a significant shift in public discourse around education. The rapid growth of evangelical schooling,[1] the court cases involving "secular humanist" tendencies in textbooks, the increasing attempts to "raise the standards" of teaching and teachers, and the calls in the literature to return to a core curriculum of a common culture all signify a deep suspicion of what is going on in our classrooms. There are very real fears—usually among right wing groups, but also to be found in official statements coming out of the federal and state governments—that for the past decade things have gotten out of control. In this vision, we are losing control both of our children and of the pace of

39

social and cultural change. We have gone too far in tilting our educational and social policies toward minority groups and women. This is not equality, but reverse discrimination. It goes beyond the bounds of what is acceptable. Not only is the search for a more egalitarian set of policies misplaced, but it fails the test of cost/benefit analysis. It is simply too expensive in practice to work and, as well, gives things to people they have not really earned.

The position is especially evident in quotes from former Secretary of Education William Bennett. In his view, we are finally emerging out of a crisis in which "we neglected and denied much of the best in American education." "For a period, we simply stopped doing the right things [and] allowed an assault on intellectual and moral standards." This assault on the current state of education, which, as I noted above, the conservatives see as being connected with attacks on the family, traditional values, religiosity, patriotism, and our economic well-being, has led schools to fall away from "the principles of our tradition."[2]

Yet, for Bennett, "the people" have now risen up. "The 1980's gave birth to a grass roots movement for educational reform that has generated a renewed commitment to excellence, character, and fundamentals." Because of this, "we have reason for optimism."[3] Why? Because:

> The national debate on education is now focused on truly important matters: mastering the basics, . . . insisting on high standards and expectations; ensuring discipline in the classroom; conveying a grasp of our moral and political principles; and nurturing the character of our young.

In essence, our educational system has become too committed to a problematic vision of equality. In the process, "our" standards, the cultural and intellectual values of the "Western tradition," our very greatness as a nation—and the "moral fiber" upon which it rests—are at risk. Just as much at risk is our economic stability and our ability to compete internationally in the global market. All of these points are part of a contradictory bundle of assertions, yet all are having real effects on education and on the language and conceptual apparatus we employ to think about its role in society.

Concepts do not remain still very long. They have wings, so to speak, and can be induced to fly from place to place. It is this context that defines their meaning. As Wittgenstein so nicely reminded us, one should look for the meaning of language in its specific contextual use. This is especially important in understanding political and educational concepts, since they are part of a larger social context, a context that is constantly shifting and is subject to severe ideological conflicts. Education itself is an arena in which these ideological conflicts work themselves out. It is one of the major sites in which different groups with distinct political, economic, and cultural visions attempt to define what the socially legitimate means and ends of a society are to be.

In this essay, I want to situate the concern with "equality" in education within these larger conflicts. I shall place its shifting meanings both within the breakdown of the largely liberal consensus that guided much educational and social policy since World War II and within the growth of the New Right and conservative movements over the past two decades that have had a good deal of success in redefining what education is *for* and in shifting the ideological texture of the society profoundly to the right.[5] In the process, I want to document how new social movements gain the ability to redefine—often, though not always, in retrogressive ways—the terms of debate in education, social welfare, and other areas of the common good. At root, my claim will be that it is impossible fully to comprehend the value conflicts underlying so much of the debate in education and the shifting fortunes of the assemblage of concepts surrounding equality (equality of opportunity, equity, etc.) unless we have a much clearer picture of the society's already unequal cultural, economic, and political dynamics that provide the center of gravity around which education functions.

Between Property Rights and Person Rights

As I have argued at considerably greater length elsewhere, what we are witnessing today is nothing less than the recurrent conflict between *property rights* and *person rights* that has been a central tension in our economy.[6] Gintis defines the differences between property rights and person rights in the following way.

> A *property right* vests in individuals the power to enter into social relationships on the basis and extent of their property. This may include economic rights of unrestricted use, free contract, and voluntary exchange; political rights of participation and influence; and cultural rights of access to the social means for the transmission of knowledge and the reproduction and transformation of consciousness. A *person right* vests in individuals the power to enter into these social relationships on the basis of simple membership in the social collectivity. Thus, person rights involve equal treatment of citizens, freedom of expression and movement, equal access to participation in decision-making in social institutions, and reciprocity in relations of power and authority.[7]

The attempts to enhance person rights partly rest on a notion of what is best thought of as positive liberty, "freedom to" as well as "freedom from." In industrial nations, this has grown stronger over the years as many previously disenfranchised groups of women and men demanded suffrage. The right to equal political participation would be based on being a person rather than on ownership of property (or later on being a white male). Further, person rights have been extended to include the right of paid workers to form unions, to organize a common front against their employers. At the same time, claims about the right to have a job with dignity and decent pay have been advanced. And, finally, there have been demands that economic transactions—from equal treatment of women and people of color in employment, pay, and benefits to health and safety for everyone—are to be governed by rules of due process and fairness, thereby restricting management powers of unrestricted use and "free contract."[8]

This last point is important since it documents a growing tendency to take ideas of civil equality and apply them to the economic sphere. Thus, "the right to equal treatment in economic relationships, which directly expresses the dominance of person over property rights, has been an explicit demand of women, racial minorities, immigrant workers, and others."[9]

This, too, has been accompanied by further gains in which the positive rights of suffrage and association that have been won by women and by minority and working class groups have been extended to include what increasingly became seen as a set of minimum rights due any individual simply by the fact of citizenship. These included state-supported services in the areas of health, education, and social security, consumer protection laws, lifeline utility guarantees, and occupational safety and health regulations. In their most progressive moments, these tendencies led to arguments for full workplace democracy, democratic control over investment decisions, and the extension of the norms of reciprocity and mutual participation and control in most areas of social life from the paid workplace and the political life of local communities and schools to the home.[10] Taken together, these movements did constitute at least a partial restructuring of the balance between person rights and property rights, one that would soon be challenged by powerful groups.

It is not surprising that in our society dominant groups "have fairly consistently defended the prerogatives of property," while subordinate groups on the whole have sought to advance "the prerogatives of persons."[11] In times of severe upheaval, these conflicts become even more intense and, given the current balance of power in society, advocates of property rights have once again been able to advance their claims for the restoration and expansion of their prerogatives not only in education but in all of our social institutions.

The United States economy is in the midst of one of the most powerful structural crises it has experienced since the Depression. In order to solve it on terms acceptable to dominant interests, as many aspects of the society as possible need to be pressured into conforming with the requirements of international competition, reindustrialization, and (in the words of the National Commission on Excellence in Education) "rearmament." The gains made by women and men in employment, health and safety, welfare programs, affirmative action, legal rights, and education must be rescinded since "they are too expensive" both economically and ideologically.

Both of these latter words are important. Not only are fiscal resources scarce (in part because current policies transfer them to the military), but people must be convinced that their belief that person rights come first is simply wrong or outmoded given current "realities." Thus, intense pressure must be brought to bear through legislation, persuasion, administrative rules, and ideological maneuvering to create the conditions right wing groups believe are necessary to meet these requirements.[12]

In the process, not just in the United States, but in Britain and Australia as well, the emphasis of public policy has materially changed from issues of employing the state to overcome disadvantage. Equality, no matter how limited or broadly conceived, has become redefined. No longer is it seen as linked to past *group* oppression and disadvantagement, it is simply now a case of guaranteeing *individual choice* under the conditions of a "free market."[13] Thus, the current emphasis on "excellence" (a word with multiple meanings and social uses) has shifted educational discourse so that underachievement is once again increasingly seen as largely the fault of the student. Student failure, which was at least partly interpreted as the fault of severely deficient educational policies and practices, is now being seen as the result of what might be called the biological and economic marketplace. This is evidenced in the growth of forms of Social Darwinist thinking in education and in public policy in general.[14] In a similar way, behind a good deal of the rhetorical artifice of concern about the achievement levels in, say, inner city schools, notions of choice have begun to evolve in which deep-seated school problems will be solved by establishing free competition over students. These assume that by expanding the capitalist marketplace to schools, we will somehow compensate for the decades of economic and educational neglect experienced by the communities in which these schools are found.[15] Finally, there are concerted attacks on teachers (and curricula) based on a profound mistrust of their quality and commitments.

All of this has led to an array of educational conflicts that have been instrumental in shifting the debates over education profoundly to the right. The effects of this shift can be seen in a number of educational policies and proposals now gaining momentum throughout the country: (1) proposals for voucher plans and tax credits to make schools more like the idealized free market economy; (2) the movement in state legislatures and state departments of education to "raise standards" and mandate both teacher and student "competencies" and basic curricular goals and knowledge, thereby centralizing even more at a state level the control of teaching and curricula; (3) the increasingly effective assaults on the school curriculum for its supposedly anti-family and anti-free enterprise bias, its "secular humanism," its lack of patriotism, and its neglect of the "Western tradition"; and (4) the growing pressure to make the needs of business and industry into the primary goals of the educational system.[16] These are major alterations, ones that have taken years to show their effects. Though I shall paint in rather broad strokes here, an outline of the social and ideological dynamics of how this has occurred should be visible.

The Restoration Politics of Authoritarian Populism

The first thing to ask about an ideology is not what is false about it, but what is true. What are its connections to lived experience? Ideologies, properly conceived, do not dupe people. To be effective they must connect to real problems, real experiences.[17] As I shall document, the movement away from social democratic principles and an acceptance of more right wing positions in social and educational policy occur precisely because conservative groups have been able to work on popular sentiments, to reorganize genuine feelings, and in the process to win adherents.

Important ideological shifts take place not only by powerful groups "substituting one, whole, new conception of the world for another." Often, these shifts occur through the presentation of novel combinations of old and new elements.[18] Let us take the positions of the Reagan administration, ones which will by and large provide the framework for the Bush administration's policies as well, as a case in point, for as Clark and Astuto have demonstrated in education and Piven and Cloward and Raskin have shown in the larger areas of social policy, significant and enduring alterations have occurred in the ways policies are carried out and in the content of those policies.[19]

The success of the policies of the Reagan administration, like that of Thatcherism in Britain, should not simply be evaluated in electoral terms. They need to be judged by their success as well in disorganizing other more progressive groups, in shifting the terms of political, economic, and cultural debate onto the terrain favored by capital and the right.[20] In these terms, there can be no doubt that the current right wing resurgence has accomplished no small amount in its attempt to construct the conditions that will put it in a hegemonic position.

The right in the United States and Britain has thoroughly renovated and reformed itself. It has developed strategies based upon what might best be called an *authoritarian populism*.[21] As Hall has defined this, such a policy is based on an increasingly close relationship between government and the capitalist economy, a radical decline in the institutions and power of political democracy, and attempts at curtailing "liberties" that have been gained in the past. This is coupled with attempts to build a consensus, one that is widespread, in support of these actions.[22] The New Right's "authoritarian populism"[23] has exceptionally long roots in the history of the United States. The political culture here has always been influenced by the values of the dissenting Protestantism of the seventeenth century. Such roots become even more evident in periods of intense social change and crisis.[24] As Burnham has put it:

> Whenever and wherever the pressures of "modernization"—secularity, urbanization, the growing importance of science—have become unusually intense, episodes of revivalism and culture-issue politics have swept over the social landscape. In all such cases since at least the end of the Civil War, such movements have been more or less explicitly reactionary, and have frequently been linked with other kinds of reaction in explicitly political ways.[25]

The New Right works on these roots in creative ways, modernizing them and creating a new synthesis of their varied elements by linking them to current fears. In so doing, the right has been able to rearticulate traditional political and cultural themes and because of this has effectively mobilized a large amount of mass support.

As I noted, part of the strategy has been the attempted dismantling of the welfare state and of the benefits that working people, people of color, and women (these categories are obviously not mutually exclusive) have won over decades of hard work. This has been done under the guise of anti-statism, of keeping government "off the backs of the people," and of "free enterprise." Yet, at the same time, in many valuative, political, and economic areas the current government is extremely state-centrist both in its outlook and, very importantly, in its day-to-day operations.[26]

One of the major aims of a rightist restoration politics is to struggle in not one but many different arenas at the same time, not only in the economic sphere but in education and elsewhere as well. This aim is grounded in the realization that economic dominance must be coupled to "political, moral, and intellectual leadership" if a group is to be truly dominant and if it wants to genuinely restructure a social formation. Thus, as both Reaganism and Thatcherism recognized so clearly, to win in the state you must also win in civil society.[27] As the noted Italian political theorist Antonio Gramsci would put it, what we are seeing is a war of position. "It takes place where the whole relation of the state to civil society, to 'the people' and to popular struggles, to the individual and to the economic life of society has been thoroughly reorganized, where 'all the elements change'."[28]

In this restructuring, Reaganism and Thatcherism did not create some sort of false consciousness, creating ways of seeing that had little connection with reality. Rather, they "operated directly on the real and manifestly contradictory experiences" of a large portion of the population. They did connect with the perceived needs, fears, and hopes of groups of people who felt threatened by the range of problems associated with the crises in authority relations, in the economy, and in politics.[29]

What has been accomplished has been a successful translation of an economic doctrine into the language of experience, moral imperative, and common sense. The free market ethic has been combined with a populist politics. This has meant the blending together of a "rich mix" of themes that have had a long history—nation, family, duty, authority, standards, and traditionalism—with other thematic elements that have also struck a resonant chord during a time of crisis. These latter themes include self-interest, competitive individualism (what I have elsewhere called the possessive individual),[30] and antistatism. In this way, a reactionary common sense is partly created.[31]

The sphere of education has been one of the most successful areas in which the right has been ascendant. The social democratic goal of expanding equality of opportunity (itself a rather limited reform) has lost much of its political potency and its ability to mobilize people. The "panic" over falling standards and illiteracy, the fears of violence in schools, the concern with the destruction of family values and religiosity, all have had an effect. These fears are exacerbated, and used, by dominant groups within politics and the economy who have been able to move the debate on education (and all things social) onto their own terrain, the terrain of traditionalism, standardization, productivity and industrial needs.[32] Since so many parents *are* justifiably concerned about the economic futures of their children—in an economy that is increasingly conditioned by lowered wages, unemployment, capital flight, and insecurity[33]—rightist discourse connects with the experiences of many working class and lower middle class people.

However, while this conservative conceptual and ideological apparatus does appear to be rapidly gaining ground, one of the most critical issues remains to be answered. How *is* such an ideological vision legitimated and accepted? How was this done?[34]

Understanding the Crisis

The right wing resurgence is not simply a reflection of the current crisis; rather, it is itself a response to that crisis.[35] Beginning in the immediate post–World War II years, the political culture of the United States was increasingly characterized by American imperial might, economic affluence, and cultural optimism. This period lasted for more than two decades. Socially and politically, it was a time of what has been called the *social democratic accord*, in which government increasingly became an arena for a focus on the conditions required for equality of opportunity. Commodity-driven prosperity, the extension of rights and liberties to new groups, and the expansion of welfare provisions provided the conditions for this compromise both between capital and labor and with historically more dispossessed groups such as blacks and women. This accord has become mired in crisis since the late 1960s and early 1970s.[36]

Allen Hunter gives an excellent sense of this in his own description of this accord.

> From the end of World War II until the early 1970s world capitalism experienced the longest period of sustained economic growth in its history. In the United States a new "social structure of accumulation"—"the specific institutional environment within which the capitalist accumulation process is organized"—was articulated around several prominent features: the broadly shared goal of sustained economic growth, Keynesianism, elite pluralist democracy, an imperial America prosecuting a cold war, anti-communism at home and abroad, stability or incremental change in race relations and a stable home life in a buoyant, commodity-driven consumer culture. Together these crystallized a basic consensus and a set of social and political institutions which was hegemonic for two decades.[37]

At the very center of this hegemonic accord was a compromise reached between capital and labor in which labor accepted what might be called "the logic of profitability and markets as the guiding principles of resource allocation." In return they received "an assurance that minimal living standards, trade union rights and liberal democratic rights would be protected."[38] These democratic rights were further extended to the poor, women, and people of color as these groups expanded their own struggles to overcome racially and sexually discriminatory practices.[39] Yet, this extension of (limited) rights could not last, given the economic and ideological crises that soon beset American society, a set of crises that challenged the very core of the social democratic accord.

The dislocations of the 1960s and 1970s—the struggle for racial and sexual equality, military adventures such as

Vietnam, Watergate, the resilience of the economic crisis—produced both shock and fear. "Mainstream culture" was shaken to its very roots in many ways. Widely shared notions of family, community, and nation were dramatically altered. Just as importantly, no new principle of cohesion emerged that was sufficiently compelling to recreate a cultural center. As economic, political, and valuative stability (and military supremacy) seemed to disappear, the polity was itself "balkanized." Social movements based on difference—regional, racial, sexual, religious—became more visible.[40] The sense of what Marcus Raskin has called "the common good" was fractured.[41]

Traditional social democratic "statist" solutions which in education, welfare, health and other similar areas took the form of large scale attempts at federal intervention to increase opportunities or to provide a minimal level of support were seen as being part of the problem, not as part of the solution. Traditional conservative positions were more easily dismissed as well. After all, the society on which they were based was clearly being altered. The cultural center could be *built* (and it had to be built by well-funded and well-organized political and cultural action) around the principles of the new right. The New Right confronts the "moral, existential, [and economic] chaos of the preceding decades" with a network of exceedingly well-organized and financially secure organizations incorporating "an aggressive political style, on outspoken religious and cultural traditionalism and a clear populist commitment."[42]

In different words, the project was aimed at constructing a "new majority" that would "dismantle the welfare state, legislate a return to traditional morality, and stem the tide of political and cultural dislocation which the 1960's and 1970's represented." Using a populist political strategy (now in combination with an aggressive executive branch of the government), it marshalled an assault on "liberalism and secular humanism" and linked that assault to what some observers have argued was "an obsession with individual guilt and responsibility which social questions are concerned (crime, sex, education, poverty)" with strong beliefs against government intervention.[43]

The class, racial, and sexual specificities here are significant. The movement to create a conservative cultural consensus in part builds on the hostilities of the working and lower middle classes toward those above and below them and is fueled as well by a very real sense of antagonism against the new middle class. State bureaucrats and administrators, educators, journalists, planners, and so on, all share part of the blame for the social dislocations these groups have experienced.[44] Race, gender, and class themes abound here, a point to which I shall return in the next section of my analysis.

This movement is, of course, enhanced within academic and government circles by a group of policy-oriented neo-conservatives who have become the organic intellectuals for much of the rightist resurgence. A society based on individualism, market-based opportunities, and the drastic reduction of both state intervention and state support, these currents run deep in their work.[45] They provide a counterpart of the New Right and are themselves part of the inherently unstable alliance that has been formed.

Building the New Accord

Almost all of the reform-minded social movements—including the feminist, gay and lesbian, student and other movements of the 1960s—drew upon the struggle by blacks "as a central organizational fact or as a defining political metaphor and inspiration."[46] These social movements infused new social meanings into politics, economics, and culture. These are not separate spheres. All three of these levels exist simultaneously. New social meanings about the importance of person rights infused individual identity, family, and community, and penetrated state institutions and market relationships. These emerging social movements expanded the concerns of politics to all aspects of the "terrain of everyday life." Person rights took on ever more importance in nearly all of our institutions, as evidenced in aggressive affirmative action programs, widespread welfare and educational activist programs, and so on.[47] In education this was very clear in the growth of bilingual programs and in the development of women's, black, Hispanic, and Native American studies in high schools and colleges.

There are a number of reasons the state was the chief target of these earlier social movements for gaining person rights. First, the state was the "factor of cohesion in society" and had historically maintained and organized practices and policies that embodied the tension between property rights and person rights.[48] As such a factor of cohesion, it was natural to focus on it. Second, "the state was traversed by the same antagonisms which penetrated the larger society, antagonisms that were themselves the results of past cycles of [social] struggle." Openings in the state could be gained because of this. Footholds in state institutions dealing with education and social services could be deepened.[49]

Yet even with these gains, the earlier coalitions began to disintegrate. In the minority communities, class polarization deepened. The majority of barrio and ghetto residents "remained locked in poverty," while a relatively small portion of the black and brown population were able to take advantage of educational opportunities and new jobs (the latter being largely within the state itself).[50] With the emerging crisis in the economy, something of a zero-sum game developed in which progressive social movements had to fight over a limited share of resources and power. Antagonistic rather than complementary relationships developed among groups. Minority groups, for example, and the largely white and middle class women's movement had difficulty integrating their programs, goals, and strategies.

This was exacerbated by the fact that, unfortunately, given the construction of a zero-sum game by dominant groups, the gains made by women sometimes came at the expense of blacks and browns. Furthermore, leaders of many of these movements had been absorbed into state-sponsored programs which—while the adoption of such programs *was* in part a victory—had the latent effect of cutting off leaders from their grassroots constituency and lessened the militancy at this level. This often resulted in what has been called the "ghettoization" of movements within state institutions as movement demands were partly adopted in their most moderate forms into programs sponsored by the state. Militancy is transformed into constituency.[51]

The splits in these movements occurred as well because of strategic divisions, divisions that were paradoxically the results of the movements' own successes. Thus, for example, those women who aimed their work within existing political/economic channels *could* point to gains in employment within the state and in the economic sphere. Other, more radical, members saw such "progress" as "too little, too late."[52]

Nowhere is this more apparent than in the African-American movement in the United States. It is worth quoting one of the best analyses of the history of these divisions at length.

> The movement's limits also arose from the strategic divisions that befell it as a result of its own success. Here the black movement's fate is illustrative. Only in the South, while fighting against a backward political structure and overt cultural oppression, had the black movement been able to maintain a *de*-centered unity, even when internal debates were fierce. Once it moved north, the black movement began to split, because competing political projects, linked to different segments of the community, sought either integration in the (reformed) mainstream, or more radical transformation of the dominant racial order.
>
> After initial victories against segregation were won, one sector of the movement was thus reconstituted as an interest-group, seeking an end to racism understood as discrimination and prejudice, and turning its back on the oppositional "politics of identity." Once the organized black movement because a mere constituency, though, it found itself locked in a bear hug with the state institutions whose programs it had itself demanded, while simultaneously isolated from the core institutions of the modern state.[53]

In the process, those sectors of the movement that were the most radical were marginalized or, and this must not be forgotten, were simply repressed by the state.[54]

Even though there were major gains, the movements' integration into the state latently created conditions that were disastrous in the fight for equality. A mass-based militant grassroots movement was defused into a constituency, dependent on the state itself. *And very importantly, when the neoconservative and right wing movements evolved with their decidedly anti-statist themes, the gains that were made in the state came increasingly under attack and the ability to recreate a large scale grassroots movement to defend these gains was weakened considerably.*[55] Thus, when there are right wing attacks on the more progressive national and local educational policies and practices that have benefitted people of color, it becomes increasingly difficult to develop broad based coalitions to counter these offensives.

In their failure to consolidate a new "radical" democratic politics, one with majoritarian aspirations, the new social movements of the 1960s and 1970s "provided the political space in which right wing reaction could incubate and develop its political agenda."[56] Thus, state reforms won by, say, minority movements in the 1960s in the United States, and the new definitions of person rights embodied in these reforms, "provided a formidable range of targets for the 'counter-reformers' of the 1970s." Neoconservatives and the New Right carried on their own political "project." They were able to rearticulate particular ideological themes and to restructure them around a political movement once again.[57] And these themes *were* linked to the dreams, hopes, and fears of many individuals.

Let us examine this in somewhat more detail. Behind the conservative restoration is a clear sense of loss: of control, of economic and personal security, of the knowledge and values that should be passed on to children, of visions of what counts as sacred texts and authority. The binary opposition of we-they becomes very important here. "We" are law abiding, "hard working, decent, virtuous and homogeneous." The "theys" are very different. They are "lazy, immoral, permissive, heterogenous."[58] These binary oppositions distance most people of color, women, gays, and others from the community of worthy individuals. The subjects of discrimination are now no longer those groups who have been historically oppressed, but are instead the "real Americans" who embody the idealized virtues of a romanticized past. The "theys" are undeserving. They are getting something for nothing. Policies supporting them are "sapping our way of life," most of our economic resources, and creating government control of our lives.[59]

These processes of ideological distancing make it possible for anti-black and anti-feminist sentiments to seem no longer racist and sexist because they link so closely with other issues. Once again, Allen Hunter is helpful.

> Racial rhetoric links with anti-welfare state sentiments, fits with the push for economic individualism; thus many voters who say they are not prejudiced (and may not be by some accounts) oppose welfare spending as unjust. Anti-feminist rhetoric . . . is articulated around defense of the family, traditional morality, and religious fundamentalism.[60]

All of these elements can be integrated through the formation of ideological coalitions that enable many Americans who themselves feel under threat to turn against groups of people who are even less powerful than themselves. At the very same time, it enables them to "attack domination by liberal, statist elites."[61]

This ability to identify a range of "others" as enemies, as the source of the problems, is very significant. One of the major elements in this ideological formation has indeed been a belief that liberal elites within the state "were intruding themselves into home life, trying to impose their values." This was having serious negative effects on moral values and on traditional families. Much of the conservative criticism of textbooks and curricula rests on these feelings, for example. While this position certainly exaggerated the impact of the "liberal elite," and while it certainly misrecognized the power of capital and of other dominant classes,[62] there was enough of an element of truth in it for the right to use it in its attempts to dismantle the previous accord and build its own.

A new hegemonic accord is reached, then. It combines dominant economic and political elites intent on "modernizing" the economy, white working class and middle class groups concerned with security, the family, and traditional knowledge and values, and economic conservatives.[63] It also includes a fraction of the new middle class whose own advancement depends on the expanded use of accountability, efficiency, and management procedures which are their own cultural capital.[64] This coalition has partly succeeded in altering the very meaning of what it is to have a social goal of equality. The citizen as "free" consumer has replaced the previously emerging citizen as situated in structurally generated relations of domination. Thus, the common good is now to be regulated exclusively by the laws of the market, free competition, private ownership, and profitability. In essence, the definitions of freedom and equality are no longer democratic, but *commercial*.[65] This is particularly evident in the proposals for voucher plans as "solutions" to massive and historically rooted relations of economic and cultural inequality.

Will the Right Succeed?

So far I have broadly traced out many of the political, economic, and ideological reasons that the social democratic consensus that led to the limited extension of person rights in education, politics, and the economy slowly disintegrated. At the same time, I have documented how a new "hegemonic bloc" is being formed, coalescing around New Right tactics and principles. The question remains: Will this accord be long lasting? Will it be able to inscribe its principles into the very heart of the American polity?

There are very real obstacles to the total consolidation within the state of the New Right political agenda. First, there has been something of a "great transformation" in, say, racial identities. Omi and Winant describe it thusly:

> The forging of new collective racial identities during the 1950s and 1960s has been the enduring legacy of the racial minority movements. Today, as gains won in the past are rolled back and most organizations prove unable to rally a mass constituency in racial minority communities, the persistence of the new racial identities developed during this period stands out as the single truly formidable obstacle to the consolidation of a newly repressive racial order.[66]

Thus, even when social movements and political coalitions are fractured, when their leaders are coopted, repressed, and sometimes killed, the racial subjectivity and self-awareness that were developed by these movement have taken permanent hold. "No amount of repression or cooptation [can] change that."[67] In Omi and Winant's words, the genie is out of the bottle.[68] This is the case because, in essence, a new kind of person has been created within minority communities.[69] A new, and much more self-conscious, *collective* identity has been forged. Thus, for instance, in the struggles over the past three decades by people of color to have more control of education and to have it respond more directly to their own culture and collective histories, these people themselves were transformed in major ways.[70] Thus:

> Social movements create collective identity by offering their adherents a different view of themselves and their world; different, that is, from the world view and self-concepts offered by the established social order. They do this by the process of *rearticulation*, which produces new subjectivity by making use of information and knowledge already present in the subject's mind. They take elements and themes of her/his culture and traditions and infuse them with new meaning.[71]

These meanings will make it exceedingly difficult for the right to incorporate the perspectives of people of color under its ideological umbrella and will continually create oppositional tendencies within the black and brown communities. The slow, but steady, growth in the power of people of color at a local level in these communities will serve as a countervailing force to the solidification of the new conservative accord.

Added to this is the fact that even within the new hegemonic bloc, even within the conservative restoration coalition, there are ideological strains that may have serious repercussions on its ability to be dominant for an extended period. These tensions are partly generated because of the class dynamics within the coalition. Fragile compromises may come apart because of the sometimes directly contradictory beliefs held by many of the partners in the new accord.

This can be seen in the example of two of the groups now involved in supporting the accord. There are both what can be called "residual" and "emergent" ideological systems or codes at work here. The residual culture and ideologies of the old middle class and of an upwardly mobile portion of the working class and lower middle class—stressing control, individual achievement, "morality," etc.—has been merged with the emergent code of a portion of the new middle class—getting ahead, technique, efficiency, bureaucratic advancement, and so on.[72]

These codes are in an inherently unstable relationship. The stress on New Right morality does not necessarily sit well with an amoral emphasis on careerism and economic norms. The merging of these codes can only last as long as paths to mobility are not blocked. The economy must pay off in jobs and mobility for the new middle class or the coalition is threatened. There is no guarantee, given the unstable nature of the economy and the kinds of jobs being created, that this pay off will occur.[73]

This tension can be seen in another way which shows again that, in the long run, the prospects for such a lasting ideological coalition are not necessarily good. Under the new, more conservative accord, the conditions for capital accumulation and profit must be enhanced by state activity as much as possible. Thus, the "free market" must be set loose. As many areas of public and private life as possible need to be brought into line with such privatized market principles, including the schools, health care, welfare, housing, and so on. Yet, in order to create profit, capitalism by and large also requires that traditional values are subverted. Commodity purchasing and market relations become the norms and older values of community, "sacred knowledge," and morality will need to be cast aside. This dynamic sets in motion the seeds of possible conflicts in the future between the economic modernizers and the New Right cultural traditionalists who make up a significant part of the coalition that has been built.[74] Furthermore, the competitive individualism now being so heavily promoted in educational reform movements in the United States may not respond well to traditional working class and poor groups' somewhat more collective senses.

Finally, there are counter-hegemonic movements now being built within education itself. The older social democratic accord included many educators, union leaders, minority group members, and others. There are signs that the fracturing of this coalition may only be temporary. Take teachers, for instance. Even though salaries have been on the rise throughout the country, this has been countered by a rapid increase in the external control of teachers' work, the rationalization and deskilling of their jobs, and the growing blame of teachers and education in general for most of the major social ills that beset the economy.[75] Many teachers have organized around these issues, in a manner reminiscent of the earlier work of the Boston Women's Teachers' Group.[76] Furthermore, there are signs throughout the country of multi-racial coalitions being built among elementary and secondary school teachers, university-based educators, and community members to act collectively on the conditions under which teachers work and to support the democratization of curriculum and teaching and a rededication to the equalization of access and outcomes in schooling. The Southern Coalition for Educational Equity and the Rethinking Schools group based in Milwaukee provide but two of these examples.[77]

Even given these emerging tensions within the conservative restoration and the increase once again of alliances to counter its attempted reconstruction of the politics and ethics of the common good, this does not mean we should be at all sanguine. It is possible that, because of these tensions and counter-movements, the right's economic program will fail. Yet its ultimate success may be in shifting the balance of class forces considerably to the right and in changing the very ways we consider the common good.[78] Privatization, profit, and greed may still substitute for any serious collective commitment.

We are, in fact, in danger both of forgetting the decades of hard work it took to put even a limited vision of equality on the social and educational agenda and of forgetting the reality of the oppressive conditions that exist for so many of our fellow Americans. The task of keeping alive in the minds of the people the collective memory of the struggle for equality, for person rights in *all* of the institutions of our society, is one of the most significant tasks educators can perform. In a time of conservative restoration, we cannot afford to ignore this task. This requires renewed attention to important curricular questions. Whose knowledge is taught? Why is it taught in this particular way to this particular group? How do we enable the histories and cultures of the majority of working people, of women, of people of color (again, these groups are obviously not mutually exclusive) to be taught in responsible and responsive ways in schools? Given the fact that the collective memory that *now* is preserved in our educational institutions is more heavily influenced by dominant groups in society,[79] the continuing efforts to promote more democratic curricula and teaching are more important now than ever.

These efforts need to be done in concert with other more political movements that wish to extend the substance of democracy in all of our institutions. Action in education is made that much more powerful, and more likely to succeed, if it is organically connected to democratic social movements in the larger society.[80] Yet, while action on the curricula and teaching that dominate our schools may not be sufficient, it is clearly necessary. It should be clear that the movement toward an authoritarian populism will become even more legitimate if the values embodied in the conservative restoration are the only ones made available in our public institutions. Building the widespread recognition that there were, are, and can be more equal modes of economic, political, and cultural life can only be accomplished by organized efforts to teach and expand this sense of difference. Clearly, there is educational work to be done.

Notes

A briefer presentation of my arguments here appears in *Teachers College Record* 90, no. 2 (1988).

1. See the excellent discussion in Susan Rose, *Keeping Them Out of the Hands of Satan: Evangelical Schooling in America* (New York: Routledge, 1988).

2. William J. Bennett, *Our Children and Our Country* (New York: Routledge, 1988).

3. Ibid., 10.

4. Ibid.

5. See Michael W. Apple, *Teachers and Texts: A Political Economy of Class and Gender Relations in Education* (New York: Routledge and Kegan Paul, 1986) and Henry Giroux, "Public Philosophy and the Crisis in Education," *Harvard Educational Review* 54 (May 1984): 186–194.

6. Michael W. Apple. *Education and Power*, rev. ARK ed. (New York: Routledge and Kegan Paul, 1985) and Apple, *Teachers and Texts*.

7. Herbert Gintis, "Communication and Politics," *Socialist Review* 10 (March-June 1980): 193.

8. Ibid., 196.

9. Ibid., 197.

10. Ibid.

11. Ibid., 194. See also Samuel Bowles and Herbert Gintis, *Democracy and Capitalism* (New York: Basic Books, 1986).

12. Apple, *Teachers and Texts*.

13. Mary Anderson, "Teachers, Unions, and Industrial Politics," unpublished doctoral dissertation, School of Behavioral Science, Macquarie University, Sydney, Australia, 1985, 6–8.

14. Ann Bastian, Norm Fruchter, Marilyn Gittell, Golin Greer, and Kenneth Haskins, *Choosing Equality: The Case for Democratic Schooling* (Philadelphia: Temple University Press, 1986), 14.

15. I wish to thank my colleague Walter Secada for this point.

16. Michael W. Apple, "National Reports and the Construction of Inequality," *British Journal of Sociology of Education* 7, no. 2 (1986): 171–190.

17. See Michael W. Apple. *Ideology and Curriculum*, 2nd rev. ed. (New York: Routledge, 1990) and Jorge Larrain, *Marxism and Ideology* (Atlantic Highlands, N.J.: Humanities Press, 1983).

18. Stuart Hall, "Authoritarian Populism: A Reply," *New Left Review* 151 (May-June 1985): 122.

19. David Clark and Terry Astuto, "The Significance and Permanence of Changes in Federal Education Policy," *Educational Researcher* 15 (October 1986): 4–13; Frances Pivan and Richard Cloward, *The New Class War* (New York: Pantheon, 1982); and Marcus Raskin, *The Common Good* (New York: Routledge and Kegan Paul, 1986). Clark and Astuto point out that during Reagan's terms the following initiatives characterized educational policies: reducing the federal role in education, stimulating competition among schools with the aim of "breaking the monopoly of the public school," fostering individual competition so that "excellence" is gained, increasing the reliance on performance standards for students and teachers, an emphasis on the "basics" in content, increasing parental choice "over what, where, and how their children learn," strengthening the teaching of "traditional values" in schools, and expanding the policy of transferring educational authority to the state and local levels (p. 8).

20. Stuart Hall and Martin Jacques, "Introduction," *The Politics of Thatcherism* (London: Lawrence and Wishart, 1983), 13.

21. Stuart Hall, "Popular Democratic vs. Authoritarian Populism: Two Ways of Taking Democracy Seriously," in *Marxism and Democracy*, ed. Alan Hunt (London: Lawrence and Wishart, 1980), 160–161.

22. Ibid., 161.

23. I realize that there is debate over the adequacy of this term. See Hall, "Authoritarian Populism: A Reply" and B. Jessop, K. Bennett,

S. Bomley and T. Ling, "Authoritarian Populism, Two Nations, and Thatcherism," *New Left Review* 147 (1984): 33–60. Authoritarian populism is, of course, a term that denotes a central tendency of a broad and varied movement, as I shall show later on in my discussion.

24. Michael Omi and Howard Winant, *Racial Formation in the United States* (New York: Routledge and Kegan Paul, 1986), 214.

25. Walter Dean Burnham, "Post-conservative America," *Socialist Review* 13 (November-December 1983): 125.

26. Hall, "Authoritarian Populism: A Reply," 117.

27. Ibid., 112.

28. Hall, "Popular Democratic vs. Authoritarian Populism," 166.

29. Stuart Hall, "The Great Moving Right Show," in *The Politics of Thatcherism*, ed. Stuart Hall and Martin Jacques (London: Lawrence and Wishart, 1983).

30. Apple, *Education and Power*.

31. Hall, "The Great Moving Right Show," 29–30.

32. Ibid., 36–37. For an illuminating picture of how these issues are manipulated by powerful groups, see Allen Hunter, "Virtue With a Vengeance: The Pro-Family Politics of the New Right," unpublished doctoral dissertation, Department of Sociology, Brandeis University, Waltham, 1984.

33. See Apple, *Teachers and Texts*.

34. Jessop, Bonnett, Bomley, and Ling, "Authoritarian Populism, Two Nations, and Thatcherism," 49.

35. Hall, "The Great Moving Right Show," 21.

36. Allen Hunter, "The Politics of Resentment and the Construction of Middle America," unpublished paper, American Institutions Program, University of Wisconsin, Madison, 1987, 1–3.

37. Ibid., 9.

38. Samuel Bowles, "The Post-Keynesian Capital Labor Stalemate," *Socialist Review* 12 (September-October 1982): 51.

39. Hunter, "The Politics of Resentment and the Construction of Middle America," 12.

40. Omi and Winant, *Racial Formation in the United States*, 214–215.

41. Raskin, *The Common Good*.

42. Omi and Winant, *Racial Formation in the United States*, 215–216. See also Hunter, "Virtue With a Vengeance."

43. Omi and Winant, *Racial Formation in the United States*, 220. For a more complete discussion of how this has affected educational policy in particular, see Clark and Astuto, "The Significance and Permanence of Changes in Federal Education Policy" and Apple, *Teachers and Texts*.

44. Omi and Winant, *Racial Formation in the United States*, 221. I have elsewhere claimed, and shall point out later, however, that some members of the new middle class—namely efficiency experts, evaluators and testers, and many of those with technical and management expertise—will form part of the alliance with the New Right. This is simply because their own jobs and mobility depend on it. See Apple, *Teachers and Texts*.

45. Omi and Winant, *Racial Formation in the United States*, 227.

46. Ibid, 164.

47. Ibid. See also Samuel Bowles and Herbert Gintis, *Democracy and Capitalism* (New York: Basic Books, 1986). The discussion in Bowles and Gintis of the "transportability" of struggles over person rights from, say, politics to the economy is very useful here. I have extended and criticized some of their claims in Michael W. Apple, "Facing the Complexity of Power: For a Parallelist Position in Critical Educational Studies," in *Rethinking Bowles and Gintis*, ed. Mike Cole (Philadelphia: Falmer Press, 1988).

48. See Apple, *Education and Power* and Apple, *Teachers and Texts*.

49. Omi and Winant, *Racial Formation in the United States*, 177–178.

50. Ibid.

51. Ibid, 180.

52. Ibid.

53. Ibid, 190.

54. Ibid.

55. Ibid.

56. Ibid, 252.

57. Ibid, 155.

58. Hunter, "The Politics of Resentment and the Construction of Middle America," 23.

59. Ibid., 30.

60. Ibid., 33.

61. Ibid., 34.

62. Ibid., 21.

63. Ibid., 37.

64. Apple, *Teachers and Texts* and Apple, "National Reports and the Construction of Inequality."

65. Stuart Hall, "Popular Culture and the State," in *Popular Culture and Social Relations*, ed. Tony Bennett, Colin Mercer, and Janet Wollacott (Milton Keynes, England: Open University Press, 1986), 35–36.

66. Omi and Winant, *Racial Formation in the United States*, 165.

67. Ibid., 166.

68. Ibid.

69. I say "new" here, but the continuity of, say, African-American struggles for freedom and equality also needs to be stressed. See the powerful treatment of the history of such struggles in Vincent Harding, *There Is a River: The Black Struggle for Freedom in the United States* (New York: Vintage Books, 1981).

70. See also David Hogan, "Education and Class Formation," in *Cultural and Economic Reproduction in Education*, ed. Michael W. Apple (Boston: Routledge and Kegan Paul, 1982), 32–78.

71. Omi and Winant, *Racial Formation in the United States*, 166.

72. Apple, "National Reports and the Construction of Inequality."

73. See Apple, *Teachers and Texts* and Martin Carnoy, Derek Shearer, and Russell Rurberger, *A New Social Contract* (New York: Harper and Row, 1984).

74. Apple, "National Reports and the Construction of Inequality." For a comprehensive analysis of the logic of capitalism, one that compares it with other political and economic traditions, see Andrew Levine, *Arguing for Socialism* (Boston: Routledge and Kegan Paul, 1984).

75. See Apple, *Education and Power* and Apple, *Teachers and Texts*.

76. See Sara Freedman, Jane Jackson, and Katherine Boles, *The Effects of the Institutional Structure of Schools on Teachers* (Somerville, Mass.: Boston Women's Teachers' Group, 1982).

77. For further discussion of this, see Apple, *Teachers and Texts*; Bastian, Fruchter, Gittell, Greer, and Haskins, *Choosing Equality*; and David Livingstone, ed., *Critical Pedagogy and Cultural Power* (Westport, Conn.: Bergin and Garvey, 1987). "Substance" in Chicago and "Chalkdust" in New York City are other significant examples of such progressive groups.

78. Hall, "The Great Moving Right Show," 120.

79. Apple, *Ideology and Curriculum*.

80. I have discussed this in greater detail in Apple, *Education and Power*.

PLURALISM AND THE
DILEMMA OF DISCORDANCE
AMONG BLACKS AND JEWS

Charles D. Blakeney and Ronnie A. F. Blakeney

America's vision of a pluralistic society rests on the hope that intergroup prejudice can be reduced through moral education. Unfortunately, prejudice is a major impediment to pluralism. Glazer (1975) and others (e.g., Takaki 1987) use models of the integration of Euro-American immigrants into the American melting pot to suggest that prejudice can be reduced through exposure, education, and assimilation. This assumes that intergroup prejudice is governed by generalized laws of social and moral psychology wherever there is intergroup antipathic interaction. It assumes that the prejudices of any one group toward the members of any other group are morally equivalent. Prejudice, after all, is prejudice. But prejudice, although it is a risk of pluralism, implies a different moral relationship between group members.

Pluralism implies membership in a community of equals, with different, but equally valued cultural beliefs and customs. Prejudice characterizes a relationship of inequality in which there is a perpetrator (the prejudiced person) and a recipient (the victim of prejudice). In a thorough historical review which outlines social, legal, and moral differences in the intergroup relations of waves of European immigrants and the intergroup relations between those Euro-Americans and America's racial minority groups, Takaki (1987) argues that the experience of racial minority groups in America is *not* the historic equivalent of the experience of Euro-American ethnic groups. In this essay we suggest that American racial minorities' historical experiences of prejudice and pluralism create the conditions for psychological discordance in the cross-racial moral judgments of minorities. Throughout this essay we use the term "majority" to denote the dominant group and "minority" to denote the subordinate group. The same relationships may or may not hold where the numerical majority is not the dominant group, and we make no claims with respect to those situations.

Prejudice and Moral Psychology

Classic studies of racism, prejudice, and anti-semitism can be loosely classified into two groups: those which look for the psychodynamic correlates of prejudice and those which examine the social structure correlates of race prejudice. The classic empirical study in the psychodynamic genre remains *The Authoritarian Personality* (Adorno et al. 1950) which outlines the correlates of prejudice in rigid constricted thinking, intolerance for ambiguity, moral rigidity, dichotomization, ambivalence toward parents, and a bent toward authoritarianism. Bettleheim and Janowitz (1964) extended the notion of a prejudiced personality type to include the ego-defensive function of prejudice for the individual in search of identity. The "Frustration/Aggression" hypothesis (Dollard et al. 1939) is within that same genre, although theoretically it is grounded in the stimulus-response theory. It suggests that personal frustration, rather than personal confusion, precipitates the aggression that grounds prejudice. Sartre (1948) looked at anxiety or fear as a psychological correlate of prejudice. What all these theories have in common is the conclusion that under certain conditions it is within the nature of the human psyche for prejudice to color some moral relationships.

On the socio-cultural side of the coin are historians and sociologists who, while not discounting individual psychodynamics, look for larger socio-cultural explanations for the phenomenon of prejudice. Some researchers look for specific features within a culture or its historical moment (e.g., Handlin 1951; Baran and Sweezey 1966). Others, particularly structuralists like Levi-Strauss (1976), see intergroup conflict and parallel ethnocentricism as a natural and necessary creative force in human development. Levi-Strauss reports that all over the world different tribes and nations have a word for the rest of the world which denigrates them, makes the Other just a bit different, a bit lower than "The Man" and "The People."

Each set of theorists (psychologists and sociologists) suggests that the other is necessary for a full understanding of why some individuals are prejudiced and not others, and why some groups are the object of such prejudice and not others, and both sets of theories share the same moral logic. They assume that, as Allport puts it: "basic conditions of human living and thinking . . . lead naturally to the formation of erroneous and categorical prejudgment." It is argued that prejudice, although it may have bad effects on the recipient of that prejudice, is a universal and natural condition among human beings living in social groups. It follows from this argument that the race or ethnic group prejudice of the minority is the psychological, if not moral, equivalent of the intergroup prejudice of the majority. Yet blacks and Jews were often specifically excluded as subjects in the generalized studies of prejudice from which our extant theories derived. Adorno et al., for example, although they included Jews and blacks in their original sample, generalize their findings to "non-Jewish, white" Americans. Forty years later, the National Science Foundation is sponsoring a major nationwide study of "racial attitudes" which uses the same narrow, asymmetrical assumption, and hence makes the same scientific error: asking black respondents who may be in the sample the same questions as they ask whites: how they feel about blacks as, for example, neighbors and coworkers (Sniderman 1989). For the past five decades the research to support generalizing theories of prejudice to the historic victims of prejudice has remained scant.

Twenty years ago, Saunders (in Ladner 1972) found no studies which specifically examined black anti-white prejudice, and we found no study since which specifically examined the moral psychology of "black racism." And although research on antisemitism was plentiful in the twenty years following World War II, we found no study of Jewish prejudice toward (or against) gentiles in America. Paradoxically, there are more studies of black anti-semitism and anti-Arab prejudice among Israeli Jews (Nissan 1985; Smooha 1987) than there are studies of black anti-white prejudice or Jewish anti-WASP prejudice.

Studies of prejudice among members of minority groups are limited almost entirely to the impact of prejudice on the personality (Kardiner and Ovesey 1964), lifestyles (Greir and Cobbs 1968), identity (Memmi 1965), and self-perception (Fanon 1967) of its victims. These studies, which examine the effects of prejudice among blacks and Jews, essentially examine racial self-hatred. In this respect, the same sad truth must be reported after fifty years of doll studies. In the 1930s Clark and Clark (1939) conducted a series of studies in which black children were presented with a family of black dolls and a family of white dolls and were asked such questions as: which they would prefer to have as friends; which were smarter (did better in school); which were prettier; which families they would prefer to live with, etc. Since the 1930s, doll studies have been used extensively to measure change over time, and to measure change in self-esteem and racial attitudes after an intervention, for example, measuring change after interracial exposure in an integrated Head Start program. Although there was some variation in the late 1960s among light-skinned middle class children, overall black children still prefer white dolls, despite positive black images on television, despite integration of the schools, despite the wide variety of black dolls now available (Porter 1971; Gopaul-McNicol 1988). With respect to Jews, Jewish self-hatred continues to be a favorite, if controversial, subject for Jewish-American novelists (Bettleheim 1979). Jewish identity continues to be tied to the experience of oppression. In 1943, Hannah Arendt (1978) wrote: "Whatever we do, whatever we pretend to be, we reveal nothing but our insane desire to be changed, not to be Jews." Nearly fifty years later Graubard (1992) described the assimilationist tendencies in the American Jewish community as evidence of continued self-hatred. He suggested a long-standing feeling of "difference" among American Jews— little changed over sixty years. He quoted Lewisohn (1928) on assimilation.

The Jews have wanted profoundly to be Americans, Germans, even Poles . . . can such things be done? Can they be done without inflicting an inner hurt, a wound to the moral fiber? Can people, in masses, as groups, repudiate their ancestry and its experiences?

Blacks and Jews attest both to the powerful intergenerational impact of prejudice and discrimination on its victims and to the continued asymmetry in their relationships to the American majority group.

The Paradox of the Prejudice of the Minority

We are left, then, with a multiplicity of studies describing the dynamics and correlates of the majority's prejudice against the minority, and a relative abundance of research and commentary on how blacks and Jews are affected by centuries of being victims of prejudice, but little scientific study to guide us in our examination of minority anti-majority prejudice. What little research there is on minority anti-majority prejudice presents a paradox which demands our attention. The seminal work in the moral psychology of prejudice remains Davidson's (1977) examination of urban and suburban children in the cauldron of school desegregation in Boston. Using Kohlberg's measure of moral judgment development (Kohlberg 1969), Davidson found that stage of moral reasoning and interracial contact both influenced the prejudice of white children. Within the sample, generally, children with higher stages of moral reasoning were less prejudiced, while lower stage moral reasoning was correlated with more prejudice. Longitudinally, white children became less prejudiced after interracial exposure than they were before that exposure. In other words, among white children, the opportunity to test their prejudicial stereotypes against actual experiences with black children reduced their prejudice. The troublesome finding for our work is that the same was not true for black children. For black children prejudice remained constant, even in the higher stages of moral reasoning, where it decreased among whites (Davidson 1976). Further, interracial contact (exposure) did not decrease prejudice among black students. On the contrary, there was a slight tendency toward increased prejudice among black Boston children who were bussed to suburban schools. This sad side note has been repeated in nearly every study which has examined the ability of interracial exposure to reduce prejudice.

Foley (1977) looked at the prejudice of black and white prison inmates in Florida. She found that exposure to blacks reduced the prejudice of whites, while exposure to whites increased the prejudice of blacks. In other words, negative prejudgments by whites toward blacks were disconfirmed and abandoned, yet negative prejudgments of whites by blacks increased. Further, as in the Adorno et al. studies, prejudiced whites were characterized by rigid constricted thinking, while tolerant whites were more cognitively complex, had greater tolerance of ambiguity, and were less authoritarian in their attitudes. Prejudiced blacks, however, did not fit the "prejudiced personality" theory. Prejudice actually increased in relation to cognitive complexity among the black subjects. It was the more narrow, cognitively simple blacks who were less prejudiced against whites.

The same "failure to conform to theory" on the part of blacks is reported in at least two other studies of the effects of interracial exposure on prejudice. In both these studies college students on interracial campuses were asked to comment on hypothetical situations where sometimes one participant or another was identified as black, and sometimes no racial identification was suggested. Both studies were directed at white students, but each had a few subjects (about 10 percent) who happened to be black. In both studies, white students' prejudice declined after interracial exposure, but black students' prejudice did not. Further, Locke and Tucker (1988) administered the DIT (Rest 1979), a modified form of Kohlberg's moral judgment interview. They found that among white college students, adequacy of moral reasoning was negatively correlated with prejudice. Like Davidson, however, they found that among black students prejudice did not decline as adequacy or complexity of moral reasoning increased. Thus, we find that among black children, black prison inmates, and black college students, "prejudice" does not follow the same "laws" as it does among white children, white prison inmates, and white college students. It does not decline as moral reasoning increases, nor as cognitive complexity increases, nor as interpersonal interracial exposure increases.

Research on moral development suggests that both cognitive complexity (Kohlberg 1973) and opportunities for social interaction as a member of a community of equals (Kohlberg 1968) are components of moral judgment development, as cognitive complexity and opportunities for interaction with the environment are necessary for cognitive development generally. A given level of cognitive complexity is a necessary but insufficient condition for stage of moral judgment, as well as for the decline of prejudice. In theory, increased opportunities for social interaction (exposure) are also related to both moral judgment development and to decline of prejudice. Thus, for whites, the correlates of moral judgment development and the correlates of a decline in prejudice are consistent. For blacks, however, the structural correlates of prejudice and moral judgment are not consistent. This may be an artifact of measurement, which we address in the current study. It may, alternatively, reflect the conceptual notion that prejudice is not a developmental construct (an altogether plausible notion which goes beyond the scope of the present study); but it may also reflect the different structural and functional relationship between moral judgment development and the prejudice of the minority toward the majority as contrasted with the prejudice of the majority toward the minority. The current study addresses those structural and functional relationships.

Measuring Prejudice

Traditionally prejudice is studied by presenting the subjects with a list of statements and asking them whether they agree or disagree, and how strongly (cf. the E Scale of Adorno et al.). In other words, prejudice is more often examined as an attitude or belief, using a five point Likert scale, rather than as a moral judgment. Moral judgments, on the other hand, are examined using an open-ended semi-clinical interview. Traditionally, subjects are presented with a series of hypothetical moral dilemmas and asked how they ought to be resolved. The responses are scored based on the underlying structure of the moral reasoning, rather than on the choice of moral action. Even in the two studies we have cited, Davidson (1977) and Locke and Tucker (1988), which examined the relationship of prejudice to moral judgment, prejudice was measured by asking the subjects to produce statements about minority group members, and then the statements were rated positive, negative, or neutral. Both ways of examining prejudice in relation to moral judgment are problematic. They provide a "content," but give us no clue as to the structure of the moral reasoning implied in a prejudgment and, hence, no way to understand its relationship to the individual's construction of the socio-moral world, or to his or her moral character. By using the clinical-developmental method, rather than traditional attitude methods, we can begin to illuminate both the structural-developmental and functional relationships between prejudice and moral judgment.

A Moral Developmental Approach
to the Moral Problem of Discordance

Kohlberg identified a sequence of six stages of moral judgment which characterize the structure of moral thinking at successively adequate developmental stages. The structures are said to be universal, although the content may vary culturally. Each structure organizes the way the person thinks about issues of justice and fairness. People all over the world use predominantly one stage of moral judgment to solve a variety of moral problems (see Table 1).

Theoretically, a schema or structure of morality requires a level of cognitive maturity, role taking, and a sense of justice. Role taking, in turn, implies a parallel sense of self. How one sees oneself is reflected in and is reflective of one's view of the socio-moral order. Moral judgments are derived from this construction of the self-other relationship. How minorities see themselves in relation to the (historical, actual or potential)

Table 1

Six Stages of Moral Judgment

Stage One: Preconventional morality, which defines right as avoiding punishment. Stage one requires concrete operational thought and ego-centric role taking.

Stage Two: The second preconventional stage, which defines right as ego-centric needs meeting. Stage two requires concrete operational thought and ego-centric, but coordinated role taking.

Stage Three: The first conventional stage, which defines right as maintaining interpersonal concordance and an image of oneself in the eyes of the other as a "good person." Stage three requires the beginning of formal operational thought and interpersonal role taking.

Stage Four: The second conventional stage, which defines right as maintaining a system of rules and order, with social roles implied. Stage four requires formal operational thought and institutional role taking.

Stage Five: The first post-conventional stage, which defines right as behaving according to self-chosen principles of justice and fairness, universally applied. Stage five requires fully formal thought and ideal role taking, as if from behind the veil of ignorance.

Stage Six: The second post-conventional stage is hypothetical at this point. It defines right in abstract terms of universalizability, reversibility, etc. It is used only heuristically and not for the purposes of measurement.

Other when that Other is considered, in Mead's (1934) term, "Antagonistic" is an important consideration in understanding both their general moral judgment and their cross-racial or intergroup moral judgment.

For conceptual clarity we distinguish what might be called the prejudice of the minority toward the majority by calling it "discordance," and retain the term "prejudice" for the intergroup prejudgments which traditionally characterize the moral reasoning of the majority toward the minority. Nothing in this essay should be construed to suggest, however, that members of minority groups cannot be prejudiced in the same way as members of the majority. We argue only that discordance is a distinct phenomenon.

Let us define the two terms conceptually. By prejudice we mean "a judgment formed without due examination and consideration of the facts" (see Allport for the history of this definition), or "a feeling, favorable or unfavorable, toward a person or thing, prior to, or not based on, actual experience" (*New English Dictionary*). Although theoretically such prejudices could be either positive or negative, thoughtful or emotional, in practice psychological research on prejudice finds about 80 percent of the faulty, inflexible definitions to be antipathic, rather than sympathic, to be negative, rather than positive. Prejudice, then, is an *a priori* moral judgment, usually negative, without basis in fact, about others or another because of their group identity.

Discordance is the impingement of minority status on the intergroup moral judgments of the historic victims of injustice with respect to the historic perpetrators or beneficiaries of that injustice. It characterizes the moral judgments of blacks and Jews toward WASPs, for example, but not the moral judgment of blacks and Jews toward one another. It accounts for but is not limited to, the consideration of actual, historical, and potential injustice toward an individual as a member of a racial or ethnic minority group. Discordance is thus an *ex post facto* moral judgment, negative or positive, about others or another, based on their membership in the class of historic perpetrators or beneficiaries of injustice. Because prejudice is an *a priori* judgment, it does not necessarily depend on the developmental state of moral judgment. An *a priori* judgment is derived from "feelings" which are not subject to cognitive scrutiny, and therefore are not integrated into the cognitive schema which are used to "figure out" or "judge" other matters. Discordance is an *ex post facto* judgment and is thus subject to cognitive scrutiny and stage of moral judgment. Because discordance considers existing facts, rather than being based on feelings alone, facts are evaluated using existing cognitive schema. Since a given stage of moral reasoning depends on a prior stage of cognitive development (Kohlberg 1984; Kuhn et al. 1977) a discordant moral judgment depends on both the cognitive and the moral stage.

The Study

Method

In order to address the methodological, psychological, and moral questions inherent in the unexplored territory of discordance we interviewed a stratified cross section of over 100 blacks and Jews, ages 7 to 77. We split the sample between middle class (college educated) and working class blacks and Jews, and between males and females. The subjects came from California (urban and rural) and from New York, with a subset of Harvard graduate students who had come from across the nation. We chose blacks and Jews for this exploration rather than other non-European immigrant groups because blacks and Jews have a cross-national experience of historically unfair treatment in common, and because as a group they differ in their current status in America with respect to prejudice, discrimination, and social status. The observation of discordance in the cross-racial moral reasoning of both Jews and blacks would suggest that discordance is a psychological phenomenon (what Cullen [1921] called a race-memory) common to a people who share a history of unfair treatment, rather than a temporal phenomenon, directly reflecting individual experience (such as post-traumatic stress). Discordance, then, might characterize the moral relationship of any group which continues to suffer injustice over a long period of time at the hands of a dominant culture. Mavis Gallent (1989), for example, described racial memory as central to understanding the antipathy between Irish-Catholic Canadian immigrants and French-Canadian Catholics. Their physical differences might disappear in two generations, she wrote, "only aversions and fear, the stuff of racial memory, are handed down intact." The current study probes the effects of "racial memory of aversions and fears" on the cross-racial moral judgments of blacks and Jews.

If discordance were the moral and psychological equivalent of prejudice we would find more discordance at lower stages of moral reasoning than at higher stages. We would find less discordance among college graduates as a result of increased cognitive complexity as a component of moral judgment development than among working class subjects as a group. If discordance were a reflection of personal experiences of discrimination then we would likely find more among blacks in contemporary America than among Jews, particularly in the postwar generations.

In our examination of discordance, we measured abstract moral judgments, scoring them by Kohlberg's Standard Scoring method, and compared them to the subjects' moral judgments on racially contextual moral dilemmas. We asked the subjects up to four dilemmas like the following:

1. If two children were drowning equal distances from you, and you could save only one, how should you choose who to save? Why that way? What if one were black (Jewish) and the other not? Why should (shouldn't) it make a difference?

2. If you were walking by three kids and saw them beating up one kid, what should you do? What if the three kids doing the beating were white/gentile and the kid being beaten up was black/Jewish? What if the kids doing the beating were black/Jewish and the victim were white/gentile?

3. Tell us your own hardest moral dilemma, and how you thought about and resolved it. (at the suggestion of Carol Gilligan)

4. (After Kohlberg's standard moral dilemma about the man stealing medicine to save his dying wife): Should it make a difference if the pharmacist who invented the medicine is black (Jewish)? What if the pharmacist is a known racist/anti-semite? The man steals the medicine and is caught. Should the judge sentence him or let him go free? What if the judge and the man are both black/Jewish?

Each of the dilemmas was scored for moral choice, (e.g., should steal/should not steal); moral stage (1–5, including transitional statements as, e.g., 2/3); criteria judgments (i.e., the moral reasons for the choice, for example, an appeal to rights, duties, consequences, equity, or equality) and discordance (whether the response varied by race at any of the three levels—content, stage, or criteria).

Results

Based on moral choice alone, 55 percent of the moral dilemmas were resolved discordantly. The number of dilemmas solved discordantly ranged from one to four for each subject, with a mean discordance score of 2.3. More than 60 percent of blacks and Jews (66 percent of blacks and 69 percent of Jews) were discordant on at least one racially contextual moral dilemma. By moral choice discordance, we mean that the subject chose one moral action as "right" in the monoracial situation, and another as "right" in the interracial situation. For example, if a subject said that it would be right to save a Jewish child being beaten by WASP bullies, but not the reverse, regardless of the reason for the moral choice, the response was scored as Content Discordant (see Table 2). We call this content choice discordance "Ethnocentric Discordance" because of its structural and functional relationship to group identity.

Table 2

Content Discordance among Blacks and Jews

	Concordance		Discordance	
Blacks	25	(40%)	37	(60%)
Jews	13	(31%)	29	(69%)
Total	38	(36%)	66	(63%)

In terms of stage of moral reasoning, 72 percent of blacks and Jews used a different stage of moral reasoning to resolve at least one of the racially contextual moral dilemmas than they used on the abstract dilemma. We call this stage discrepancy "Structural Discordance." There was no statistically significant difference between blacks and Jews, men and women, college and no college with respect to structural discordance. There were 183 discordant responses out of a possible 326 dilemmas. When we say that these subjects used a different stage of moral reasoning to resolve contextual dilemmas than they used to solve abstract dilemmas, we mean that, for example, a subject relied on stage four, the systems maintenance orientation, to solve the abstract Heinz dilemma, then solved the racially contextual dilemma by reference to either interpersonal relations (stage three) or abstract principles of justice (stage five). In practice, the contextual shift was always one stage higher or lower than the abstract stage, and almost as frequently higher as lower (55 percent of those who changed stage were higher, +1; 45 percent were lower, -1). We call the discordance *structural* when it includes differences based on stage alone, or differences in both moral choice and moral reason. For example, if a subject argued to save the black child "because you'd be a hero in the community" and to save the white child "because his dad would give you a reward" we scored it "discordant" because he used stage three moral reasoning (concern with reputation and the perception of others) to solve the monoracial dilemma and stage two (egocentric needs meeting) to solve the interracial dilemma.

Unlike prejudice, which declines as stage of abstract moral reasoning increases, there was no statistically significant relationship between abstract stage of moral reasoning and discordance (see Table 3).

This confirmed the observation of Davidson (1977) and Locke and Tucker (1988) that among black students, race remains a factor in moral judgment at higher stages, and extends this observation to Jews.

There are several provocative, but nonsignificant trends within the data which we will discuss. First, discordance increased to 78 percent among college graduates, and 80 percent among college graduate women. There was also a nonsignificant tendency for there to be more discordance among those whose abstract dilemmas were scored "in moral stage transition" than among those who were firmly rooted in a particular moral stage.

Discordance and Moral Judgment Development

The results of this examination support the hypothesis that discordance is different from prejudice in its relationship to moral judgment development. The data lend support to

Table 3

Discordance by Stage of Abstract Moral Reasoning
(183 dis/326 total)

Stage	Concordance		Discordance	
1	9	(48%)	10	(52%)
1/2	1	(16%)	5	(84%)
2	29	(69%)	13	(31%)
2/3	17	(36%)	31	(64%)
3	34	(47%)	38	(53%)
3/4	19	(24%)	29	(76%)
4	16	(32%)	34	(68%)
4/5	11	(39%)	17	(61%)
5	7	(54%)	6	(46%)

(Abstract standard Kohlberg dilemma is extracted from the total since it was used to calculate "stage".)

the formulation of discordance as racial memories of aversions and fears which are reflected in the cross-racial moral judgments of blacks and Jews. According to Davidson (1977) prejudice declines as stage of moral reasoning increases; but discordance crosses all stages of moral judgment development with no statistically significant differences, but a trend toward slightly more discordance at stages 4, 4/5 and 5. This suggests that discordance has a different relationship to moral judgment development than does prejudice. Discordance does not decline among college graduates, but rather has a tendency to increase. This suggests discordance is a more cognitively complex phenomenon than prejudice. There was a slight tendency for discordance to increase among those subjects who were in developmental transition. This suggests that discordance is related to a tolerance for ambiguity, because it is in developmental stage transition that people reevaluate competing moral frameworks. There was no significant difference between blacks and Jews on the amount or type of discordance. This suggests that discordance is more a function of racial memory than of personal experience. Although prejudice has never been well examined through a developmental lens, discordance is clearly a developmental phenomenon. The discordant moral judgments are themselves stage-related. They become increasingly complex, hierarchically integrated, and prescriptive as they vary by stage of moral judgment. In the next sections we describe the structural and functional relationship between discordance and moral judgment development.

Moral Judgment Discordance and How It Grows

In this section we describe how considerations of race effect the structure of moral judgment at each moral stage from pre-conventional, egocentric, needs-meeting stage two to post-conventional, principled stage five.

Stage two: "If I save her, she will play with me." At egocentric moral stage two racial concordance or discordance depends on its individual needs-meeting capacity. Listen to Bette (age 8), Marilyn (age 10) and Juanita (age 11) on the Drowning Dilemma:

> Just save whoever you can because if you help her, she might be your friend, and you'd have somebody to play with.
> (Scored Concordant)

> I'll save the black one. She might do me a favor someday if I'm drowning.
> (Scored Discordant)

> I'll save the white one. That would be right because lots of black kids play with me, and if I save the white one, she might play with me too, and be my friend.
> (Scored Discordant)

Color sometimes enters into moral judgments, then, even among small "unprejudiced" little girls, to the extent that it reflects their egocentric needs and their predictions, given their social experience. At this stage and age, discordance may be indistinguishable from prejudice. The fundamental differences between us and them, if any are noted, are concrete, and there is little construction of a group identity.

Stage three: The fundamental difference between Us and Them. Beginning at stage three, however, there are considerations of social conventions. At stage three moral judgments are guided by the importance of maintaining interpersonal relationships, and one's image of oneself as a good person in the eyes of others within significant interpersonal relationships. Individuals have differentiated special obligations to significant others. At stage three we find that discordance imposes special obligations toward members of one's ethnic group which are ordinarily reserved for kinship groups. One 19-year-old college sophomore told us that it was like the difference between running over a jack rabbit on the freeway and running over a pet rabbit you had raised in your yard. In both cases you feel bad, but in the case of the pet rabbit "there's a closeness or attachment" that takes longer to overcome.

Hattie and Anna, working class women aged 47 and 75 respectively, exemplify the sense of special obligations as deriving from fictive or extended kinship groups.

> I'd save the black one. I think you should take care of and help your own. He or she is mine. My race, and may be related down the line, you never know. (Scored Discordant)

> I'd take my own kind. I just feel closer to my own kind. Each group should take care of their own kind. So I'd hide the Jew, because he's one of ours. You take care of your own. (Scored Discordant)

Here the discordance is at its most benign. It is an ethnocentrism which is at the same time an extension of family and a prescription for pluralism. Group membership engenders special obligations to fellow members. This does not so much disparage the other (as prejudice does), nor even ennoble one's own group. Rather, it describes a world of benign ethnocentrism. This is the Levi-Strauss world of intertribal relations. But even at stage three the discordance is not always so benign.

At each stage of moral reasoning there is a conflict for about one out of three subjects over whether to include race as a consideration in moral reasoning. Danielle, a 17-year-old New Yorker, argued that the question of race in a drowning dilemma is itself unfair. 'There's no difference between a black person and a white person," she argued. On probing, however, she suggested that if she could only save one:

> I suppose I should save the black man. He's one of my kind. And if I had to, I'd justify it by saying: Well, look how they treated us—even though that doesn't really make a difference to me. The reason would be that they just didn't care about us. And really, if they saw one of us in the water, drowning, even if there was only one person drowning and that person was black, would he jump into the water to save him? To save me? He probably wouldn't save me. I feel that white people are just more prejudiced. I know some blacks are prejudiced, too. But whites just have more prejudice than we do. So if anybody's gonna save the black drowning person, I guess it probably would have to be another black swimmer.

Even though Danielle considered herself unprejudiced, and argued that it would be wrong to consider race in deciding who to save, she acknowledged, grudgingly, the racial memory of a fear that gives rise to a race-based moral prescription: on some level one ought to take into account the statistical likelihood of whites' having more prejudice, and therefore, the greater likelihood of the black person not getting rescued. Danielle's tension is between her ideal world with the morality which would hold sway there (a world where people are perceived and treated equally and fairly, without regard to racial classification) and her accommodation to the world in which she actually lives, which is not only imperfect, but also peopled by prejudiced whites. In his examination of the moral judgments of Israelis, Nissan (1985) called this accommodation a "limited acceptable morality."

We might think of the conflict between accommodating to the world as it is and acting as if the world were "more moral" as serving the function of facilitating a developmental transition. In other words, the cognitive conflict which is generated for Danielle might help her to grow, morally. Since cognitive moral conflict is conducive to growth (cf. Power, et al. 1989), then perhaps the experience of such conflict is adaptive. While longitudinal research is necessary to accurately assess this question, the current cross-sectional study is illuminating. For many subjects, the tension associated with cross-racial moral judgment was a conflict well into middle and old age. If subjects had resolved the conflict developmentally at earlier stages we would see less discordance among older subjects and less discordance at the higher stages. The rather large proportion of older black and Jewish men who retained predominantly stage three moral reasoning suggests that the discordance may itself have limited development, rather than enhance it. Alternately, each new moral stage may bring with it a new vision of race/ethnic conflict or tension such that at a given time a given subject may have come to terms with the role of race in moral reasoning, but be troubled by it again at a later developmental stage. This could help to account for the trend among higher stage college students to have more discordance. Longitudinal research is necessary to examine the impediment vs. enhancement hypotheses, but we can observe that tension associated with racial discordance colored the moral judgments of half the discordant subjects. Jacob, age 59, is one example of a middle aged man who is struggling with the logical and moral conflict of living in an unfair world. Like Danielle, Jacob described a sociomoral world which is peopled by prejudiced Others, and like Danielle, it makes him angry. His own hardest moral dilemma was "Bigotry."

The mere fact that you can't accomplish what many other people can accomplish, merely because you're Jewish. You're limited, regardless of what they say in this country. There's only so far you can go. How many Supreme Court Justices have we had? How many Jews working for presidential administrations? And every time somebody comes into the store, what's the first thing that they say? "I'm gonna Jew you down," Not, "I'm gonna chisel you down," or "talk you down," "I'm gonna Jew you down." I mean, these are prominent people, college graduates.

When you get somebody angry the first thing out of their mouth is "dirty Jew" or "Jew bastard." I've seen it too many times. When I was younger I used to deal with it by smacking somebody in the kisser. But now, I just try to overlook it, things that would normally aggravate you. To a certain extent you're always thinking about it, but you can't let it aggravate you all the time.

There is a basic assumption that one's day-to-day interactions have to take into account the probable prejudice of the "Antagonistic Other." Jacob, too, carries a "race memory of aversions and fears." In this way WASPs are seen as different from blacks and Jews. They are more prejudiced than we are. By extension, we are more caring, kind, and long-suffering, even Christlike (Fullinwider 1969).

Stage four: Being a part of history: Having a place in the vast world. The problem of discordance becomes even more difficult for those who primarily use stage four moral reasoning. Moral reasoning requires a parallel stage of role taking. Role taking is the developmental process of coordinating increasingly complex perspectives of the Other, with one's own moral point of view. By taking another person's perspective we can consider their moral claims, even when those claims conflict with our own. At stage four the Other, whose perspective is being coordinated, is the larger social system. To paraphrase DuBois (1903), how can we expect a man to honor the moral claims of the majority group by taking into account the perspective of a society whose "million fellow citizens half despise him?" To take the role of a social system, a system of laws and regulations which denigrates you as a member of your birth-group, is to argue for your own limitations, circumscriptions. As Jacob put it: "There's only so far you can go:" a glass ceiling. Yet to fail to see the larger social perspective is to deny a reality in which minorities live. As Valjean agonized, after hiding his convict status under the goodness of respectability: "On the one hand I'm condemned; on the other, I'm damned."

At modal stage four, the system's perspective, we find two apparently discrete ways of resolving what Gilligan and Murphy (1979) called "the dilemma of the fact": the conflict between an ideal morality and a morality which compromises with the real world context with all its complicating little details and imperfections. The first way is a developmental extension of the ethnocentric discordance we first met at stage three. At stage four, with ethnocentric discordance, it is possible for blacks and Jews to create mini-worlds, governed by social institutions, expectations, and traditions which exist not geographically, in space, at one point in time, but chronologically, through space, connecting the past to the future of the group through the self and the personal obligation to perpetuate the traditions, the values, and the group itself. We found this among both blacks and Jews who grew up with strong family traditions, particularly in multigenerational church/synagogue-based communities. These subjects made references to "the oral tradition of the slave grandmother Mafundi" (storyteller) and to the grandparents' Sabbath songs. These subjects dealt with the potential developmental conflict of maintaining "the system" when that system circumscribes your opportunities for full participation by virtue of your group membership, by denying the existence or importance of the larger social world.

Erikson (1968) described a phenomenon wherein members of one adolescent group discount all others outside their moral universe, a universe within which there are mutual rights and obligations and mutual respect. Others are reclassified as something less than "us," maybe less than human. Erikson called this phenomenon "pseudospeciation," creating a false species within humanity, in much the way antebellum anthropologists classified African Americans. Ethnocentric discordance is its least malignant and most ego-defensive form. In this way, ethnocentric discordance maintains a group identity which ties racial discordance both morally and psychologically to a parallel ethnocentrism. It differs from ethnocentrism generally in that it cannot be coterminous with "the Nation." Indeed, unlike Levi-Strauss's ethnocentrism where "my people" are "The Man," in black America "The Man" refers euphemistically to the white social system and its representatives. We might think of the relationship of ethnocentrism to ethnocentric discordance by using the example of the Japanese. Ethnocentric discordance might characterize the ethnocentrism of Japanese Americans (*nisei* and *sansei*) but not the ethnocentrism, chauvinism, or nationalism of Japanese in Japan.

As long as I fear persecution. The developmental alternative to this separatist, pluralist world which denies or denigrates the importance of the larger society is to acknowledge the unfair power of the antagonistic Other over one's self and one's own group. Minority group members who acknowledge the contradictions between the morally ideal world and the perceived actuality of racial injustice wrestle to balance the tension which amplifies that which we first heard at stage three: How do I remain unprejudiced and yet take into account the prejudice of the antagonistic Other? At stage three that antagonistic Other is fundamentally different from the self as individual WASPs are different from individual blacks and Jews: They are more likely as individuals to be prejudiced against us, than we are as individuals to be prejudiced against them. At stage four the antagonistic Other is reconstructed as the American (or Western) social system as a whole. Individual WASPs may or may not be prejudiced, but the system itself is unfairly biased. The moral question at stage four is the conscious elaboration of "Why be Just in an Unjust world?" At stage four subjects with structural discordance ask how they should account for the institutional unjust Other and still be fair, objective, unbiased and dignified. A Jewish law student and a black university professor demonstrate the difficult balancing act required at stage four. Both these subjects grew up in large, extended families, in racially mixed working class neighborhoods, and were the first generation in their families to complete college. Both said that they never particularly thought of themselves as black or Jewish until they went away to college. Each had been hailed for his/her own particular talents throughout school, and each believed in "equality." We will call them Tom and Jerry, and describe the tension in the sense they have made of their minority status, given their moral stance. Tom said:

> There should be no difference between our rights. . . . I thought I was good until I found out that black was bad according to society's norms. The white students were supposed to have academic prowess, and I was supposed to have athletic prowess. I soon realized the social norm. I asked myself for the first time: 'If he is good, then what am I? I must be bad. How will I prove myself to be good?' That's where the battle started. Not at birth because I didn't know then what I was to encounter later on. The white man has set up the norm.

If there's a hierarchy of color, there's a hierarchy of power, which is in conflict with the Constitution's claim that every man was born with inalienable rights, but anytime you're different in this society, you're subordinate. . . .

My dream, my driving force, is to make the way easier for my sons growing up in America. And we have that right, because our blood was shed on this continent just like anybody else's. We were fighting for this country from the time Columbus came, and maybe your grandfather was lynched, and maybe we'll be lynched. The ideology, the norms are the same. And they're based on race, and they're based on color. Were Jesus' eyes blue? No. Was his hair blonde? No. He was a Jew. Are they blonde haired and blue eyed? No. How many were killed? Why were they killed? I'll tell you. The same norms, the same hierarchy. You have to teach them what happened, you have to teach the children not just what happened in the last five minutes, but in the last 500 years. Race is real, and prejudice and discrimination are real. They're a part of the American system, and maybe the white man's psyche. I can deal with it, day to day. I can get along with white folks, too, as long as they respect my dignity. But you have to have dignity to live on this earth. That's the bottom line.

At stage four Tom balances his sense of the ideal world with his experience of the world as it actually is. He looks at the system's unfair treatment of minorities, people of color (in which he includes Jews), and derives from that a sense of special obligations to other blacks, particularly as part of the continuity of generations. This special obligation does not come from ethnocentric pluralism, as it did at stage three, but from a shared experience of injustice within the social system, and a concomitant moral obligation to right historic wrongs.

Jerry, too, has a sense of special obligations derived from a shared history of injustice. Her hardest moral dilemma was "The Middle East Question."

When I'm confronted with that dilemma, I have to back off, because I'll say Israel's right every time, even though sometimes I'm on the side of the Arabs logically. I'm really not sure that it's fair for Israel to have that land exclusively, but I guess that I fear that someday it won't, and that all that persecution will come up in my face, and I won't have anywhere to go. I can't take part in any academic or logical debate about it, because I feel prejudiced. I mean any old WASP can look at these questions objectively, although they may have prejudices that they're unaware of, too. I mean, they could be anti-semitic and side against Israel. But for me its more emotional than logical. Being pro-semitic when you're Jewish is more emotional than being anti-semitic when you're not Jewish, but what's worse is that I feel bad. I mean, I feel sorry for those damn Palestinians who are trying to annihilate my people. They have no place to go. Nobody wants them. They have a claim to the land, but their claim is in opposition to the people I feel an obligation to. And I know that it's really personal. I would feel an obligation to Namibia if it promised to admit any Jew if the need arose again. And I know that it's wrong to let those feelings get in the way of what you know, logically, objectively to be more fair, but *as long as I fear persecution* I can't resolve this problem.

For Tom, the special obligation to both blacks and to justice comes from anger. For Jerry the special obligation comes directly from fear, which comes from her racial memory of persecution and the potential for that same persecution to occur at any time. Her stance is something like that of a mother porcupine who recognizes that sometimes she unfairly unleashes her powerful defense mechanism when she spots a possible intruder who indeed may not have meant her offspring any harm. In this way discordance may serve an ego-defensive function in that it prevents the "unconserved" "illogical" feelings from toppling the whole moral structure. Jerry's self-protective, defensive stance on the Middle East Question is very much like Tom's stance on The American Question, except that Tom *lives* in America, Jerry does not live in the Middle East. That is, Jerry's tension is morally disequilibrating when she thinks about the Middle East, or the history of persecution which has trailed Jewish communities for two millennia. Tom's tension disequilibrates his day-to-day life, colors his daily moral decisions: how to educate his children, how to accommodate to racism in his work, where to live, what social and political activities to engage in. For both Tom and Jerry, and for many of the college graduates in our sample, discordance created a sense of disequilibrium, a sense that they could not actually live up to their own moral codes without compromising either their ultimate personal safety or their special obligations. Their group identity and feelings *as minority persons* and their integrity *as moral persons* remained in conflict. Their commitment to a world in which justice exists for all is both magnified and diminished by their need to compromise with the world as it is: historically, actually, and potentially unjust.

Stage five: "I'm beginning to think it comes from me." Moral judgment development moves through a sequence of increasingly adequate moral stages. By "increasingly adequate" we mean that each successive stage solves moral problems which are posed by the prior stage. In theory, moral judgment stage five ought to resolve the questions posed at stage four. Since the disequilibrating problem posed for minorities at stage four is a moral problem, it should be resolvable with the capacity for stage five moral reasoning. Yet, recall from our data that one third of the dilemmas posed to stage five subjects were resolved discordantly and 70 percent of the stage five subjects resolved at least one moral dilemma discordantly. How does post-conventional moral reasoning allow principled minorities to make sense of the social convention (some might say social fiction) of race in America? Let us first clarify our claim that race is a social convention, if not a social fiction. With respect to black Americans we must first note that racial designation is based neither on genetic differences nor chromatic ones. Historically, America had to create mulattos, quadroons, and octoroons to account for the various admixtures *within* black America, particularly in the nineteenth century. By the twentieth century, *by convention* in both black and white America, people who are "a little bit black" are either black or "passing" for white, and people who are "a little bit white" (or even mostly white) are black, too. In black America as well as white America, by social convention, those people who are of black and white admixture who claim to be white are "denying their blackness," yet rarely might it be argued that the mass of "black Americans" who are of historically mixed racial heritage are "denying their whiteness." With respect to Jews, although nearly half of the Jews in America consider themselves "unaffiliated" (Goldfarb 1989), which is to say non-practicing, nevertheless they are still considered (and usually consider themselves) Jews. So how does a person who is subject to the reality of the social convention make post-conventional sense of that convention?

David is a 34-year-old graduate student and former Naval officer, who was reared in a segregated city and then was sent to integrate a formerly white Catholic seminary. He was fairly representative of the stage five subjects in this study. On the whole, they seemed to have thought through the dilemmas of being black/Jewish in America and what it means to them. They seem to have made a considered judgment to choose to acknowledge their group membership while at the same time acknowledging their uniqueness and individuality. In other words, they take moral responsibility for their own minority status, while not denying the social pressure for doing so, both from the unjust, antagonistic system, and from their own group. David talked about the tension in being what he called "quote Black in America unquote." He said:

> It's difficult for me to cast myself as independent of black people. It's difficult to address the question of what it feels like to be black in America because it sort of demands that I recognize being black as a sort of experience I share with all other blacks. I don't think I share that. My experience is not the same as all other blacks, so it's difficult for me to think of myself as like other blacks in terms of the shared experience, and difficult for me to think of myself as independent because I'm aware of the things that I do share in common with all other blacks.

[What are those things?]

> Well, the external things I respond to, the sense of alienation, a sense of being 'other than,' other than whatever makes up the mainstream of American society, I feel excluded from that.

[And where does this feeling of being excluded come from?]

> *I'm beginning to think it comes from me.* When I was small I thought we were the norm and *they* were different. We had to treat them kindly, not be cruel. Then in seminary I began to

feel like I was different, like there were things about me that I would have to overcome. It's like it was a game or a contest, and I'd been dealt a bad hand. Then, as I got older, I realized *they* were cheating. By the time I went into the Navy I had figured out that if they had to cheat to win, there must be some advantage I had somewhere. Otherwise, why would they be cheating? I don't think I articulated it quite that way then, but it's how I *felt*. Now, I know that sometimes the hatred of other people that I feel may be because of my race or their racism, but it may not, and you can never really know.

In the Navy I had to compromise myself, my integrity, do a little tap dance just to get along with this guy. He was one of the few genuine rednecks I have ever met. And I really didn't dig myself doing that little tap dance, but he had all the social support. I was the most junior officer on the ship. I couldn't beat him on his own terms. He had all the power.

[What was the hardest thing about tap dancing for you at that time?]

Being aware that I was tap dancing as an expedient. I couldn't live the lie, and I couldn't have the confrontation. The moral dilemma is survival, and doing it in a morally correct way. The result for me was recognizing that there is a morality that is specific to blacks, as opposed to the general morality. Being black you have to apply a sense of humor to understanding why a person is doing wrong.

Among black people there is more likely to be a conflict between individual morality and the shared or general morality of the group. Individual morality has to do with living up to your own principles, asking yourself: 'What kind of a person would I be if I did this?' Shared morality has to do with a concern over what's good for the group. So, the struggle to survive in a morally correct way has to do with reconciling these two moralities.

Unlike the stage four subjects, who asked: Why be just in an unjust world? David poses his own moral question: How to be just in an unjust world, and abide by one's principles? His answer balances the universal and the particular, the consideration of the unjust, antagonistic other, and the special obligations not only to one's group, but also to the world, as a member of a minority group which has a special relationship to issues of justice. David's abstract moral reasoning reflects this balance, this integration of ethnocentrism and structural discordance, the universal and the particular. He says:

> Society has laws because laws represent a standard, a sort of goal for the collective philosophy of the people. It's not that laws are exactly a standard, they provide a framework within which it is thought that people can best function without infringing upon the interest of other people. You know I think that laws attempt to do something like that. And, because laws are laws and laws don't always consider morality, that's why you have judges—like the original Platonic notion that you have to have laws because people are inconsistent, but you have to have people because laws are insensitive. And morality, at least the public morality, exists somewhere between the two. Society wants to promote moral behavior, and the closer society can come to creating an ideal moral atmosphere, then the better society has reconciled the law and the people.

Thus, in both his abstract moral reasoning and in his racially contextual moral reasoning David has achieved a balance which considers abstract principles of justice (the framework, the ideal goals), the historical actuality of injustice, and the psychological reality of group identity. The group identity engenders special obligations for David not in the "link in the chain" way it does at stage four, but in a more ecological sense. "It is my source and I feel a need to replenish it" David says, chuckling. "Nothing exotic. I just might need it again." For David, the "black community" is a weight, a burden that keeps him from being free to choose in the existential sense, but at the same time "working with black kids," giving back to the source, invigorates and renews him.

Discordance and Disequilibration

Across the sample of college-educated blacks and Jews we found that experiences with racism and anti-semitism, either personal or distant, either day-to-day or life-changing, created disequilibrating feedback to a nonracist, unprejudiced mental moral structure in such a way as commonly to lead to a discordant reconstruction of the moral stage. That is, whether the person grew up in an integrated neighborhood or a stucco or gilded ghetto, rich or poor, many of our subjects claimed to have had no conflict about racial identity or interracial interaction until. . .and then they told us a story. Let two such examples suggest the disequilibrating dynamic. The first is a 37-year-old black college administrator who grew up in Connecticut. The second is a 32-year-old Jewish social worker who grew up in New York.

> You know, I didn't really ever think about what it meant to be black until one day, I was really just a kid, and I was watching the news and I saw the dogs attacking school children. The police were siccing German shepherds on school children. And I started retching, man, started physically throwing up. I mean when I realized that the police had released those dogs on those children because they wanted to go to an all-white school, and they were Black. I mean to this day I feel sick to my stomach when I see a German shepherd. I mean, I was a black school kid then, too. It could have been me. No matter how I tried I couldn't understand why that was happening.

> I remember very well when it first hit me what it meant to be Jewish. It was really the first time I left New York. We were driving to California, and were in New Orleans for Mardi Gras. I mean, I just couldn't believe it. We were watching the parade, and there I was. I mean, the kid was only three or four years old, and I was so shocked, so doubtful of my own ears, that I asked the father, standing next to me, what the child had said. And he repeated: 'Them Jews is too cheap to throw candy off a float—throw more candy cheap Jews.' And I was left shaking. I got dizzy, my legs wouldn't support me. I had to get out of that town. But now I know why no Jews live between New York and Los Angeles. How could anybody live in a community where anti-semitism is fed to the children with candy!

For these two young professionals, their formerly unbiased moral structures were toppled, disequilibrated, by the irrefutable evidence of a deep layer of prejudice within America. This disequilibration suggests a major ontogenetic difference between prejudice and discordance with respect to moral judgment development. Prejudice is said to be a part of the moral structure or personality which expresses a "faulty and *inflexible* generalization toward a group or a member of a group... not merited by his own misconduct" (Allport 1958, 10). Discordance in these cases arises not from the inflexibility of moral prejudgments of antipathy, but rather in the way the experience of the others' *actual* "misconduct" confronts and dislodges the individual's prior, unprejudiced moral balance. When a person who is prejudiced is confronted with contradictory evidence he reframes the data to fit his theory. An example of this kind of garden variety prejudice being reframed comes from a prejudiced black subject of this study who said:

> I always thought that white people were mean and uncaring, I never trusted them or made friends with them. Then one summer I had a job at the recreation center, and I met this counselor who was cool. She was really all right, and I couldn't figure it out. She was white, but she wasn't mean. Then I found out that her parents were both deaf, so I knew, she was just like us, a minority.

In Piagetian terms, prejudice is characteristically over-assimilative: The data are made to fit the existing schema. Discordance, on the other hand, imposes itself on an unprejudiced moral stance—the data force the individual, dizzy and retching, to modify the way he sees the world.

Conclusions

We have demonstrated that discordance differs from prejudice in its structural relationship to moral judgment development. Discordance itself is a developmental phenomenon, which requires increasing complexity in both its logic and in its role taking. Discordance also serves a different function with respect to group identity, individual development, and social or moral values.

Group identity. Bettleheim and Janowitz suggest that prejudice serves the function of defining the "non-self" by fighting against something, providing, insulating and protecting a group identity. This function may be positive or negative. Group identity is the basis and reason for pluralism. According to Bettleheim and Janowitz, the value of group identity depends on whether the identity construction (a) denigrates the non-self; and (b) aims toward something of social value. The Greenies, for example, might have a sense of themselves as advocates for the environment without denigrating non-Greenies. Group identity is thus of positive value. When the Greenies begin to advocate harassment of non-Greenies, the value of their group identity is limited by the extent to which it limits others' freedoms. Both prejudice and discordance are functionally related to group identity. Prejudice creates an identity which denigrates the outgroup, does not elevate one's own group, and in the end creates nothing of social value. With discordance we observed two somewhat distinct types of group identity. The first type, which is statistically associated with content discordance, does not denigrate the outgroup. We called this Ethnocentric Discordance. The second type, associated with Structural Discordance has as its aim, universal justice, a social value.

Ethnocentric discordance includes both ethnocentricism and a moral judgment derived therefrom. The moral judgment imposes special obligations toward one's own group as of primary moral importance. Members of other groups are not entirely ruled out of the moral universe, but given their own special place with their own intra-group special obligations.

Structural discordance implies a group identity derived from the group's special relationship to justice, as the historic recipients of injustice, often at the hands of, or to the benefit of the outgroup. One's own group is construed as the Just, and the outgroup is construed as the Unjust. There are important developmental implications here for the difference between prejudice and discordance. Group identity associated with prejudice does not necessarily impede moral development. (Lincoln's notion that blacks were not the equal of whites does not mean he was not principled, in the Kohlbergian sense.) Having an anti-minority prejudice does not affect taking the perspective of the larger social system in the way that we have described for discordance.

The Moral Function of Discordance

The group identity which is associated with discordance is functionally different from prejudice in that it allows two avenues for development which might otherwise be incompatible with taking the perspective of the larger social system which excludes or denigrates the minority status individual by virtue of her group membership. Ethnocentric discordance does this by creating a smaller socio-moral world. Structural discordance does this by accommodating the tension in the use of two modes of moral thinking: the abstract and the contextual, the universal and the particular, casting that tension as an energetic force, a mission ideology which becomes clear at stage five, where special obligations are universalized, and where minorities are construed to have a special obligation to fight for justice (or peace, or brotherhood). The identification with the downtrodden, and the concomitant commitment to justice serves as the developmental counterbalance to the special burdens of minority status. It is inherent in the dual meaning of "The Chosen People" which we hear among both Jews and blacks: We (blacks/Jews) are chosen to carry God's special burdens, and to be His special messengers. Anna, born just after the turn of the century, had practiced pediatrics in Third World countries for much of her life. She told us:

> From what I know of history, Jews were born to suffer. It's the suffering that makes us great. Purifies us like steel in the flame. You've got to be beaten down to wait for the Messiah. It's the suffering that makes us continue. And we continue because God wants us to have a good heart. There's no use to continue if people are to be mean. God wants us all to have a good heart, and that's all He asks of us.

The suffering is in service of the good heart, which is in service of bringing about the messianic age of peace, justice and brotherhood.

Jonathan is a 39-year-old school district administrator in the northeast. He told us that:

> My whole identity, my whole sense of being, is tied up to this sense of injustice as it's experienced by black people. I think for me being black means, well, if you've had certain advantages and you're in a position like I am, it means I have a special

responsibility to do what I can to improve the quality of life for other people who are subjected to the atrocities of the system even more than I am.

Both Jonathan and Anna share a mission ideology which comes from their group identity and prescribes their life's work as the struggle for a better world. This is the developmental function of discordance. Here, suffering at the hands of injustice is reconstructed to the Good in a way reminiscent of Nat Turner's response to his captors. Recall that Turner led a rebellion in 1831. His captors asked him, now that he was to be hanged and his revolution had failed to end slavery, if he could not admit the moral wrong in his actions. Turner refused to "confess his sins," and replied: "Was not Christ crucified?" For Turner and many of our higher stage subjects, the discordance may serve some developmental function for the self, and also some social function in bringing about positive change. Discordance may not always serve a developmental aim. Discordance, we have suggested, may limit a minority subject's social world horizontally, or may pose an unresolvable conflict which acts to forestall development, particularly between moral stages three and four. Further, the dilemmas of discordance may not be resolved developmentally, and may yield "unconserved affect." Piaget (1981) describes moral judgment as a way of conserving or organizing feelings in a hierarchy of values. When those feelings cannot be conserved into that system of values, it results in a rage which, while it might be organized into some practical schema, may also be a disintegrating force, running counter to development and counter to logic itself. The fierce fighting of Israeli soldiers against Palestinian children and the uprisings in America's central cities are often described as related to the unconserved fear and rage. In 1966, after several sweltering summers of inner city conflagrations, a group of black ministers reported to the *New York Times*:

> We, an informal group of Negro churchmen in America, are deeply disturbed about the crisis brought upon our country by historic distortions of important human realities in the controversy about "Black power." What we see shining through the variety of rhetoric is not anything new, but the same old

problem of power and race which has faced our beloved country since 1619.

The conscience of Black men is corrupted because having no power to implement the demands of conscience, the concern for justice in the absence of justice becomes a chaotic self-surrender. Powerlessness breeds a race of beggars. We are faced with a situation where powerless conscience meets conscienceless power, threatening the very foundations of our nation. . . . Without the capacity to participate with power, i.e., to have some organized political and economic strength to really influence people with whom one interacts, integration is not meaningful. . . . We must not apologize for the existence of this form of group power, for we have been oppressed as a group and not as individuals.

The discordance, then, can take several forms, but for most of the blacks and Jews we interviewed across genders, social classes, and experiences, we found that race continued to be a concern which intruded on abstract moral judgment in the way that the light of day intrudes on one's dreams.

The discordance phenomena illuminate two ways that moral judgment may be effected by varying the "context." The first way, suggested by Gilligan and Murphy (1979) and supported by Selman and Jacquette (1978) and others (cf. Nissan 1985), is that the social context itself may affect the application of one's own highest stage of moral reasoning to a particular problem, in this case, a cross-racial moral dilemma. This is undoubtedly the case for many of our subjects. Some had difficulty predicting the actions of the other in cross-racial role taking. Others simply imposed the special obligation rubric. A second explanation for the discordance in cross-racial moral reasoning is the role of affect. When a situation or dilemma creates unconserved affect, race memories which cannot be integrated into existing mental schema, then there is discordance in cross-racial moral reasoning. This hypothesis was proposed by Locke and Tucker (1988) to account for racial variations by blacks on interracial dilemmas. Our data suggest that for some people the context becomes a defining criteria, while for others the affective intrusion accounts for the discordance.

Pluralism and Moral Education:
The Dilemma of Discordance

Each of the two explanations for discordance have different implications for moral education in a pluralistic society. First, a word about prejudice, discordance, and pluralism. Discordance in the cross-racial moral reasoning of minority group members with respect to the majority can be understood as the complement of prejudice. Discordance is how minorities account for prejudice in their moral reasoning. If there were not an unfair distribution of power associated with prejudice, there would not be discordance, but only ill-will between equals. Both prejudice and discordance are downside risks of pluralism. While pluralism may be possible among groups of equal status, wherever there is a hierarchy of power, pluralism requires a prior moral task. From the point of view of structural developmental moral psychology, prejudice is developmentally prior to pluralism. Prejudice implies a complementary relationship of unequal power. There is the perpetrator (or beneficiary) of prejudice, and there is the recipient, or victim. In Piagetian terms prejudice implies a morality of constraint. Pluralism, on the other hand, implies symmetrical relationships among groups of equal value and status, co-members of a community of equals. In Piagetian terms, pluralism implies morality of cooperation.

Implications for Moral Education

The discordance phenomenon suggests two considerations for those who would develop programs to foster a viable pluralistic society. First, it is important to understand the difference between the prejudice of majority group children toward the minority (and of some minority group children as well) which often comes from lack of knowledge and seems to respond to exposure and the discordance of minority group children which serves to insulate identity against assaults from veridical but denigrating observations of unfair treatment in the larger society. We cannot assume that programs which are designed to reduce prejudice among majority group members will be effective in reducing discordance among minority group members. Our second observation is that discordance varies by developmental stage. This means that the way adults think about cross-racial differences is very different from the way children think about cross-racial differences, and that the way adults think about cross-racial differences itself varies by developmental stage. Knowing that children think differently from adults about race, however, does not mean that they do not think about race and group differences. It means that they have their own ways of understanding what those differences are, and their implications for relating to people of different groups. As always the developmentalists' caution must be applied to the moral education of discordant children and adolescents: First, we must understand what minority status means to them.

In the end, just knowing that minority status has different implications for cross-racial moral judgment than does majority status should facilitate pluralism. As long as we ignore or minimize group differences, race memories, we fail to integrate them into the process of change. We cannot denigrate the valid moral claims of the historic victims of injustice as long as those claims remain a part of racial memory if we are ever to achieve the dream of a pluralistic society in which people respect group differences as contributing to a just and caring community of equals.

References

Adorno, T. W., E. Frenkel-Brunswik, D. Levinson, and R. M. Sanford. 1950. *The Authoritarian Personality*. New York: Harper & Bros.

Allport, G. 1958. *The Nature of Prejudice*. Garden City, N.Y.: Doubleday Anchor.

Arendt, H. 1978. *The Jew as Pariah*. New York: Grove Press.

Baran, P., and P. Sweezey. 1966. *Monopoly Capital*. New York: Holt.

Bettleheim, B. 1979. *Surviving and Other Essays*. New York: Knopf.

Bettleheim, B., and M. Janowitz. 1964. *Social Change and Prejudice*. London: Free Press of Glencoe.

Candee, D. 1977. *Final Report: National Institute of Education's Life Outcomes Study*. Cambridge, Mass.: Harvard University Center for Moral Education.

Clark, K. and M. Clark. 1939. "The Development of Consciousness of Self and the Emergence of Racial Identity in Negro Preschool Children." *Journal of Social Psychology* 10: 591–599.

Cullen, C. 1921. *Color*. New York: Harper.

Davidson, F. H. 1976. "Ability to Respect Persons Compared to Ethnic Prejudice in Childhood." *Journal of Personality and Social Psychology* 34 (no. 6): 1256–1267.

———. 1977. "Respect for Persons and Ethnic Prejudice in Childhood: A Cognitive Developmental Description." In *Pluralism in a Democratic Society*, ed. M. H. Tumin and W. Plotch. New York: Praeger.

Dollard, J., L. Doob, N. E. Miller, D. H. Mowrer, and R. R. Sears. 1939. *Frustration and Aggression*. New Haven, Conn.: Yale University Press.

Dubois, W. E. B. 1903. *Souls of Black Folk*. New York: Doubleday.

Erikson, E. 1968. *Identity, Youth, and Crisis*. New York: Norton.

Fanon, F. 1967. *Black Skin, White Masks*. New York: Grove.

Foley, A. 1977. "Personality Characteristics and Interracial Contact as Determinants of Black Prejudice toward Whites." *Human Relations* 30 (no. 8): 709–720.

Fullinwider, S. P. 1969. *The Mind and Mood of Black America*. Homewood, Ill.: Dorsey.

Gallent, M. 1989. *The New Yorker* (November).

Gilligan, C. and M. D. Murphy. 1979. "Development from Adolescence to Adulthood: The Philosopher and the 'Dilemma of the Fact'." In *Intellectual Development Beyond Childhood*, ed. D. Kuhn. San Francisco: Jossey-Bass.

Glazer, N. 1975. *Affirmative Discrimination: Ethnic Inequality and Public Policy*. New York: Basic Books.

Gopaul-McNicol, S.-A. 1988. "Racial Identification and Racial Preference of Black Preschool Children in New York and Trinidad." *Journal of Black Psychology* 14 (no. 2, February): 65–68.

Graubard, A. 1992. *Saving Remnants: Feeling Jewish in America*. New York: Macmillan's Free Press.

Grier, W., and P. Cobbs. 1968. *Black Rage*. New York: Basic Books.

Handlin, O. 1951. *The Uprooted: The Epic Story of the Great Migrations That Made the American People*. Boston: Little, Brown.

Hughes, L. M. 1959. *Selected Poems*. New York: Knopf.

Kardiner, A., and L. Ovesey. 1964. *The Mark of Oppression*. Cleveland: World.

Kohlberg, L. 1968. "Montessori with the Culturally Disadvantaged: A Cognitive-Developmental Interpretation." In *The Challenge of Early Education: Current Theory, Research, and Action*, ed. R. Hess and R. Bear. Chicago: Aldine Press.

———. 1973. "Continuities in Childhood and Adult Moral Development Revisited." In *Life-Span Developmental Psychology: Personality and Socialization*, ed. P. B. Bates and K. W. Schaie. New York: Academic Press.

———. 1984. *Essays on Moral Development*, vol. 2, *The Psychology of Moral Development*. San Francisco: Harper & Row.

Kohlberg, L., A. Colby, J. Gibbs, B. Speicher-Dubin, and F. C. Power. 1977. *Assessing Moral Stages: A Manual*. Cambridge, Mass.: Harvard

University Center for Moral Education. (The forerunner of the recently published scoring manual.)

Kuhn, D., J. Langer, L. Kohlberg, and N. Haan. 1977. "The Development of Formal Operations in Logical and Moral Judgment." *Genetic Psychology Monographs* 95: 97–188.

Ladner, J. 1972. *Tomorrow's Tomorrow: The Black Woman.* New York: Doubleday.

Levi-Strauss, C. 1976. *Structural Anthropology.* Vol. 2. Chicago: University of Chicago Press.

Lewisohn, L. 1928. *The Island Within.* New York: Harper.

Locke, D. C., and D. O. Tucker. 1988. "Race and Moral Judgment Development Scores." *Counseling and Values* 32: 232–235.

Mead, G. H. 1934. *Mind, Self, and Society.* Chicago: University of Chicago Press.

Memmi, A. 1965. *Colonized and Colonizer.* Boston: Beacon Press.

Messner, G. (ed.). 1970. *Another View: To Be Black in America.* New York: Harcourt, Brace, & World.

Nissan, M. 1985. "Limited Morality: A Concept and Its Educational Implications." In *Moral Education: Theory and Application*, ed. M. Berkowitz and F. Oser. London: Erlbaum.

Piaget, J. 1981. *Intelligence and Affectivity: Their Relationship during Child Development.* Palo Alto, Calif.: Annual Reviews.

Porter, J. D. R. 1971. *Black Child, White Child: The Development of Racial Attitudes.* Cambridge, Mass.: Harvard University Press.

Power, F. C., A. Higgins, and L. Kohlberg. 1989. *Lawrence Kohlberg's Approach to Moral Education.* New York: Columbia University Press.

Rest, J. 1979. *Revised Manual for the Defining Issues Test.* Minneapolis, Minn.: Minnesota Moral Research Projects.

Sartre, J. P. 1948. *Anti-Semite and Jew.* New York: Schocken Books.

Selman, R. and D. Jacquette. 1978. "Stability and Oscillation in Interpersonal Awareness: A Clinical/Developmental Analysis." In *Nebraska Symposium on Motivation*, ed. C. B. Kessey. Lincoln, Neb.: University of Nebraska Press.

Smooha, S. 1987. "Jewish and Arab Ethnocentrism in Israel." *Ethnic and Racial Studies* 10:1.

Sniderman, P. 1989. Personal communication, November 18.

Takaki, R. (ed.). 1987. *From Different Shores: Perspectives on Race and Ethnicity in America.* Oxford: Oxford University Press.

Tucker, D. O., and D. C. Locke. 1986. "The Manipulation of Race in Moral Dilemmas: Implications for Moral Education and Human Relations." *Educational and Psychological Research* 6: 99–106.

FACING THE THIRD MILLENNIA: EVANGELICAL CHRISTIANS AND PUBLIC SCHOOLS

William Reese

"Election '88 brought on some headaches for those who value religious liberty and church-state separation that all the aspirin, Tylenol, and ibupropen in the world won't relieve." Thus wrote Ed Doerr in the *Humanist* in early 1989. The chairperson of the Board of the American Humanist Association and the Executive Director of Americans for Religious Liberty, Doerr argued that President George Bush, like his predecessor, lacked respect for the sound doctrine of separation of church and state. He warned civil libertarians and all defenders of the public schools to brace themselves for another round of battles over such issues as aid to private schools, public school prayer, and abortion rights. Liberty as enshrined in the Bill of Rights and protected by the Constitution required defending as right wing religious and political groups again prepared for combat.[1]

It is difficult to quarrel with Doerr's contention that religious issues will continue to inform public policy disputes generally or educational legislation specifically. The last twenty years witnessed the rise of several thousand fundamentalist Christian day schools, assaults on the teaching of evolution in the public schools, non-violent and not so gentle protests about what textbooks children should read, what books school libraries should own, and whether "secularism" and "humanism" had forever undermined traditional moral values in the neighborhood school. These quarrels will continue since they touch deep and important issues concerning

103

who should control education, define its shape, and thus prepare youth for the future. What is less clear is whether the rise of conservative evangelical movements has reached its modern-day peak. Are these movements destined to decline and lose power as the West proceeds to the Third Millennia? Perhaps an understanding of the ties between evangelical Protestantism and school Policy in the American past may illuminate these issues.[2]

The connection between various Protestant groups and education and schooling has been an intimate one throughout the course of American history. Public schools as we recognize them today were unknown before the American Revolution, yet the ties between religion and education were strong. The Puritans of New England, like other Protestant groups in the colonies, emphasized the importance of literacy and especially reading, largely though not exclusively for religious purposes. Reading the Bible, in addition to the catechetical instruction provided by one's parents and minister, promoted a more godly life and hopefully led one along the path to personal salvation. The town schools of eighteenth-century Massachusetts and the district schools of the hinterland often used the Bible as a basic reading text and taught the principles of Protestantism through successive editions of the ubiquitous *New England Primer*. "In Adam's Fall, We Sinned All," many children quickly learned as schools reinforced the lessons of parents and ministers.[3]

But even in the colonial period, no consensus existed over the propriety of a particular brand of religion in education. Quakers, Catholics, Puritan —and many other groups, including atheists—brought enough diversity to public discussions to preclude any easy agreement on important educational matters. Puritan Boston, for example, saw the emergence of a strong commercial class in the late seventeenth century that often eschewed orthodox Calvinist values in their lives. Secular public reading and writing schools for boys, for example, were founded in towns such as Boston that challenged the monopoly of older Latin grammar schools, as middle class families pressed for more attention to more practical, somewhat less religious, education. Private schools for boys and even some girls whose parents could pay for the tuition opened in response to this secular demand. Navigation, penmanship, foreign languages, and dancing were available for whatever prices the market might bear.[4]

Thus, there was more to education than Puritan ministers even in historic Boston might have desired. By the early eighteenth century, religious leaders there lamented the "decline" in the spirituality of the people, reflected in the presence of more luxury goods, finer homes, and often more secular instruction than seemed common in the previous century. A strong Protestant tone informed the Anglo-American world of colonial America, and prayer, Bible reading, and the like shaped the consciousness of generations of settlers and their children. Controversy was nevertheless always present, elders generally thought the new generation somewhat insolent, and the preservation of sound religious influence upon educational practice problematic. The so-called Great Awakening of the 1730s and 1740s spread across the land as a testimony to the perception among many that the place of religion in life had to be restored and redefined.[5]

The success of the American Revolution did not necessarily produce a completely harmonious educational and religious state. The commercial middle classes that helped to finance the American Revolution hardly turned their backs on profits after the victory at Yorktown. The values of Yankee traders threatened still further the pieties of religion and the power of local ministers; the expansion of the country westward opened new avenues to material and not necessarily spiritual gain; and the popularity of the ideas of the Enlightenment hardly seemed propitious to the faithful. The skepticism of a Voltaire, the scientific views of a Jefferson, the radicalism of a Paine, and the continued power of secularism in life led to a decline in church membership and attendance. The stage was set for another Great Awakening.

By the early 1800s, evangelical awakenings emerged that had lasting effects on American culture and education. It is not an exaggeration to say that evangelical movements became part of the mainstream of American Protestantism. The rise of faith in human reason, progress, and the perfectibility of humanity proved attractive to groups such as the Unitarians, but overall more familiar and conservative themes received greater public recognition among older and newly expanding groups such as the Methodists and Baptists. To many evangelical Protestants, the terror of the French Revolution sufficiently countered the assumptions of the Enlightenment about humanity's inherent nature. Evangelicals were unable to prevent the gradual, formal separation of church and state—the established Congregational Church of Massachusetts was the last to fall in 1833—yet they still left a visible, and quite controversial, imprint on basic American institutions such as the emerging public schools.[6]

Protestant ministers—best remembered for their camp meetings and urban revivals—played a seminal role in the establishment of Sunday schools and the creation of public schools in nineteenth-century America. All of their actions were controversial and their successes obvious though incomplete. Like previous religious activists, however, they were an essential part of all dialogues about the fate of American education. Religious denominations had always been interested in the formal and informal instruction of children and youth. What was new in the early 1800s was the growing interdenominational Protestant support for common, public school systems. The success of interdenominational Protestant groups such as the American Bible Society (1816) and the American Sunday School Union (1824) heralded the coming of even greater things by mid-century.[7]

In startlingly rapid fashion, most Protestant groups after the 1830s began to promote the establishment of common, state-controlled public schools. Early in the 1800s, many philanthropic Protestant reformers had banded together to build free charity schools in major urban areas to educate the children of the unchurched poor. Within a few decades, however, as Catholic immigration increased and the revival movements intensified, a broad-based Protestant effort to build state-sponsored schools triumphed. The majoritarian Protestants saw the public schools as a bulwark of mainstream values, a defender of a common faith against infidels, atheists, agnostics, Catholics, Jews, and others. Historian Timothy Smith has succinctly written: "An evangelical consensus of faith and ethics had come to so dominate the national culture, that a majority of Protestants were now willing to entrust the state with the task of educating children, confident that education would be 'religious' still. The sects identified their common beliefs with those of the nation, their mission with America's mission."[8]

Anti-Catholicism served as a unifying belief among most Protestant denominations throughout the 1800s. The links between Protestant leadership and school policies in the early years were numerous. For example, the earliest state school superintendents were often ordained Protestant ministers. Countless teachers were devout "Christians," meaning Protestants who had had a religious conversion. Many single women served as teachers beginning in the nineteenth century, often recruited by religious organizations hoping to save the West for God, or to convert manumitted slaves. Many of these teachers often saw their role in essentially religious terms. More due to custom rather than legislation, teachers often began school days with a non-denominational Protestant prayer and a reading (often without comment) from the King James version of the Bible. Anti-Romanism ran riot.[9]

The successful linkage of Protestant values with the new public school system could be seen in the teaching staff, curriculum, and attitude of ministers toward the enhanced role of the state in the educational sphere. Wrongly assuming that Protestants would long remain dominant, these reformers could not foresee that the state might become more secular and ultimately might infect schools with irreligious beliefs. Most Protestant groups—except for some Lutherans, Seventh Day Adventists, and some small denominations—supported the state system and thus lacked strong systems of denominational schools to counter this possible development. And, as the nineteenth century progressed, the Industrial Revolution added even higher levels of materialism to the American scene, adding further possibilities that secular, worldly values would undermine the power of religion and shape basic social institutions.

Besides Protestant holdouts from the broadly Protestant state system of schools that emerged, Catholics, Jews, nonbelievers, and other dissenters often attacked the development of public education. Opponents supported education and schooling but often denounced the state systems of instruction that emerged. Catholics slowly built a competing system of parochial schools after their efforts to share the tax fund were defeated in the 1840s. They condemned the public school texts that disparaged the culture of immigrants and Catholics and that openly ridiculed the papacy. That all "Christians" were Protestants struck Catholics and others as ludicrous, just as it would to many citizens in the next century. But the allegiance of evangelical Protestants to the public schools remained powerful, and the easy equation of Protestantism, Americanism, and public schooling was understandable given the power of majorities to define reality.[10]

The early twentieth century witnessed a continual struggle by evangelical Protestants to control the destiny of American education. As prescient observers sometimes predicted, the belief that the state would remain tightly bound with Protestant values was an overly optimistic one. That is, secularism and materialism were strongly nourished by the intensification of marketplace values in the late nineteenth century, and the religious complexion of the country grew as millions of immigrants, especially Catholics and to a lesser extent Jews, came to America in the new century. Protestants still were dominant on school boards, in much of the teaching force, and especially prominent in shaping school policy in small towns and villages across the country. But professional administrators in the growing schools, especially in cities, while usually Protestant, increasingly supplanted the ministers so influential in state government and local school control in the nineteenth century. Like an echo from the past, Protestant ministers and lay activists condemned the decline of school and society.[11]

Efforts were continually made, of course, to guarantee that a set of homogeneous, pan-Protestant values still dominated schools serving an increasingly heterogeneous people. But the Scopes Trial, which discredited fundamentalist ideas among many citizens, undermined Darwin's theory of evolution about as successfully as Prohibition ended the drinking of bourbon. Yet the fight over evolution was part of a larger crisis facing the faithful. Evangelical and fundamentalist Christians even before the 1920s well understood that a creeping secularism grew larger in the wake of America's emergence as an industrial and world power. Evangelist Billy Sunday attacked the rise of vocational education programs in the schools in the early 1900s, since he realized that material gain was increasingly becoming an important motive behind the expansion of schools in general and the high schools in particular. Despite these complaints against what were seen as dangerous features of modern education, destined to obscure the moral mission of the schools, vocational programs became common and often flourished. How to prepare for the world of work came to define for many the goals of public schools.[12]

Evangelical Protestants won the battle in Tennessee in the 1920s over the teaching of evolution in the schools, since the U.S. Supreme Court did not reverse bans against the teaching of evolution until 1968. Early in the century, prayers in schools were increasingly mandated by law to ensure compliance with the older Protestant faith. But these individual victories did not constitute any ultimate winning of the war. The early twentieth century witnessed a continual movement of mainstream Protestant churches toward liberalism. Some Protestant ministers who advocated the social gospel even became prominent Christian Socialists, calling for various forms of public ownership of the means of production. Such liberalizing tendencies reflected changes within Protestantism itself as certain leaders confronted the challenges of immigration, urban and industrial growth, and the problems of poverty in metropolitan areas.[13]

Evangelical Protestants countered all this by leading impressive revivals, passing legislation requiring prayers in the schools, and fighting atheists and evolutionists wherever they found them. The essential beliefs of anti-modernist sentiment surfaced between 1910 and 1915 in a remarkable set of writings called *The Fundamentals*, whose sixty-four contributors reemphasized the basic evangelical creed: the divinity of Christ, the inerrancy and infallibility of the Bible, human depravity, and the life, death, and resurrection of the Lord. In the 1920s fundamentalists opposed the Catholic Al Smith in his bid for the presidency. In this and subsequent decades they built an impressive array of Bible colleges,

Bible institutes, and other institutions to combat the growing secularization of American life. Many evangelical Christians became well known for their anti-bolshevik, patriot, and pro-American views.[14]

Conservative evangelical Christians of the last decades of the twentieth century continued to face the challenges of America's expansive materialism, secularism, cultural pluralism, and deep social change. America was the world's leading economic and military power after World War II, and the spread of markets abroad and the consumption of goods and services at home became notable national preoccupations. The civil rights movement, women's rights movement, and Great Society programs by the 1960s, plus the war in Viet Nam, brought new social issues to the fore for all citizens. Crucial to conservative evangelical thinking about the place of education in society was the fateful decisions of the U.S. Supreme Court in 1962 and 1963 that banned state-sponsored school prayer. Although the decisions were often ignored and such prayers continued, many conservative Protestants saw this symbolic blow against tradition as a sign of deeper problems in American culture and the public schools.[15]

One notable response to these changes was the creation of independent Christian day schools. Many of the early private elementary and secondary Christian schools founded in the late 1950s and 1960s were direct responses to court-ordered racial integration and busing. Yet their creation also reflected a deeper fear of social change and overall suspicion of the drift of public school policy. Busing plans often stimulated and accelerated the movement to build independent "Christian" day schools. Still, many evangelical Protestants in the last decades of the twentieth century built their own institutions for a variety of reasons. The tendency of American policy in the twentieth century was to build large, centralized, professionally managed school systems that offered an increasingly secularized curriculum that was oriented to the labor market. Gone was the faith in the type of moral or religious training represented by McGuffey Readers, Protestant school prayers, and Bible readings. Many evangelicals in the 1970s and 1980s would continue to fight for what they perceived to be Christian values in the public schools and in their own emerging private schools.[16]

The separation of a minority of evangelical Protestants from the public schools in favor of their own independent Christian day schools was indeed a notable phenomenon in the late twentieth century. By the early 1980s, approximately four to five thousand of these schools existed, enrolling perhaps a million students. Conservative evangelical Baptists and other smaller Protestant groups in large cities as well as in rural America constructed havens from what they saw as a frightening world of competing values in the public schools. In their own, relatively small schools, parents and evangelical teachers presented children absolute biblical truths, a Christian curriculum, patriotic values, and traditional discipline. Many evangelical Christians thought they were simply creating the values of the old-time public school. When asked in 1975 why so many parents were choosing Christian schools over public schools, an Indianapolis private school administrator responded: "They express a felt need for an old-fashioned school that teaches basic things and from a Christ-centered point of view."[17]

In the 1970s and 1980s, a host of evangelical Christians portrayed public schools in the most distressing terms. They assailed public schools for their blind acceptance of secular values, exemplified by the teaching of evolution, the legal exclusion of prayer, the materialist philosophies undergirding the curriculum, the increase in school violence, teacher strikes, and the like. Often many evangelical Christians painted an unreal portrait of public schools that only highlighted their many flaws and necessary compromises to reach new student populations in a changing world. Reading evangelical attacks on the schools, one would think that most students were drug addicts who routinely assaulted teachers and lacked any commitment to academic instruction or moral values. Some evangelicals blamed "secular humanists" for the "decline" of the public schools, as human needs replaced the deity at the core of the public school mission. Some ministers attacked public schools for their "pagan philosophy" of instruction; others said humanists had "turned our public schools into a jungle in which any kind of animal can do anything it wants."[18]

The withdrawal of conservative evangelical Protestants from support for the public schools was never complete in the late twentieth century. Only a minority of evangelical Protestants send their children to private schools, and many Baptists and other activists formed and joined many conservative political action groups to advance far reaching social reforms. After the reaction against the civil rights movement and anti-war movement in the late 1960s, America entered an era in which the presidency would be held almost unbrokenly (save for the conditions created by Watergate) by Republicans. From Nixon in 1968 to Bush in 1988, Republicanism was nearly invincible. Conservative evangelical Christians especially in the 1970s and afterward were not unafraid to build their own educational institutions while simultaneously trying to restore, as they saw it, some of the tradition to the public school system.

Throughout the 1970s and 1980s famous political pressure groups such as Moral Majority and less well-known but potent local and state lobbying organizations used modern communication systems to advance their conservative causes. Christian television programs grew dramatically, and they brought the messages from conservative pulpits throughout the nation into the homes of the curious and faithful. Jerry Falwell and other ministers often presented forceful statements about the fall of public morality and the decline of the public schools in sermons that reached millions of listeners and voters. Computer-assisted mailing campaigns helped raise money for conservative political candidates, and the presidential aspirants became quite aware of the influence of this minority force in the political arena. Evangelicals did not completely withdraw from the battle over the public schools but often remained committed combatants.[19]

Conservative evangelical Protestants fought secularism and humanism on several fronts as far as schools were concerned. Some, though not all, conservatives pressured for tuition tax credits to help aid private school expansion. Even more fought, often quite successfully, to limit state power in school accreditation and the licensing of teachers in private schools. Bible colleges trained teachers for the rapidly expanding fundamentalist schools, and Christian educators developed school curricula with a Bible-centered orientation. Christian school activists often withdrew their children from the world to protect them from the evil teachings of the public schools, but they were also often quite savvy politically in their attempts to shape other people's children.[20]

Evangelical activists fought against what they saw as the most disturbing trends in the public schools. They always, of course, attacked school violence, low academic standards, and falling test scores. All this they linked to the decline of moral and religious values in public education, a product of the liberalism of the 1960s. Conservative evangelicals remained quite active in many campaigns designed to extend their influence in the public schools. First of all, they often placed huge pressure on state textbook commissions in important states such as Texas and California to select materials that best conformed to their worldview. History texts that seemed to impugn American values or biology texts that taught evolution as fact and ignored biblical facts about creation were often targeted for extinction. Few evangelical Christians believed that the absolute truths of the sort found in the *New England Primer* would ever again be found in the schools. Yet, they worked to hold the tide of secular humanism and perhaps partly to reverse it.[21]

The late twentieth century also saw the revival of older battles over creation. Creation science research centers were formed to distribute supposedly scientific research confirming the truths of Genesis. Christian publishing houses assailed the flaws in evolutionary theory, and lobbyists pressured state education officials and secular publishers to provide equal time for biblical theories of creation in biology textbooks. Presidential candidates, like local figures running for office, were often forced to state their positions on whether prayer should be "restored" to the public schools. When state legislatures passed laws permitting school prayer, and judges ruled them unconstitutional, evangelicals then pressed for moments of silence to allow time for the faithful. Even in a world awash in consumer and material goods, hope remained strong that America would see a return of that old time value system.

As conservative evangelical Protestants faced the end of the twentieth century, it was unclear whether the conservative movement had peaked or still had life. The modern day great awakening seemed to have its greatest public recognition politically during the presidencies of Ronald Reagan. While Reagan often espoused evangelical positions—the return of "voluntary" school prayer, aid to private schools, the teaching of creationism, and so forth—his administration had very few major legislative accomplishments in these areas. Some successes were registered, but overall evangelicals still in the fray have been unable to enjoy clear victories. The plight of the homeless, the budget deficit, drug wars at home and abroad, and the dissolution of the Soviet empire have taken precedence in public debate as the century enters its final decade.

The history of American education cannot be understood at any moment apart from evangelical Protestantism. From the beginning, Protestants left an indelible religious imprint on the shape and character of the nation's schools. Public schools were in many respects an outgrowth of the second great awakening of the early to mid-nineteenth century. Protestants filled the classrooms, ran the state departments of education, wrote the textbooks, and infused the system with their values. Like their colonial predecessors, however, evangelical Protestants over the past two centuries have had to combat the continual force of materialism, secularism, and cultural diversity that has helped overall to define the American people. Those who champion absolute moral values based on their view of the Bible or who believe that public schools should save souls rather than shape minds or prepare youth for the labor market will have tough going as they approach the Third Millennia.

Notes

1. Ed Doerr, "Election '88," *Humanist* 49 (January-February 1989): 37.

2. See William J. Reese, "Soldiers for Christ in the Army of God: The Christian School Movement in America," *Educational Theory* 35 (spring 1985): 175–194.

3. See Bernard Bailyn, *Education in the Forming of American Society* (New York, 1960); and Lawrence A. Cremin, *American Education: The Colonial Experience, 1607–1783* (New York, 1970).

4. See especially Jon Teaford, "The Transformation of Massachusetts Education, 1670–1780," *History of Education Quarterly* 10 (fall 1970): 287–307; Robert F. Seybolt, *The Public Schools of Colonial Boston, 1635–1775* (Cambridge, 1935); Robert F. Seybolt, *The Private Schools of Colonial Boston* (Cambridge, 1935); and Henry F. Jenks, *Catalogue of the Boston Public Latin School, Established in 1635 With an Historical Sketch* (Boston, 1886).

5. Teaford, "The Transformation of Massachusetts Education," 287–307; Emit Duncan Grizzell, *Origin and Development of the High School in New England Before 1865* (Philadelphia, 1923), chap. 1; Robert Middlekauf, *Ancients and Axioms: Secondary Education in Eighteenth-Century New England* (New York, c. 1971); Douglas Sloan, ed. *The Great Awakening and American Education: A Documentary History* (New York, 1973); and a basic introduction to the Great Awakening in Sydney E. Ahlstrom, *A Religious History of the American People* (Garden City, N.Y., 1975).

6. Donald G. Mathews, "The Second Great Awakening as an Organizing Process," *American Quarterly, The Life of the Mind in America* (New York, 1965); Timothy Smith, *Revivalism and Social Reform* (New York, 1957); and William G. McLoughlin, *Revivals, Awakenings, and Reform* (Chicago, 1978), chap. 3.

7. John R. Bodo, *The Protestant Clergy and Public Issues* (Princeton, 1954), 168–169; and Lawrence Cremin, *American Education: The National Experience, 1783–1876* (New York, 1980), chap. 2.

8. Timothy L. Smith, "Protestant Schooling and American Nationality, 1800–1850," *Journal of American History* 53 (March 1967): 687.

9. Lloyd P. Jorgensen, *The State and the Non-Public Schools* (Columbia, Mo., 1987); David B. Tyack, "The Kingdom of God and the Common School: Protestant Ministers and the Educational Awakening in the West," *Harvard Educational Review* 36 (fall 1966): 450; Ruth Elson, *Guardians of Tradition: American Schoolbooks of the Nineteenth Century* (Lincoln, Neb., 1964); and Ray Billington, *The Protestant Crusade, 1800–1860: A Study of the Origins of American Nativism* (New York, 1938).

10. Carl F. Kaestle, *Pillars of the Republic: Common Schools and American Society* (New York, 1983), chap. 7.

11. David B. Tyack and Elisabeth Hansot, *Managers of Virtue: Public School Leadership in America, 1820–1980* (New York, 1982), Part II.

12. On Billy Sunday, see McLoughlin, *Revivals, Awakenings, and Reform.*

13. David B. Tyack, "Onward Christian Soldiers: Religion in the American Common School," in *History and Education*, ed. Paul Nash (New York, 1970): 212–255; Henry F. May, *Protestant Churches and Industrial America* (New York, 1949); and William J. Reese, "The Public Schools and the Great Gates of Hell," *Educational Theory* 32 (winter 1982): 9–17.

14. David F. Wells and John D. Woodbridge, eds., *The Evangelicals* (Nashville, 1975); Winthrop Hudson, *Religion in America* (New York, 1981), chap. 14; Ernest Sandeen, *The Origins of Fundamentalism* (Philadelphia, 1968); and Ed Dobson and Ed Hindson, *The Fundamentalist Phenomenon: The Resurgence of Conservative Christianity* (Garden City, N.Y., 1981), 13–14, 110–111.

15. Reese, "Soldiers for Christ," 175–194.

16. An earlier critique of the Christian School movement for its racial exclusiveness was by David Nevin and Robert E. Bills, *The Schools That Fear Built: Segregationist Academies in the South* (Washington, D.C., 1976). Important articles from different perspectives include: James C. Carper, "The Christian Day School Movement," *Educational Forum* 47 (winter 1983): 135–149; and James C. Carper, "The Christian Day School in the American Social Order, 1960–1980," in *Religion and Morality in American Schooling*, ed. Thomas C. Hunt and Marilyn M. Maxson (Washington, D.C., 1981), 79–101.

17. Very M. Haley, secretary of the Christian Academy, cited in Harley M. Bierce, "Faith-Oriented Schooling Shows Rapid Growth Among Protestants," *Indianapolis Star* (11 July 1975), 109. Other examples are cited in Reese, "Soldiers for Christ," 176–180.

18. Pastor Clyde Winegar, quoted in Joan Richardson, "Education—According to the Gospels," *Peoria Journal Star* (30 October 1977), C1; and Dick Ulmer, "Christian Schools Buck Trend," *Omaha World Herald* (16 August 1981), B10. Also see Jerry Falwell, *Listen, America!* (New York, 1980); and Tim LaHaye, *The Battle for the Public Schools* (Old Tappan, N.J., 1983).

19. An introduction to the literature would include Alan Crawford, *Thunder on the Right* (New York, 1980); Thomas McIntyre, *The Fear Brokers* (Boston, 1979); plus the books cited previously by Falwell, Dobson, and Hindson, and any number of articles in journals such as *Christianity Today* in the 1980s.

20. James C. Carper, "The *Whisper* Decision: A Case Study in State Regulation of Christian Day Schools," *Journal of Church and State* 24 (spring 1982): 281–302; "Christian Schools: Learning in the Courtroom," *Christianity Today* 22 (September 22, 1978): 36–37; and Edward E. Plowman, "Alarmed at Government Intrusion, Religious Groups Close Ranks," *Christianity Today* 25 (March 13, 1981): 72–74.

21. See the previous articles by Reese, Carper, and the various books and articles by religious leaders themselves.

CATHOLICISM AS INTEGRAL HUMANISM:

CHRISTIAN PARTICIPATION IN

PLURALISTIC MORAL EDUCATION

Michael J. Himes

In his Confessions, Augustine paid eloquent testimony to what he had learned from various neo-Platonic writings which were highly regarded by Christian intellectuals of the fourth century.[1] But he noted that, amid all that he read in these books which was in accord with Christian teaching, one doctrine, and that the key one, was absent, "I read there that God the Word was born not of flesh or blood, not of the will of man or of the will of the flesh, but of God. But that the Word became flesh and dwelt among us, that I did not read there."[2] For Augustine, at least in the 390s when he wrote his Confessions, the unique doctrine of Christianity which distinguished it from even the loftiest speculations of classical philosophy was the incarnation.

The hallmark of Christianity is incarnationalism, the claim that the Absolute Mystery which lies at the root of all existence which we call God has been fully expressed in the life, death, and destiny of a particular human being, Jesus of Nazareth. That claim is scandalous. From the very beginning of Christianity it was recognized that it would be regarded as "foolishness" by many and would prove a "stumbling block" precisely to those who appreciated the absoluteness of the Mystery called God (1 Corinthians 1:23). A claim so deeply rooted in a tradition as rich as Christianity is multifaceted. This central incarnational claim allows, indeed demands, development in many directions. One of these directions, explored even from the earliest centuries of Christianity, has been an extraordinarily rich humanism.

The central contention of this essay is that the Catholic tradition understands Christianity as authentic humanism and, as such, should be able to interact fruitfully with much of the humanist agenda in moral education for participation in our society. This is, I recognize, by no means the position of much of the Evangelical tradition within Christianity. That is why I am a Catholic and not an Evangelical.

The recognition that the Catholic and Evangelical perspectives are not the same immediately raises an important consideration. Pluralism is not only the condition of the society within which Christianity attempts to make itself heard it is an internal mark of Christianity itself. Great religious traditions are woven of multiple strands. Buddhism, Islam, Judaism, all contain strands which have emphasized particular elements of the core experience of those traditions. Christianity, too, is a far richer tapestry than many of those who describe themselves as Christians readily acknowledge. The collection of foundational Christian documents called the New Testament includes related but quite distinct accounts of Christian self-understanding. The communities which produced the various documents clearly had different understandings of Jesus' teaching, different ways of describing the significance of his life and destiny, different visions of their missions, and different styles of community life and organization.[3]

Despite attempts to distinguish some particular position as *the* Christian view, Christians should candidly admit the fact of considerable pluralism within the tradition and observe a becoming modesty about canonizing any one strand. By no means should this be construed as a license to subsume any and every opinion under the rubric "Christian" simply because its proponents claim the title.[4] Some elements of the tradition are so central that any attempt at formulating a Christian response to a question which omits or diminishes them is thereby disqualified.

Stephen Sykes has argued that the attempt to discern the essence of Christianity by isolating particular elements in order to demonstrate the unity of the tradition over time is futile. He offers the provocative suggestion that Christian theologians appropriate W.B. Gallie's notion of an "essentially contested concept."[5] The "crucial question" then becomes "what it is that constitutes the fact that the players are all playing in a single game, and that the participants in the dispute are contending about the same matter."[6] Sykes concludes that "the contestants who disagree about what Christianity is, are, despite all their differences, disagreeing about the nature of a single 'performance'," which he identifies as "the life, death and resurrection of Jesus Christ."[7] He then notes that "it is manifest, therefore, that this *formal* characteristic of one who is a contestant about the concept of Christianity contains a statement about the status of Christology for a Christian."[8] Christianity remains centrally concerned with Jesus' question to his disciples, "Who do you say that I am?" (Mt. 16:15, Mk. 8:29, Lk. 9:20), although Christians may differ among themselves on how it is to be answered.

The Incarnational Principle as the Foundation of Christian Humanism

To explore the depth of the incarnational claim in the Christian tradition, another key symbol must first be explored, creation. However much they differ on the details of narrative, the two creation myths in Genesis (1:1–2:4a and 2:4b–25) agree on the central place which humanity occupies in the divine plan for the cosmos. In the first of these stories, God is depicted as creating all things by the mere speaking of his command that they be: "Let there be light," "let there be a firmament," etc. (1:3, 6, 9, 14, 20, 24). But when God comes to the creation of the human beings on the afternoon of the sixth day, for the first time God deliberates before the act of creation: "Let us make the human being in our image and likeness" (1:26). God has a model according to which the human being will be fashioned, and the model is God's self. God confers on humanity dominion over all creatures: "Let the human being have dominion over the fish of the sea and the birds of the sky, the cattle and all the wild animals, and all the creatures that creep upon the earth. . . . God also said, 'See, I give you for your food every seed-bearing plant on earth and every tree which bears fruit'" (1:26 and 29). Three points should be noted in this first creation myth. First, creating human beings requires more planning than creating the firmament or the sun, moon, and stars, more than separating the waters and the dry land, more than making all plants and fish and birds and animals. The human being is placed last in the order of creation in the story because it is the culmination of God's creative action. Humanity is God's masterpiece and has received God's fullest attention. Second, being human is the image and likeness of God. Third, since God has dominion over all creation, the part of creation which is like God must have dominion over all other creatures. Thus, humanity is given authority like God's.

The second creation myth reverses the order of events. God fashions the first human being before plants and animals and fish and birds (2:7). All the rest of creation is designed to meet the human being's needs. Instead of being the culmination of creation, humanity is first in order of creation, that for which everything else comes into being. The dominion given humanity over creation is expressed in the divine permission for the human being to give names to all the other creatures, i.e., determine their nature (2:19–20). Both myths are in agreement, however, that humanity holds a unique place in the cosmos, that it is God's greatest work, and that all else receives its purpose from its relationship to humanity.

But there is another point to be observed in both stories in Genesis. According to the first story, "God created the human being in God's image; in the divine image God created the human being, male and female God created them" (1:27). In the vision of this first of the creation myths, being in the image of God means being sexed. Sexuality means relatedness, incompleteness without the other. And that is part of being "like God," for God in the Hebrew scriptures is always the God of the covenant, the God who is related to his creatures. The notion of God "in God's self" is foreign to the scriptures. The only God the scriptures know is God in relation to creation. If being human is being "like God" then being human is being in relationship. The second myth's way of making this same point is the divine recognition that "it is not good that the human being should be alone" (2:18). And it emerges that nothing is a fit companion for a human being (2:22–23). Humanity is not "right" outside of community.

The themes of these two creation myths find echo in and provide the context for the story of "the fall" and the introduction of evil into the divinely created cosmos.[9] The repeated divine judgment in the first of the creation stories is that "God looked [at what God had made] and saw that it was good" (1:4, 10, 12, 18, 21, 25), and the story concludes with the statement that "God looked at everything that God had made and saw that it was very good" (1:31).[10] The first temptation is precisely that this judgment be rejected. The motive advanced by the serpent for disregarding the divine command not to eat the fruit of the tree of the knowledge of good and evil is that, if the first man and woman do so, they "will become like God in knowing good and evil" (3:5).[11] But the first creation myth claimed that they are "like God," that God has created them "in God's image." The presupposition of the first temptation is that the divine judgment that human being is "very good" was false. The serpent invites the human being to reject the goodness of humanity by denying that being human is being "like God." And the first sin is the acceptance of that invitation.

Thus the origin of evil in the Genesis story of the fall is the denial that humanity is in the image of God and the rejection of the goodness of being human. The entry of evil into the world which God had proclaimed good is the first human beings' loss of faith in the goodness of their existence. The first sin in this mythic account is neither disobedience nor pride; it is despair, the rejection of the goodness of finite, specifically human, being. And significantly the first result of this sin is the collapse of relationship. The first man and woman now hide when God comes to stroll with them in the garden in the cool of the evening (3:8). The man who had greeted the woman with joyous recognition when he first encountered her (2:23) now blames her for having given him the forbidden fruit (3:12). The woman, in turn, places the blame on the serpent whom she had trusted shortly before (3:13). Human beings, who are only truly human in relationship with one another according to the creation stories, now turn on one another in mutual reproach. The erosion of trust and communion continues through the myths of prehistory in the first eleven chapters of Genesis. The fall story ends with human beings alienated from God. Shortly they become alienated one from another—the murder of Abel by Cain (4:1–15)—and then find themselves living in mutually alienated groups, symbolized by the collapse of communication—the tower of Babel story (11:1–9).[12] And the root of this ever widening evil is the denial of the goodness of human being.

Against this background, the doctrine of the incarnation in Christian tradition can be seen as the startling claim which it was intended to be. Perhaps its strongest statement is also one of the earliest, the hymn in Paul's letter to the Philippians (2:6–11). In the second chapter of the letter, Paul quotes a hymn, presumably one already known to the Christians in Philippi. If the letter is authentically Pauline, then it predates the composition of the gospels. Assuming that the letter was written sometime in the late fifties or very early sixties of the first Christian century and that the hymn quoted in it is earlier, this song could well be the earliest extant literary expression of the Christian community's faith concerning the person of Jesus, the now risen Christ.

> Although he was in the form of God,
> he did not think that being equal to God was something
>   to be held in grasp,
> but rather he emptied himself
> to assume the condition of a servant
> and became a human being
> and was like all other human beings. (2:6–7)

This hymn has enormous importance for the Christian understanding of Christ, but its importance for Christian anthropology should not go unnoticed. When read against the background of the Hebrew scriptures, the hymn celebrates the archetype's having at last become one with the image. But this primitive Christian hymn states this in an extraordinary manner: the one who is in the form of God does not deem being Godlike as something which is to be retained but wills to become a human being exactly like all other human beings. This is the most sweeping claim concerning the goodness and dignity of creaturely being, and specifically of human being, which the Christian tradition has made: the Creator has chosen to become a creature, God has chosen to become a human being.

Nicholas Lash has written that

the real difficulty in saying that christianity, or theology, is about God and man, the real difficulty in *verus Deus et verus homo*, consists not in knowing what we mean by *God* or what we mean by *man* (though these are no small questions), but in the difficulty of knowing what we mean by *and*.[13]

Whatever "and" means in this christological usage, it does not mean "in addition." The classical Christian claim about Christ does not simply juxtapose divinity and humanity. Jesus of Nazareth is not divine "and also" human. The peculiar meaning of "and" in classical Christian doctrine might be rendered "in light of" or "because of." The doctrine asserts that in Jesus we see revealed true divinity insofar as we see true humanity, and that we see true humanity insofar as we see true divinity. The key to the understanding of classical christological doctrine is that divinity and full humanity are not in competition. The relationship between divinity and humanity revealed in the incarnation is one of direct, not indirect proportion, i.e., the fuller the expression of God, the richer the humanity which receives the expression, *and* the more fully and richly human one is, then the more perfectly one receives God who is always self-gift.

This incarnational principle is closely connected to the symbol of creation. The religious significance of *creatio ex nihilo* is not only cosmological, it is also teleological; it makes a claim about the purpose of creation. Creation has no intrinsic ground. It gives nothing to God, not even glory. God needs nothing from creation. Therefore the only reason for the existence of anything other than the Absolute Mystery which we name God can only be that God gives something to creation. But anything which God would give to creation other than God's self would be part of creation. Creation exists so that it can be gifted, and the gift which it is given is God's self. Everything which is exists so that God can communicate God's self to it. There is no other ground for being but the self-communication of God. Human *being* is that point in creation at which creation becomes capable of self-knowledge and self-acceptance, i.e., capable of recognizing the divine self-gift and accepting it gratefully. Humanity exists in order to be filled with the self-gift of God.

Pope's famous admonition, "Know then thyself, presume not God to scan; / The proper study of Mankind is Man,"[14] is correct, but not in the way that he thought. For if the incarnational claim of Christianity is taken seriously, then to know human being is also to know God in part. Humanity exists in order to be the recipient of the self-giving of God. The exploration and development of the receiver leads to some grasp of the gift. Every creature, insofar as it is seen to be a creature, i.e., to exist as the object of God's gift of self, is a sacrament, a symbol which by being what it is points to the presence of God. To know anything as created is to know it as referred to God. The ability of a thing to refer us to something else depends on our noticing it and appreciating that it is. The more a thing is, the more it refers. The primary requirement for being a religious symbol is simply being. A true religious symbol does not stand for something else; it reveals that something else by being itself. This is the true symbolism which, in the words of Goethe, "is where the particular represents the more general, not as a dream or a shadow, but as a living momentary revelation of the Inscrutable."[15] Goethe made this the crux of the distinction between poetry and allegory: the latter "seeks the particular for the general," whereas poetry "sees the general in the particular." The very nature of poetry is that "it expresses something particular, without thinking of the general or pointing to it."[16] If Goethe is correct—and surely he is no mean authority on poetry—then the incarnation is the poetry of God. For the humanity of Jesus does not point to or stand for the fullness of the divine self-gift; that would reduce the incarnation to allegory. It is by being fully, totally, and completely human that divinity is given expression—poetry of the highest order! If one is to symbolize God, one must be human; if one is to symbolize God so perfectly that one is God, then that one must be perfectly human.

Not only are full divinity and full humanity not in competition, the latter is the symbol—or in classical Catholic terminology, the sacrament—of the former. The Catholic tradition maintains that the Absolute Mystery is never directly graspable, that the self-communication of God is always mediated, never immediate, that "no one can see the face of God and live" (Exodus 33:20).[17] This is the sacramental principle which is so deeply rooted in Catholicism and so intimately related to the doctrines of incarnation and creation. And the ultimate sacrament, the religious symbol which is always primary in the life of every human being, is the self. The discovery of the self in its intrinsic relatedness to other selves is the way in which we come to "know" God.

This incarnational base has grounded much of what has been richest in Christian theology from Augustine's insight that to speak of God he would first have to speak of the restlessness of his own heart[18] to Karl Rahner's insistence that all theology begins with anthropology. For the human being has been created for the self-giving of God. In Rahner's term, the human being exists in order to be a "hearer of the Word":[19] "We could now define man, within the framework of his supreme and darkest mystery, as that which ensues when God's self-utterance, his Word, is given out lovingly into the void of god-less nothing."[20] Thus, recognizing that the Absolute Mystery which is God remains sovereignly *mystery* and so can never be adequately grasped in any human constructs or concepts, one can speak of the divine self-gift only by exploring that which is created precisely to be the recipient of the gift, the human person. In this sense Rahner's claim is correct: "all theology is therefore eternally an anthropology."[21] To speak about God who is gift is to speak about the human being who is the object of the giving; to know the Word is to know the one who is called into being in order to hear the Word.

Taking this incarnational principle with maximal seriousness, it follows that the Christian life requires the fullest possible development of the human person in all aspects of his or her being. Integral Christianity is integral humanism. For if divinity and humanity are in direct, not indirect, proportion, then the more fully human one becomes, the more like God he or she becomes. Consequently, it is the duty of Christians who appreciate and believe in the radical import of the incarnational principle to work for the full humanization of all persons. Only by full humanization can human beings become more "like God," for God has not only created humanity in the divine image, God has become a human being "like us in all things but sin."

Christian Humanism Is Intrinsically Pluralistic

An obvious question must be posed: what is full humanization? How does one determine what constitutes integral humanism? Is not the point of so much dispute in our pluralist society precisely the meaning of the term "human"? How then does the Catholic insistence on taking the incarnational principle with maximal import advance the discussion? And the plain truth is that it does not and cannot immediately answer these questions. What the Catholic tradition's incarnationalism and sacramentalism does do, however, is to make the question a religiously relevant one for believers. No Christian who gives to the incarnation the weight which the Catholic strand within Christianity has given it can simply dismiss the concerns of humanism as mistaken or unimportant for his or her faith. If humanity is what we share with God, which is certainly one of the implications of the doctrine of the incarnation, then as believers in the incarnation, we must approach the question of the development of full humanity with nothing less than religious reverence. From the Alexandrian Fathers of the second and third centuries with their interpretation of Christ as the *paidogogos* of humanity and of Christianity as the ultimate stage of the divine *paideia* by which God leads creation to its full stature[22] through the rise of the medieval universities to John Henry Newman's classic statement of the ideals of liberal education, *The Idea of a University*,[23] the Catholic tradition has recognized the intimate connection between the Gospel and the process of humanization, as that has been variously understood. Education, taken in its richest sense as the formation of the human person in the full and harmonious exercise of all his or her capacities, is a religious act for those who believe that humanity is what they and God have in common.

But what constitutes integral humanism is not answerable by Christianity alone. The claim that in Christ we see the one who is *verus Deus et verus homo*, as Nicholas Lash notes, raises the question of the meaning of "and" and sets guidelines for its answer but it does not claim to resolve the questions of what we mean by God and what we mean by human.[24] The Christian tradition has something to say to both these questions, but it claims—or should claim—no final answer to either of them. Any attempt to insist on a final definition of God is blasphemous. And any attempt to insist on such a definition of the human person is, at best, presumptuous.

The first commandment of the decalogue warns against idolatry, the besetting sin of religion (Exodus 20:3–5 and Deuteronomy 5:7–9). The temptation for religious persons and communities is always to identify God with their highest, purest, richest image of God. Deeply ingrained in the religious genius of the Hebrew tradition, to which Christianity is so much indebted, is its suspiciousness of all attempts to make an image of God. All images of God, all concepts of divinity, are in danger of becoming idols, for no image can be identified with God, no matter how traditionally sanctioned, scripturally based, doctrinally orthodox, or ecclesiastically approved. Idols must be smashed periodically, i.e., religious people must remind themselves that the "God" they imagine when they worship is not *God*. Catholic theology has tried to be faithful to this anti-idolatrous principle of the Jewish and Christian traditions by maintaining that God is always Mystery. The absolute transcendence of God means that God can never be grasped in any conceptual formula or doctrinal definition. Such formulae and definitions may have something true to say about the Mystery, but they never exhaust it. Only God can express God's self perfectly, can speak a Word which is absolute self-expression to the point where Speaker and Word are one (John 1:1). If another is to hear that Word, that other must be fashioned by God to be an apt hearer of the Word. One biblical way of expressing this is the prohibition of images "made by hands." For only God can make an image of God—and that image has been made: the human being.

The hallmark of true humanity, then, for the Christian tradition is its capacity to receive the self-communication of

God. But that capacity presumes the ability of the human being to transcend itself, i.e., to go beyond itself. It is the "open-endedness" of humanity, its capacity, for self-transcendence, which makes the human person the point in creation to which the divine self-communication can be made in an unsurpassable manner. It is this quality which the doctrine of the incarnation presumes. Thus, the one point regarding human being upon which Christianity must insist is precisely the inability finally and absolutely to limit human being. The very definition of the human person for Christianity is that it is the creature which cannot be defined. As the image of God and the hearer of the Word, the human person is also mystery.

Thus, the Catholic tradition within Christianity insists that the fostering of integral humanity means, first and foremost, that no preconceived limitations can be put on the meaning of humanity. Any form of humanism which imposes an absolute blueprint on the human person is not true or integral humanism. At its best (and it is not always at its best), Catholicism recognizes that no formula, including none of its own formulae, can be made the final definition of true humanity. Catholicism should be—and sometimes is—*catholic*, i.e., it acknowledges and respects other perspectives on the human person, so long as none makes pretensions to absoluteness. It realizes that no community of faith, however divinely founded, no tradition of thought, however rich, no strand of experience, however fruitful, can give a final answer to the question, "What is a human being?" Integral humanism, therefore, is open-ended and necessarily dialogic.

If faithful to its own convictions, Catholic Christianity not only encourages pluralism, it demands it. It is, in H. Richard Niebuhr's phrase, "radical monotheism" which he contrasted with polytheism and henotheism. Polytheism is the denial of ultimacy to any value. It is pluralism degenerating into mere plurality, for the guiding maxim of polytheism is *de gustibus non disputandum*. Henotheism is "that social faith which makes a finite society, whether cultural or religious, the object of trust as well as of loyalty and which tends to subvert even officially monotheistic institutions, such as the church."[25] Henotheism exalts a historically and culturally conditioned view of reality (and all views of reality are so conditioned) into Reality. But radical monotheism is that social faith in which "the value-center is neither a closed society nor the principle of such a society but the principle of being itself; its reference is to no one reality among the many but to One beyond all the many, whence all the many derive their being, and by participation in which they exist."[26] Christianity's radical monotheist insistence that only God is God relativizes all other values. Any attempt to absolutize any perspective, any doctrine, any political or social system, is idolatrous, a collapse into henotheism. If God is the fullness of truth, then nothing else is. But God is always Absolute Mystery, which means that no perspective or doctrine can be enshrined as the final and complete formulation of truth and no perspective or doctrine can simply and immediately be dismissed as false. The radically monotheist Christian believer in Mystery must approach those who are not Christian believers with respect and attention. For since the Christian knows that no one can lay claim to absolute possession of the Truth, the Christian must allow for partial truths in unexpected places. This is not what Niebuhr termed polytheism, for it does not shirk the obligation to weigh all positions carefully and to reject what is found inadequate. What most clearly renders a position inadequate is any claim to total adequacy. The Catholic Christian tradition, when it is faithful both to its radical monotheism and to its incarnational principle, must enter into conversation with all those who seek full human development. Only two dialogue partners are ruled out: "polytheists" for whom real conversation is impossible since no truth exists, and "henotheists" for whom real conversation is unnecessary since truth is already theirs.

In fidelity to its own deepest elements, therefore, Catholic Christianity should enter into free and open collaboration with all who seek full human development, even when understandings of "human" differ. The Catholic tradition ought not to fear pluralism. Indeed, its commitment to the absoluteness of the Mystery which is God and the transcendence of the human person demand pluralism. Sadly, the Catholic tradition has not always been consistent with its own deepest beliefs. As for all religious communities, idolatry has been a temptation for Catholicism and not always a successfully resisted temptation. There have been and are occasions when the Catholic community slides into henotheism. It has identified its notion of God with God, absolutized its dogmatic formulations as immune to history, and elevated its practice to being the only genuinely human life. When it has done so, it has suffered and caused others to suffer. But at its best, Catholic Christianity embraces the relativizing of all doctrines, practices, and forms of worship which the acceptance of God as Mystery entails. It then recognizes, in light of the incarnational principle, that to be human is the way to be like God and that the definition of the human is the point in creation to which God communicates God's self.

Integral Humanism Requires the Education of the Whole Person

The seriousness with which Catholicism takes the incarnational principle that the more richly developed humanity is, the more fully God can communicate God's self leads to its characteristic concern for a propaedeutic to the Gospel. The divine self-gift does not violate humanity, for humanity exists in order to receive that gift. The more fully one has explored and cultivated one's capacities as a human being, the readier one is to hear the Gospel, the Word which is God's self. This cultivation, this process of humanization, cannot therefore be a matter of indifference to the Catholic Christian tradition. Indeed, insofar as humanization is necessary for the hearing of the Word, it is an essential part of the mission of Christianity. This care for the development of the whole human person as part of the necessary propaedeutic to the Gospel includes the intellectual, physical, social, political, and economic well-being of the person. Once the incarnational principle is accepted in depth, the Christian finds that he or she must say, *homo sum: humani nil a me alienum puto*.[27]

Thus, in the Catholic Christian perspective, religion involves the education of the person as an integral human being. Since a religious act is an act of the person, religion affects and is affected by every element in the formation of the person. Although this conviction has run through the Catholic tradition, no one has said it more strongly in this century than Friedrich von Hügel in his great work, *The Mystical Element of Religion.*[28]

In the course of that long and complex book, von Hügel described three elements of religion which he called by various names. The most general designation he gave of the three is the Historical-Institutional, the Intellectual-Speculative, and the Experimental-Mystical elements. Each corresponds, von Hügel argued, to an aspect of the human person which must be developed if one is to attain full maturity. These aspects develop in accord with stages of personal growth. Thus, a child's religious life is marked by the Historical-Institutional element. The appeal experienced by the child of some religious stimulus "would generally have been externally interpreted by some particular men and women, a Mother, Nurse, Father, Teacher, Cleric, who themselves would generally have belonged to some more or less well-defined traditional, institutional religion."[29] The child's religion is marked by the presence of religious authority working through the senses and the imagination of the child. "And at this stage the External, Authoritative, Historical, Traditional, Institutional side and function of Religion are everywhere evident. . . . Religion is here, above all, a fact and a thing."[30] In the healthily developing person, this reliance on authority provokes questioning and promotes a certain tension between the Historical-Institutional and the Intellectual-Speculative elements.

> Direct experience, for one thing, brings home to the child that these sense-informations are not always trustworthy, or identical in its own case and in that of others. And, again, the very impressiveness of this external religion stimulates indeed the sense of awe and wonder, but it awakens curiosity as well. The time of trustful questioning, but still of questioning, first others, then oneself, has come. . . . Religion here becomes Thought, System, a Philosophy.[31]

But, von Hügel maintains, the human person is preeminently "a creature of action, even more than of sensation and reflection."[32] Action and interaction provide the possibilities of full growth and of self-knowledge for the mature human being.

Man's emotional and volitional, his ethical and spiritual powers, are now in ever fuller motion, and they are met and fed by
the third side of religion, the Experimental and Mystical. Here
religion is rather felt than seen or reasoned about, is loved and
lived rather than analyzed, is action and power, rather than
either external fact or intellectual verification.[33]

Central to von Hügel's thought is the contention that,
although these three elements of religion may be linked to
stages in personal development (and even, he argues, in the
historical development of Western culture[34]), they do not simply succeed one another. In the mature person, the three
elements co-exist, but not in simple juxtaposition. All are necessary, but they are in "almost inevitable mutual hostility."[35]
Furthermore, his hyphenated designation of each of the three
elements—the Historical-Institutional, the Intellectual-Speculative, and the Experimental-Mystical—reflects their "dou-
bleness," i.e., that within each are present two modes of living
out the element. In the first there is the contrast "between
Institutionalism and History,—the Present and the Past, a
direct Sense-Impression and Picture and a Memory"; in the
second, " between Criticism and Construction,—Analysis and
acuteness of mind, and Synthesis and richness and balance of
imagination, head, heart, and will"; and in the third, "between
Mysticism and Action, as respectively Intuitive and quiescent
and Volitional and effortful."[36] Thus, multiple combinations
are possible and necessary. For the mark of authentically religious person is ever re-achieved creative tension among these
double elements.

While religion, "where genuine, is ever the deepest, the
central life,"[37] von Hügel insisted that the religious dimension of life can attain its greatest richness only when all other
aspects of human life are equally well developed. As true religion depends on the maintenance of healthy tension among
its constitutive elements, so full humanity depends on the
maintenance of the interplay of all the forces which it embraces, including religion.

And indeed—and this is the point which specially concerns
religion—the soul cannot attain to its fullest possible spiritual

development, without the vigorous specific action and differentiation of forces and functions of a not directly religious character, which will have to energize, each according to its own intrinsic nature, within the ever ampler, and ever more closely-knit, organization of the complete life of the soul.[38]

Von Hügel' s developmental psychology is out-moded and one might well quarrel with his naive cultural history, but his book remains a classic statement of Catholic Christianity as integral humanism. Religious maturity requires human maturity, and vice versa. To the extent that any aspect of the human person is underdeveloped, to that extent the person's religious life is stunted. Thus personal relations and family life, physical health and nutrition, the study of the humanities, the rigorous pursuit of the sciences, engagement in politics, construction of the social order, involvement in commerce and the production of goods, all are of the greatest concern to Catholic Christianity, because all are aspects of the whole person and in their interplay, sometimes harmonious, sometimes contentious, full humanity emerges.

Von Hügel's is an authentically Catholic vision in its strong insistence that human life cannot be compartmentalized. *Homo sciens, homo faber, homo ludens, homo communalis, homo religiosus* are all first and foremost *homo*. The person is not a collection of faculties; the human being is not made up of a reasoning part, a volitional part, an aesthetic part, a religious part, etc. The whole person reasons, then chooses, the whole person plays, the whole person acts, the whole person prays. Every act of the person is an actualization of the whole person. One cannot be a Christian believer in isolation from being a responsible and intelligent late twentieth-century man or woman with all the opportunities, problems, and pressures that this entails. Consequently, any attempt at responsible moral education which does not take the religious dimension into account will prove to be education in the abstract. It will not deal with the person as he or she exists in the concrete. And it will accordingly be a failure, albeit a well-intentioned one.

Moral education in our society has come to a critical moment for several reasons. One and by no means the least is that the Enlightenment attempt to deal with religion as a purely private reality has irretrievably collapsed. When it became obvious after the Reformation that religion could no longer function as a glue to hold society together, that rather it had become a source of bitter internecine conflict, the Enlightenment relegated religion to a matter of individual conscience. This meant that the individual's religious beliefs were not to be subject to external coercion. But neither were they to be admitted into the circle of public conversation. Religion was an affair of the heart, the family, and the hearth. It had no place in the forum or the marketplace. The Enlightenment solution prevented public religious conflict—a boon that is not to be despised. But it did so by making both the believer and the citizen into abstractions. An abstraction never endures; reality always wins.

The emergence of the religious right in American political and social life is simply the most striking instance of the breakdown of the Enlightenment solution to religious pluralism. There is scarcely any significant ethical issue in public debate which can be understood while ignoring the religious presuppositions of at least some of the participants in the debate. The abortion debate is an obvious instance of this fact. But the growing discussion of "the right to die," of the new technologies of conception, of health care allotment, of homosexuality and "gay rights," of responses to the AIDS epidemic, of welfare reform, of censorship and government sponsorship of art deemed obscene by some citizens, of tax policy, of nuclear deterrence—all are unintelligible without the recognition that explicitly religious reasons lie behind claims advanced in the public forum. Prohibit the voicing of such reasons within the debate, and the debate will simply become a shouting match.

A slogan which is almost always applauded in American life is "the separation of church and state." And deservedly so. The union of church and state has again and again proven to be the corruption of both. But too often the separation of church and state is equated with the separation of religion and politics. "Church" and "state" are institutions; "religion" and "politics" are aspects of individual and communal human life. The first pair can and should be separated to the benefit of both. The second pair can be distinguished but must not be separated under pain of producing disintegrated persons. One and the same human being votes, earns a living, produces goods, invests in the stock market, marries, raises children, and prays. Try to separate any of those acts from the others, and you lose the reality of the person. Attempt to educate for one of those roles while bracketing the others, and you educate an abstraction, not a human being. One cannot deal with the person as citizen or as member of a profession or as participant in the marketplace and ignore the religious dimension of his or her life. For when all is said and done, the citizen, the professional, the businessman or -woman does not exist. Only the person exists.

Thus, moral education which abstracts from religion abstracts from reality. This does not mean that moral education must embrace a particular religious perspective. But it does mean that the moral educator who thinks that ethics can be taught while simply prescinding from the religious formation of the person will of necessity fail in assisting the development of a moral person, because he or she will not be addressing the whole person. The attempt to deal with religion as a factor in moral education in our pluralistic society greatly complicates the educator's task, of course. But who ever claimed that reality is tidy?

On the other hand, the pluralist society in which religious believers find themselves in the United States and increasingly in the world at large places the obligation on believers to enter into public discussion responsibly. Fideism of any sort is not a responsible stance in the pluralist forum. As religion should not be disqualified from civic conversation, so it should not expect a privileged place in such conversation. Religious believers must observe the standards of rational civic discourse. When religious reasons are advanced in support of ethical positions, believers must be willing to submit those reasons to scrutiny and to give warrants for finding those reasons compelling. *Credo quia absurdum* has never found acceptance within the Catholic tradition as a compelling ground for faith; it will certainly not be effective in the public forum as a cogent warrant for any position under discussion.

The Catholic Christian tradition should not shrink from entering upon the public debate. And, as part of that entry into public debate, it has no reason to demur from moral education which it does not control in a sectarian context. Its own intrinsic pluralism, rooted in its acknowledgment of the absolute Mystery of God, should free it of credal absoluteness which would preclude genuine interaction with those who stand in other religious traditions or no religious tradition. The centrality of the incarnational principle within Catholic Christianity should allow it to converse fruitfully with any form of humanism, including that often cited but ill-defined bugbear of some religious spokespeople outside the Catholic tradition, secular humanism. So long as humanism is open in principle to the mystery of being human, it may actually emerge that Catholic Christianity has more in common with it than it does with other forms of Christianity which are less insistent on the radical quality of the incarnation.

In *Redemptor hominis*, his first encyclical, Pope John Paul II gave a remarkable definition of the Catholic understanding of Christianity.

> In reality, the name for that deep amazement at the human person's worth and dignity is the Gospel, that is to say: the Good News. It is also called Christianity.[39]

That is Catholic Christianity as integral humanism. "Deep amazement at the human person's worth and dignity" is not only the best place to begin moral education in a pluralist society. It might well be the best possible goal.

Notes

1. Augustine had read these *libri Platonici*, neo-Platonic works translated into Latin by Victorinus, even before he was recommended to do so by Simplicianus who regarded them as propaedeutic to belief in God and God's word, *Confessions* 8, 2, 3. That these texts should have been praised so highly by Simplicianus, the "father" of Ambrose, is an indication of the esteem in which they were held in some Christian circles.

2. *Confessions* 7, 9, 14.

3. See *inter alia* Raymond E. Brown and John P. Meier, *Antioch and Rome: New Testament Cradles of Catholic Christianity* (New York: Paulist Press, 1983); Raymond E. Brown, *The Churches the Apostles Left Behind* (New York: Paulist Press, 1984); and Raymond E. Brown, *The Community*

of the Beloved Disciple: The Life, Loves, and Hates of an Individual Church in New Testament Times (New York: Paulist Press, 1979).

4. Pluralism, not only as the context within which theology is carried on but as a condition intrinsic to Christian theology itself, is a much discussed issue; see esp. David Tracy, *The Analogical Imagination: Christian Theology and the Culture of Pluralism* (New York: Crossroad, 1981), and the same author's *Blessed Rage for Order: The New Pluralism in Theology* (New York: Seabury Press, 1975).

5. Stephen Sykes, *The Identity of Christianity: Theologians and the Essence of Christianity from Schleiermacher to Barth* (Philadelphia: Fortress Press, 1984), 250–276. The term "essentially contested concept" appears in W.B. Gallie, *Philosophy and the Historical Understanding* (London: Chatto and Windus, 1964).

6. Sykes, *Identity of Christianity*, 254.

7. Ibid.

8. Ibid., 255.

9. The most acute attempt at reading the "fall" story in Genesis 3 precisely on the level of symbol is that of Paul Ricoeur, *The Symbolism of Evil*, trans. Emerson Buchanan (Boston: Beacon Press, 1967), 232–260. His insistence on the need for such a reading of the text is well taken: "The harm that has been done to souls during the centuries of Christianity, first by the literal interpretation of the story of Adam, and then by the confusion of this myth, treated as history, with later speculations, principally Augustinian, about original sin, will never be adequately told. In asking the faithful to confess belief in this mythico-speculative mass and to accept it as a self-sufficient explanation, the theologians have unduly required a *sacrificium intellectus* where what was needed was to awaken believers to a symbolic superintelligence of their actual condition" (p. 239).

10. Ricoeur notes that the "fall" myth is integrated into the context of the creation myths in Genesis. He makes the point, however, that the story of the introduction of evil in chapter 3 is connected with the second creation story, that of 2:4b–25, not the first (1:1–2:4a) in which is found the explicit judgment that everything which has been created is "good" (pp. 244–245). While this may be true and important from the perspective of source-criticism, it should not be forgotten that we are dealing with the text as it has stood for twenty-five centuries, and it is that final text which has shaped the Jewish and Christian traditions and which we must seek to interpret. Ricoeur admits this elsewhere; see p. 249, n. 8.

11. There is some ambiguity in this famous verse. The term translated here as "God" is *elohim*, a plural form used throughout the Hebrew scriptures to refer to the one God. It is possible that the plural "gods" is intended here. Thus the phrase would be translated, "You will become like gods," i.e., celestial figures; see E. A. Speiser, *Genesis*, Anchor Bible (Garden City, N.Y.: Doubleday, 1964), 23, note 6; also Bruce Vawter, *On Genesis: A New Reading* (Garden City, N.Y.: Doubleday, 1977), 78. In either case, the temptation is a rejection of the goodness of the human being as it exists.

12. See Ricoeur, 248–249, n. 8: "The decisive argument, in my opinion, is the place of this story at the head of this series formed by Genesis 1–11. The sin of Adam is the first, in the sense that it is at the root of all the others: Adam breaks with God, as Cain separates himself from his brother and the men of Babel are confounded."

13. Nicholas Lash, *His Presence in the World: A Study in Eucharistic Worship and Theology* (London: Sheed and Ward, 1968), 4f.

14. Alexander Pope, "An Essay on Man in Four Epistles," Epistle II, 11. 1–2.

15. Johann Wolfgang von Goethe, quoted in René Wellek, *A History of Modern Criticism*, 2 vols. (New Haven, Conn.: Yale University Press, 1955), 1:211.

16. Ibid.

17. Indeed, the Absolute Mystery remains incomprehensible even in the union of the saints with God, traditionally called the beatific vision; see Karl Rahner, "An Investigation of the Incomprehensibility of God in St. Thomas Aquinas," *Theological Investigations* 16 (New York: Seabury, 1979), 244–254; also in the same volume, "The Hiddenness of God," 227—243.

18. Augustine, *Confessions*, 1, 1, 1.

19. Karl Rahner, *Hearers of the Word* (New York: Herder and Herder, 1969). This phrase appears often in Rahner's work.

20. Karl Rahner, "On the Theology of the Incarnation, *Theological Investigations* 4 (London: Darton, Longman and Todd, 1966), 116.

21. Ibid.

22. For the centrality of *paideia* to the whole of classical culture, see Werner Jaeger, *Paideia: The Ideals of Greek Culture*, trans. Gilbert Highet from the 2nd German ed., 3 vols. (New York: Oxford University Press, 1939, 1943, 1944); for the appropriation of this idea by Christian writers in antiquity, e.g., Clement of Alexandria, Origen, and the many subsequent Fathers of the Church who were influenced by them, see *inter multa alia*, Henry Chadwick, *Early Christian Thought and Classical Culture: Studies in Justin, Clement, and Origen* (New York: Oxford University Press, 1966) and Werner Jaeger, *Early Christianity and Greek Paideia* (Cambridge, Mass.: Belknap Press of Harvard University Press, 1961); for the same train of thought among the Latin Fathers, see Charles Norris Cochrane, *Christianity and Classical Culture: A Study of Thought and Action from Augustus to Augustine*, rev. ed. (New York: Clarendon Press, Oxford University Press, 1944).

23. John Henry Cardinal Newman. *The Idea of a University Defined and Illustrated* (London: Longmans, Green, and Company, 1896).

24. Lash, *His Presence in the World*, 4f.

25. H. Richard Niebuhr, *Radical Monotheism and Western Culture, With Supplementary Essays* (New York: Harper and Row, Torchbooks edition, 1970), 11.

26. Ibid., 32.

27. Terence, *Heauton timorumenos*, 1. 77

28. Baron Friedrich von Hügel, *The Mystical Element of Religion as Studied in Saint Catherine of Genoa and Her Friends*, 2d ed., 2 vols. (London: J.M. Dent and Sons, 1923).

29. Ibid., 1:51.

30. Ibid.

31. Ibid., 1:52.

32. Ibid.

33. Ibid., 1:53.

34. Ibid., 1:3–49.

35. Ibid., 2:387.

36. Ibid., 2:392f.

37. Ibid., 2:393.

38. Ibid.

39. John Paul II *Redemptor hominis* (Washington, D.C.: United States Catholic Conference, 1979), #10, p. 28. The translation of *hominis* has been rendered here as the more accurate and gender-inclusive "human person" rather than the official English translation's "man."

THE MORAL PART OF PLURALISM AS THE PLURAL PART OF MORAL EDUCATION

Dwight Boyd

Without meaning to sound cynical (because I suspect the problem may be in principle unavoidable), I want to suggest that there is a relationship between the importance of a social issue and confusion in use of language in public discourse about that issue. And, unfortunately, it's a direct relationship: the more important the issue, the more confusion in how people talk to each other about it. If this suggestion resonates with your own observations, then surely you will be sympathetic to anyone facing the need to communicate unambiguously to an audience on the topic "Moral Education in a Pluralistic Society." What we mean by "pluralism" and by characterizing a society as "pluralistic" is a communicative hurdle of considerable proportions: pluralism has multiple meanings, or at least multiple connotations (Pratte 1972; Bullivant 1984). As if this were not enough, anyone even marginally acquainted with public (including academic) discussion of "moral education" will surely recognize that the same can be said of this phrase, perhaps even to a greater degree, if that is possible. When we put them together the task is daunting, to put it mildly. But put them together we must—because it is their conjunction that represents what I think is one of the linchpins of viability of any post-modern society. In short, if we cannot put them together, I am not sure such society can be cohesive—and I shudder at the prospect of its increased balkanization should we fail.

My intention in this essay then is to get into this confusion—and hopefully through it—via several successive, cumulative linguistic and conceptual maneuvers with regard to what I think should orient our moral concern(s) when we navigate the issue of pluralism. I want to use my entrance into and passage through the cluster of notions contributing to this confusion in such a way that a sort of escape velocity is attained in the direction I think we should be going in conceiving what is necessary for moral education in a pluralistic society. This direction will gradually emerge, in part because of the nature and difficulty of this very problem.

Circumventing Some Conceptual Confusions for Some Metaphorical Leverage

How are we to identify the direction of our concern when we juxtapose "moral education" with "pluralism"? I suspect there are several different, and equally legitimate, directions one might take, but I want to identify what seems to me the crucial one from the point of view of a philosophical interest in the nature and justification of moral education. To do so I would note first that I assume that it is not just any notion of pluralism that is problematic in this context, but rather, we are using "pluralism" elliptically to refer to "cultural pluralism." It is something about the importance of culture to human beings, conjoined with variability of that notion, that properly focuses our attention. This is only minimal help, however, because as Pratte (1972, 61) has pointed out, "almost as common as the use of CP ['cultural pluralism'] is its lack of definition." After noting two different, historically important senses, Pratte eventually seeks to clarify our contemporary discussion by analyzing how we tend to use this notion in "ordinary language" today. He points out that

> there are two basic ways in which the term CP is literally used. First, the term is used in a purely descriptive sense to characterize the coexistence of many political, racial, religious, ethnic, geographical, age, etc. groups living together in such a way which allows the social system to function and maintain itself. The term is descriptive of a situation in which any number of subgroups in the total society retain their identity and culture while functioning with each other.... Second, we use

the term CP not only to convey descriptive data but to evaluate as well; the term is thus "mixed," serving both to describe and evaluate. Hence, for some, the term carries a positive or "hurrah" connotation:

> . . . It seems to me that the "mixed" use of CP connotes at one and the same time a theoretical construct and a programmatic value position. (68)

Assuming that Pratte is right here, and I believe he is, we need then to be alert to what we are saying "hurrah" to—and how this might get confused with only a factual claim.

When we are alert to this danger, what we can see more clearly is a second leverage point for determining our direction, also camouflaged in the rhetoric of discourse about cultural pluralism. In one of the few explicit juxtapositions of cultural pluralism and moral education that I have found, J. Theodore Klein (1974, 683–693) has identified this second point both directly and succinctly:

> A culturally pluralistic society is one in which there is value pluralism. I will define a society where value pluralism is present as a society in which people have a variety of values and can express these values through the institutions in society. (684)

I think (at least for my purposes here) Klein is right to finger "value pluralism" as the main focus of attention in our "mixed" notion of cultural pluralism. We are indeed thinking of differences among groups within a society, but these are not superficial differences. They are, rather, value differences. As Klein goes on to say,

> The units of a culturally pluralistic society would not be interest groups but cultural communities. There would be a plurality of values, including a plurality of moral values, due to the plurality of cultural communities. Within each cultural community would be a unique set of values, including a unique set of moral values. (1974, 685)

It is not unusual for this essential turning point to be missed in public discussions of cultural pluralism and in the subsequent political and educational policy that results from this discussion. As Brian Bullivant, one of the leading theorists on multiculturalism, has noted, "Factually, cultural pluralism or diversity is almost invariably thought of as applying only to differences in lifestyles" (1984, ix). Whereas it is much easier to gloss over this deep problem and focus on the more superficial and often quite literally visible differences such as food preferences, clothing styles, music and dance forms, etc., Klein's blunt way of putting it points to differences that have moral significance.

However, how we make this move, as reflected especially in the rhetoric we use to keep it in front of our collective consciousness, has serious implications for where we go from here. The danger at this point hinges on the connotations of "pluralism" when it is conjoined with "value"—and we fail to keep in mind the previously noted danger of the way in which "cultural pluralism" has "mixed" senses, both descriptive and presumptive. In short, what seems to get lost is any acknowledgment of, and willingness to face, the prescriptive side. I suspect that the way this works is that there is something about the term "pluralism" that psychologically leads in this skewed direction. It is as if the mere perception of the factual existence of "many values, all so different" is itself turned into a virtue, indeed, the only prescriptive element of cultural pluralism that can be seen. Thus, the result is an insidious slide from the fact of cultural pluralism to the supposed "fact" of ethical relativism (anything "cultural" is OK) as the only possible response—despite the fact that the latter move bids to undercut why one should be morally worried about the first real fact (and despite the fact that the seemingly natural appeal to tolerance for grounding policy claims is itself undercut).

So what if we do not use "pluralism" as our entry point? Although the same problem eventually arises, I think approaching from another direction *does* help to focus it in a more manageable form. In order to demonstrate this possibility—to swing around "pluralism" to orbit a different cluster of rhetorical notions—*and* in order to ground the direction of subsequent theoretical concern in reality, I am going to locate my concerns through an explicit focus on the Canadian scene. My subsequent recommendations for the directions we need to go, however, will be intended as quite generalizable.

In Canada, the rhetorical coin is "multiculturalism," not "cultural pluralism." This is not to say that the latter phrase never occurs, but it *is* the case that the former term is the common, accepted reference point. One reason is that it is enshrined in federal law and policy. In 1971 the Canadian Parliament initiated a new policy labeled "Multiculturalism within a Bilingual Framework." The rhetoric used by the Prime Minister in the very announcement of the policy moved very fast to identify "multiculturalism" as the approved Canadian way of referring to the issue of cultural pluralism:

> We believe that cultural pluralism is the very essence of Canadian identity. Every ethnic group has the right to preserve and develop its own culture and values within the Canadian context. To say that we have two official languages is not to say we have two official cultures, and no particular culture is more official than another. A policy of multiculturalism must be a policy for all Canadians. (Mazurek and Kach 1986, 116)

With due haste prompted as much by political expediency (e.g., nodding to Quebec Francophone claims while waving to a variety of other well-established ethnic groups loudly claiming their rights) as be deep-felt ideological commitment (Mazurek and Kach 1986), the government immediately put money and people behind the policy, claiming that government action would be guided by the following principle: "The Government of Canada will support all of Canada's cultures and will seek to assist, resources permitting, the development of those cultural groups which have demonstrated a desire and effort to continue to develop" (quoted in Kach and DeFaveri 1987, 231, from "House of Commons, *Debates*, 8 October 1971, 8581). Although for jurisdictional reasons concerning the relation between the federal government and the ten provincial governments much of the projected work according to this principle would have to remain the responsibility of the provinces (e.g., education is almost entirely in the hands of each individual province),[1] a public image of the nature of Canadian society rapidly gained visibility (and considerable popular acceptance) through the metaphor of the *"multicultural mosaic."* As an aspect of a (continually questioned) Canadian national identity, part of the popularity of this image has stemmed from a sense of a national intention to pursue a different direction from that taken by the U.S. in terms of how a society deals with the influx of diverse cultural and ethnic groups (Troper 1978). That is, in the U.S., at least in the formative years of the country, such differences were to be submerged and blended in the "melting pot" of forming an American identity. In Canada, however, through the explicit multiculturalism policy such differences are (supposed) to be acknowledged, respected, and even celebrated as unique and indispensable pieces of the overall, coherent picture of Canadian society—as a *mosaic* is made up of inlaid small pieces of variously colored and textured material which combine to form an overall pattern or design.

Although the metaphor of a "multicultural mosaic" has not been popular in discussions of pluralism in the U.S.,[2] as it has been used in Canada as a rhetorical device, I think it is useful for two different reasons. The first reason is that I think it facilitates keeping the prescriptive side of the "mixed" use of "cultural pluralism" in focus. It is being explicitly offered as an ideal, something toward which a society should strive. Part of the prescriptive leverage contained in this mosaic image is located in the necessity to recognize the integrity of the different individual pieces making up the whole mosaic: "value pluralism" is then metaphorically captured by the sense that each cultural community has unique worth within the whole mosaic of society. But this is only part of the ideal identified by the metaphor. Another part, somewhat in tension with the first, is located in the fact that individual pieces of a mosaic are not unrelated to each other, just a random jumble of differently colored pieces. Rather, despite the preservation of their separateness and unique worth, a society made up in the form of a "mosaic" of cultural communities can exist only insofar as *together* these pieces make sense in terms of some overall coherent pattern. I think both prescriptive uses of the multicultural mosaic metaphor identifies an important positive moral aim, and taken in conjunction they accurately capture the complexity of integrating the two aims.

The second reason I find the multicultural mosaic metaphor useful is that it can help us see certain theoretical *problems* which must be faced if moral education in a pluralist society is to be coherent and legitimate. Thus, in what follows, I will focus on two such problems, one each related to the positive moral aims just noted. I want to focus on these two problems more in the spirit of illuminating their difficulty than in hope of offering solutions. However, by taking them in sequence and emphasizing the latter, I intend to identify the direction I think we should be proceeding in order to come to grips with them as essentially problems of *moral education*.

Facing Problems of Perspective

The first problem that the multicultural mosaic image helps us see better pertains to the nature of the diversity that concerns us. To put it in terms of the components of the metaphor, if the mosaic is made up of separate pieces, how many pieces are there? and what is to *count* as a piece? To give you some sense of the richness of the context within which these questions must be addressed in Canada, I am going to relate some facts about the current scene in Ontario. Although these facts are hardly representative of all areas of the country, since one-third of Canada's population lives in Ontario (and one-half of the yearly immigrants to Canada end up residing there), they *are* illustrative of a set of conditions facing the country as a whole.

Perhaps the most revealing statistic to note here is that there are over 85 ethnocultural groups now in Ontario![3] Of course, these groups are represented to widely different degrees, but what this means in the context of Toronto' s (approximate) three million residents are things such as the following:

> One Toronto radio station broadcasts in thirty languages, including announcements on arrival delays for flights from "back home." There is a Toronto TV station that survives simply by broadcasting programs in a multiplicity of languages aimed at specific ethnic communities, including movies in Urdu (with English subtitles). That city's municipal government must prepare its annual property tax notices in six languages: English, French, Chinese, Italian, Greek, and Portuguese. (Malcolm 1986, 67)

The attempt to accommodate different language and cultural traditions is also evident in educational policy. In a recent public statement the Chair of the Toronto Board of Education put the Board's commitment this way:

> Children from all over the world attend our schools. . . . The Toronto Board of Education is dedicated to communicating with its many communities in their first language. Written communications are regularly prepared in eight languages plus English and interpreters are always available for parents who need them. [These languages are: French, Chinese, Greek, Italian, Polish, Portuguese, Spanish, and Vietnamese.] (Crewe 1987)

What this can mean at the level of individual schools and classrooms—where education takes place—is perhaps even more amazing. For example, when I talk to teachers in my classes at the Ontario Institute for Studies in Education (OISE) about their experiences, it is not unusual for someone to say something like, "Oh yeah, last year I had a class of 29 third-graders. . . and there were 21 different ethnic/cultural/racial backgrounds represented." Diversity at the school level is sometimes very wide. For example, last September the "Multicultural Committee" of a high school (Lester B. Pearson Collegiate Institute) in Scarborough, a city adjacent to Toronto, initiated a study of the school's student population. When it issued its report, among the findings were the following items: (1) Almost half of the students were born outside of Canada, coming from *58 countries.* (2) Only 58 percent of the students came from homes where only English was spoken, and there was a total of *48 languages* being spoken in these homes, the most common, after English, being French, Gujarati, Urdu, Punjabi, Hindi, Chinese, Spanish, and Tagalog. (3) Almost half of the students identified cultural origins *not* of (some version of) the Judeo-Christian tradition; and, in fact, there were at least 9 different religious orientations noted[4] (Cheng 1988). Finally, through the province's Heritage Language Programme "there are now 90,000 primary school students studying 58 different languages (from Swedish and Lithuanian to Urdu, Arabic and Cantonese) in more than 70 boards of education across Ontario" (Ellwood 1989, 25).

I could go on with such examples, but these should suffice to illustrate the actual complexity facing us. But it is even
more important to note that the "facts" do not just present
themselves as given. On the contrary, hidden in any way
of identifying these kinds of facts are theoretical (and ultimately, potentially *moral*) interpretive assumptions. For example, what is to count as a "cultural" difference of relevance
here? And what other criteria might be used in addition to,
or in place of, religious affiliation? How are these pieces to be
differentiated from those found by looking at ethnicity? Similarly, how does identifying either of these two interact with—
and perhaps obscure—the sociodynamically sharper lines of
race? Finally, the problem is not only how to identify which
surface "pieces" are to count, but also how not thereby to
lose sight of those divisions which lie underneath, e.g., class,
gender, and differential access to institutional structures of
power. Certainly some part of the answer to these questions
calls for straightforward conceptual clarity. But I would
strongly suggest that the days of supposedly "pure" conceptual analysis are now clearly behind us: the meaning of these
concepts and the nature of their interrelationships change
over time, according to historical and material conditions (and
perhaps also according to the standpoint of those interpreting
the meaning) (Yinger 1986).

The need to identify relevant aspects of the complex diversity hidden by general abstract terms such as "pluralism"
or "multiculturalism"—metaphorically, the number and nature of the "pieces" constituting the mosaic—is, then, the first
of the two problems that I think this metaphor helps us to
face. My observation that the pieces cannot be picked out
of the social jumble of modern life without theoretical tools,
and perhaps ideological commitments, leads directly to the
second problem. As I noted earlier, for the pieces—however
identified—conjointly to form a *mosaic* they must be related
to each other in some meaningful sense. A mosaic is not just
a random collection of such pieces, but one that forms a systematic, coherent picture or pattern of some sort. To me, this
requirement is part of the power of the image. But it also
points to another problem, one which is instructive for any
concern about moral education raised at the level of the whole

society. In short, the problem is this: how do we identify, understand, and *legitimate* the point of view that can be and should be taken to give the multicultural mosaic meaning? It is clear that the individual constitutive pieces do not contain this perspective because it is their *relationship to each other* that is at issue. But, the mosaic only "works" if the relationship can be seen and is coherent. Where do we stand for this vision?

For this second problem to be fully appreciated it is essential to keep in mind the more reflexive question, "What are we looking for when we seek this meaningful perspective for the multicultural mosaic?" It will be remembered that our first vector in this direction came from recognizing that "cultural pluralism" carries "mixed" senses in ordinary language, both descriptive and prescriptive. Further, it was also suggested that turning more in the direction of "multiculturalism talk" might give us leverage for escaping the pull of a self-defeating ethical relativism—for escaping the danger of endlessly orbiting around the blackhole of ethical relativism. The window of escape from the powerful clutches of this danger is opened exactly at this point. That is, to keep our bearings in traversing the void of moral education in a pluralistic society where pluralism is interpreted as entailing *value* pluralism, we have to keep our analytic gyroscope steady on a *moral* orientation. No amount of explanatory analysis, whether historical or political, whether sociological or psychological, whether conservative or radical, will suffice here. Understanding as much as we can about the situation we find ourselves in and how we got there will certainly help— but it must not occlude our attention to what is in essence *a moral quest*.

By explicitly choosing a Canadian rhetorical route to this point I do not mean to imply that our problems are solved if we just attend to what is happening north of the 49th parallel. I must acknowledge that I have glossed over all kinds of complicating factors which would need attention to account accurately for the actual place of multiculturalism policy and practice in Canada. But I have done this *in order to* identify more clearly and unequivocally the moral aspect of what we face in the topic of this volume. Indeed, as far as I have been

able to discover in the Canadian literature on multiculturalism, it is usually the case that this aspect is, at best, implied
but left unstated or undeveloped.

For example, there is now a thriving and active national
organization called the Canadian Council for Multicultural
and Intercultural Education (CCMIE) with "established constituent organizations in each province or territory" (McLeod
1987, "Acknowledgement"). In 1984, with the financial support of the Canadian Government's Multicultural Sector of
the Department of Secretary of State, this organization sponsored an international conference on multicultural education,
and subsequently published a collection of papers from this
conference (McLeod 1987). In this important collection there
is not a single paper that explicitly tackles the problem of
identifying and legitimating the moral stance necessary for
seeing a coherent, viable picture within the mosaic. To the
extent that it *is* acknowledged, it is so only by implication
or elliptically—as if stating a belief handles the problem. For
example, as is apparent in the name of this organization, the
mere diversity implied by "*multi*culturalism" has now been
modified to include the implied need for connection and com-
monality through "*inter*culturalism."

To capture the current understanding of this *tension*—
and the lack of pursuit of its implications—I will quote from
the introductory comments in this collection from Keith
McLeod, the President of the CCMIE at the time of the
conference:

> The Canadian Council for Multicultural and Intercultural Ed-
> ucation (the name itself is an inclusive compromise) adopted
> the following comprehensive statement on the "meaning" of
> multiculturalism in May 1984. Multiculturalism fosters a so-
> ciety and a Canadian identity in which people and groups of all
> cultures are accepted. Multiculturalism promotes human and
> group relations in which ethnic, racial, religious, and linguistic
> similarities and differences are valued and respected.
>
> The principles or tenets that are inherent in multiculturalism
> are:
>
> 1. Equality of status of all cultural and ethnic groups within
>   the framework of our official bilingual country.

2. The freedom of all individuals and groups to the retention and development of their cultures as part of the Canadian identity.
3. Equality of access by all individuals and groups to employment and promotion, services, and support.
4. A commitment to sharing our cultures within the mainstream of Canadian society.
5. An undertaking to participate in Canadian citizenship and the democratic process in terms of both rights and responsibilities.
6. A belief that individuals have the freedom to choose the particular cultural attributes they prefer within the framework of our democratic principles.
7. Respect for and observance of human rights and civil liberties as exemplified in the Canadian Charter of Rights and Freedoms, the common law, and human rights codes.

Multiculturalism includes all Canadians and is for all Canadians (pp. viii–ix).

What is interesting in this statement, for my illustrative purposes here, is what is *not* said. What is *not* said is anything about what is to be done when Nos. 1 or 2 come into conflict with Nos. 5, 6, or 7—particularly 7. That is, unless there is something legitimately overriding in Nos. 5, 6, or 7—or in some other form of appeal to transcultural moral claims— we are right back in the clutches of "value pluralism" in the previously identified dangerous sense of ethical relativism. As McLeod himself has argued elsewhere, what is needed (at least *in part*) is an understanding of our aim in terms of "capabilities that will enable people to live in a pluralistic society, producing individuals who will be capable of *transcending* the boundaries of their own ethnic culture" (McLeod 1984, 37). Writing about the needs of teachers' in-service training, Ouellet agrees with McLeod and adds the following interpretation: ". . . I believe that intercultural education can best be defined as the promotion of mutual understanding and communication between people of different cultural and religious backgrounds." He hastens to add however, "Our knowledge of the means of promoting such noble values is very scant"[6] (Ouellet 1987, 131). A clear recognition that what we are after here is fundamentally a matter of moral education is, in my opinion, at least to orient ourselves in the right direction. But even Ouellet fails to acknowledge that this "right direction" cannot be reduced to a lament about ignorance of pedagogical means, but rather, that this orientation itself requires clear analysis and *justification* of what the means are to serve.

Focusing in a Difficult Direction

What then can we say when we are, finally, clearly oriented in this direction? I think the first thing we should acknowledge is that it is hard to overestimate the difficulty of proceeding in this direction. Perhaps that is why so much of the theoretical literature—to say nothing of policy and practice—floats around the issues, but never seems to come to rest on them. Indeed, I must admit that I am not confident that the problems encountered along this line of inquiry have anything like what would normally be recognized as "solutions." They may be instances of that kind of human-cum-philosophical problem in which the "solution" exists more in the continual effort to grapple with it than in any residue of such activity. In that spirit I intend to continue. It should not be surprising, then, that at this point I have mostly questions. Getting them off my chest may serve both to indicate where I think we should be going and to illustrate the complexity of the journey. Then I will come back to take some critical, concrete steps in this direction.

Ultimately, as I have implied by analyzing the strengths and problems of the multicultural mosaic metaphor, a viable and justifiable program of moral education in a multicultural context cannot be conceived without addressing this core question: What is the moral point of view that grounds our disposition to take multicultural/intercultural education seriously—as something that is morally good, perhaps even required? Then: What are the basic value/moral commitments constitutive of this point of view? Are they coherent? How do they work together to give us more insight—and "bite"? Then, how formal are they? Do they provide sufficient content to *fuel*, as well as to motivate, moral education efforts? Can this point of view be meaningfully and substantively interpreted outside the particularities of a specific cultural reference point—as the moral part of the perspective that "makes sense" of the multicultural mosaic? Can it then be justified in some way that will have meaning and moral appeal to the various pieces of the mosaic? Does it then give us sufficient grounds for making the hard moves required if we are to reject ethical relativism at this level without undercutting the prescriptive dimensions of value pluralism that initiates our quest in the first place?

It is not exactly true that these questions, or others aimed at the same set of problems, do not appear in the literature on multiculturalism. But it does seem to me that the usual mode of treatment is something like answering-by-mentioning. For example, in 1985 the British Government's Committee of Inquiry into the Education of Children from Ethnic Minority Groups published its lengthy conclusion of several years of study, now popularly known as the "Swann Report." In a systematic review of this Report, Monica Taylor quotes a passage directly relevant to the issue at hand:

> It is essential, we feel, to acknowledge the reality of the multiracial context in which we now live, to recognize the positive benefits and opportunities which this offers all of us and to seek to build together a society which both values the diversity within it, whilst united by the cohesive force of the common aims, attributes and values which we all share. (1986, 77)

However, Taylor immediately adds the critical observation, "Unfortunately, the Report makes no attempt to specify what these shared values are" (p 77). Another example, going a little bit further, can be found in the work of James Banks, one of the leading figures of the "multiethnic education" movement in the U.S. In his explanation of and argument for what he identifies as "the multiethnic ideology" (as contrasted to "the cultural pluralist ideology" on the one hand, and "the assimilationist ideology" on the other hand), Banks paints the following picture:

> In the multiethnic, open society envisioned by the multiethnic theorist, individuals would be free to maintain their ethnic identities. They would also be able and willing to function

effectively within the common culture and within and across other ethnic cultures. Individuals would be free to act in ways consistent with the norms and values of their ethnic groups as long as they did not conflict with overarching national idealized values, such as justice, equality, and human dignity. All members of society would be required to conform to these values. *These values would be the unifying elements of the culture that would maintain and promote societal cohesion.* (1988, 124, italics in original)

This is definitely to the point, but one looks in vain for any further elaboration of the list of "overarching national idealized values," to say nothing of a coherent theoretical perspective which would not only show how these values might be interrelated in a coherent moral point of view, *but also* articulate how such a point of view could work in the way required.

Finally, I want to note one similar example from my Canadian home turf, since this served as my rhetorical entry point. In a recent, philosophically candid paper entitled "What Every Teacher Should Know about Multiculturalism," Nick Kach and Ivan DeFaveri (1987) focus directly on the tension between the interpretation of multiculturalism which leads to a self-defeating ethical relativism and the need to understand and own the moral position which must ground multiculturalism as an educational prescription. Starting from a clear recognition that "multicultural statements and policies...should promote not tolerance *simpliciter*, but tolerance when appropriate," (234) the authors do not just opt out by making a vague reference to a list of "shared values," but rather, appeal to a classic liberal, Kantian moral position of respect for persons as *that which should be the moral position behind multiculturalism.* For example, they make the following strong argument:

> The child's right to an education must be seen as more fundamental than the parents' right to transmit their view of the world. Children must be seen as ends in themselves, and not merely as a means to satisfy the parents' cultural ambitions. That human beings should be seen as ends in themselves and not merely as means to other people's ends is a moral principle more fundamental than any other, and we should not

lose sight of it on those rare occasions when it means sur-
rendering some other cherished belief. Those cultural groups
that see children merely as a means of perpetuating their culture and not as ends in themselves must be seen as morally
flawed. (135)

Though I do not *personally* disagree with Kach and De-
Faveri's claims here, I think it is crucial that they be recognized as assertions rather than an argument. It is clear,
for example, that a particular view of the human person, one
which emphasizes a notion of rational autonomy, rests at the
core of this moral position. Is there a good argument to show
how and why this view, and only this view, *must* underlie
multiculturalism? The problem here is that there are alternative interpretations—*culturally based* interpretations—that
can be given to general notions such as respect for persons
(Fernhout 1989). To simply opt for one interpretation, when
we know it will have serious implications for at least some
pieces of the mosaic, runs the risk of forfeiting too much of
our underlying commitment to pluralism.

Reconceiving a Philosophical
Problem as an Educational Task

I certainly do not want to minimize the difficulty of the
problems I have just identified, in particular, the last one.
Indeed, if anything, I want to emphasize it, because in so doing we can use this fact itself to propel us in the direction
now established, *when we appreciate its educational dimension.* That is, recognizing that we are not likely to "solve"
this problem, or set of problems today, or tomorrow, or even
next year, helps us to see that there is an active temporal
dimension to what we are after. To put this in terms of the
image explored in the previous section, the pattern of the
multicultural mosaic is not something for us to *discover*, like
archaeologists who are somehow independent of any influence on what it looks like except through methods of exposure; rather, we are more in the position of artists working
together on different sections of the picture. *What we will see
is what we construct.* This kind of constructivist activity takes

collaborative effort through time. Moreover, the pattern that we construct to make sense of the mosaic can change, and probably must change to meet successfully the demands of changing material and historical circumstances. It may well be, as Kach and DeFaveri suggest, that any moral point of view that can serve and ground multicultural education will have to be created around the hue and texture of respect for persons. But the picture still has to be constructed in terms of variations on this hue and texture, plus some synthesis of the form of these variations and their relationship, etc. When we take this seriously, I think our moral educational concerns get a significant push in two ways. In short, I think that both *students'* and *teachers'* roles get insufficient attention in discussions of multicultural education that do take the moral dimensions as central; and attention to both gains us ground. I will look first at students, in a way that illuminates what we need to keep in mind about the teacher's role.

My first suggestion then is that we need to think much more about the recipients of any moral education in this context—the students. If we take seriously the points just made, *how* we think of students is transformed, and this, in turn, says something about what kind of moral education is needed, or at least where we should start in thinking about this question. In short, the problem of how to construct the moral point of view which makes the pieces of the multicultural mosaic work together is not just *our* problem, *but necessarily that of succeeding generations as well.* It is not the sort of thing that can be solved once and for all, and the solution passed on. Whatever we say about it now *must* include the future actions of current students as part of its solution. In short, I am proposing to refocus the question, not to think only in terms of ourselves and the current situation, but to think of what the students will need in order to continue to work on the problem *with us*, and then we can work backwards from this to say what we need in moral education today.

Certainly some of this must be thought of in terms of value/moral commitments and the concomitant dispositions and abilities to act in accordance with them. As I have already indicated, it is not an easy matter how to identify these. However, my proposal is that when we consider this question we keep in constant mind the need for collaborative effort, not only now, but also in the future. In something reminiscent of R. S. Peters's "transcendental argument" in *Ethics and Education* (1966) over twenty years ago, I think certain moral commitments can be seen to constitute the grounds of possibility for taking seriously the question, "What ought we to do about this problem?" Peters, of course, was not concerned with the problem of multiculturalism. (Indeed, there is a disturbing "classist" flavor permeating much of what he says). Moreover, he thought he could generate the transcendental move monologically, i.e., through the effort of a single epistemic subject taking seriously the question, "What ought I to do?" Even with this restricted starting point, however, Peters makes a plausible case for a substantive interpretation of consideration of interests, liberty, equality, respect for persons, and fraternity as necessary moral presuppositions of the activity of answering this practical question. If we overlook the problem that this kind of move may never approximate an air-tight deduction, which I for one am certainly willing to do, then I think it can get us something of what we need. That is, what we can construct are those commitments that make it possible to talk *through* our cultural diversity about how we should make sense of it together—and these are not something for us alone today, but also for the next generation to talk to us and to each other in the continual activity of *making* this sense. In the words of Ouellet noted earlier, what we are trying to construct are those very things that make *possible* a "mutual understanding and communication." The problem of moral education in a multicultural society is *how to keep this question an open one*, not just for us, but also for those to come.

    Although, as I have suggested, this step is somewhat reminiscent of Peters, there is also at least one essential difference. In short, I want to emphasize the dialogical, communicative dimension of this activity much more than Peters does. "Mutual understanding and communication" can never be a monological matter. It is always, rather, *we* who are working on this problem *together*. Something like an active striving together toward approximating what Habermas has identified as the conditions of an "ideal speech situation" is the only way that truly intercultural communication has a chance (McCarthy 1978). Equality of position for the purpose of putting forward solutions and participating in their discursive redemption, and the avoidance of force of any kind in this activity, are some of the essential ingredients of this aim. However, what I want to emphasize here in this context is that part of our understanding of communication within this ideal is that moral statements must always be made from within what Habermas calls the "performative attitude" (Habermas 1983). They are not static truth claims warranted only by how closely they reflect reality according to some privileged epistemic position. Rather, they are *claims made to others* about the best means of regulating overlapping and competing needs and interests for the purpose of a *mutual* "redemption" of their validity. In this sense the locus of what warrants them as better or worse can be found only through the quality of the dialogic activity among persons. If this is correct—*and* the moral point of view that we should see in the multicultural mosaic is to remain an open question for future generations—what moral education *must* include is the aim of getting students on the inside of this performative understanding and use of moral discourse.

But then, where does this leave us? Although this may at first seem like quite a jump, my second positive suggestion is that we must *as a result* take a much closer look at the role of the *teacher*, something which also seems to me to get too little attention in this context. In order to get at what I think is crucial about the role of the teacher in the context just identified—in particular, the aim of getting students on the inside of the performative use of moral discourse, *whatever* their particular cultural embeddedness—we need first briefly to come to grips with the nature of that which organizes teaching behavior in the ideal sense, namely, *education*. Putting aside for a moment the concern for moral education in the sense of an *area* or *field* of educational theory and practice, I am going to elaborate an understanding of education itself as necessarily moral, as a moral relationship maintained and mediated by the activity of teachers. It is, then, in this general context that we need to appreciate the place of moral education in the more narrow sense and the crucial role of the teachers who engage in this kind of activity within a multicultural setting.

Constructing the Meaning
of the Multicultural Mosaic through the
Moral Conversation of Education

It should not be news that education is commonly thought to be a good thing. Indeed, it is such a good thing that, according to the United Nations, it is something that we all have a right to. Of course, views of exactly what education is and why it is good vary considerably. For example, at the philosophical level the range is from Plato to Peters, from Socrates to Skinner, from Montessori to Martin, from Buber to Bloom. It should be clear, in addition, that this variation is not an artificial problem found only at the level of theory. There is often substantial disagreement evidenced in the political discussion of what education should look like within a particular educational jurisdiction, and this disagreement is almost inevitably increased in degree to the extent that the jurisdiction is attempting to reflect its multicultural nature. Given this state of affairs, teachers are out on a moral limb. They are in the middle of all this disagreement, insofar as they are the ones primarily responsible for effecting education, however conceived. In my view, this is not something to be lamented and circumvented—because it is *necessarily so*. But it *does* need to be understood better and appreciated more. And moral education in a pluralist society must be grounded in this conception.In a nut shell, I want to claim that *education itself is a moral claim, extended performatively through time via the activities and role of teachers*. In what follows I will briefly try to explain this claim and its implications for moral education in the narrow sense.

When I say that education itself is a moral claim, my first intention is to locate conceptions of education themselves within the intentional sphere of human action. Education is not just something we stumble upon and then get blindly caught up in (though undoubtedly it seems that way to most children). Rather, education is more properly understood as something through which we try to *do* something. In short, education is one of the main ways we have as humans to define our humanity, to practice our humanity, to maintain our humanity, and to change our humanity. It is how we seek to connect ourselves today to ourselves of the past, and it is how we project ourselves into the future. The function of education is to maintain a kind of cultural state of dynamic homeostasis in the relationship between our current understanding of ourselves within the world around us and our seemingly open-ended potential. It is clear that we have been shaped *by* our past, and that contemporary institutions, traditions, attitudes, practices, etc., are at the same time enabling strengths and deliberating constrains. The plasticity of humanity is *perhaps* not infinite. But surely we know now even from looking backward through the lens of cultural anthropology that the variability in the development of human personhood is literally astounding—in much the same way that the infinite is astounding. And I see no reason to believe that the boundaries of such development are within sight today, or even that they could, in principle, ever be in sight.

What I am getting at here is the notion that education is essentially a constructive tool developed *by* human beings *for the development of* human beings. As Alan Tom (1984) has said:

> education is not one of the givens of the universe. Human beings—not some supernatural being or set of underlying natural regularities—cause education to be the way it is. (97)

Tom wants to emphasize, as I do also, the fact that education is a "socially constructed phenomenon" (97).[8]

It is through education, at least in part, that human beings work together to realize the visions we have of what sort of creatures we should be as human beings. When we make educational claims, despite how "factual" they may sound, we are never simply describing something, but *prescribing* it. Educational aims are not accounts of something that *is*, but of something that we want *to be*. Education is not just a convenient way of getting somewhere which we know to exist before we set out, something like a comfortable car that we can drive down a clearly marked road to a scenic picnic place, according to some travel club's map. Rather, it is something closer in kind to a free-for-all family discussion of whether, where, why, and how we might want to go somewhere, views of what scenic places look like and what would be desirable to do there, combined with suggestions about what direction one might travel to find such a place, combined with expressions of what mode of transportation would be the safest, most convenient, comfortable way of getting there.

In likening education to a "family discussion" I am trying to capture the idea that education itself is a kind of long-term moral claim needing to be made from within the "performative attitude" as previously identified. That is, it is a way of making known to others, both of this generation and of following generations, our vision of human development, and it is a way of maintaining that vision as essentially contestable, requiring on-going communal consideration, critique, confirmation, etc. It is the way we have constructed to be self-reflexive together, *through time*, about what it means to be human. It is a kind of long-term conversation, one whose point is its own maintenance. In much the same way that a conversation exists *because* the participants have different things to say, differing visions of what it means to be human are not something to be circumvented, but rather, that which gives education its meaning and *raison d'etre*. That we must deal with this difference if the conversation is to continue is what makes *moral education* a necessary core of any general conception of education.

If education is analogous to a conversation in these ways, who is doing the talking? *Teachers are*. It is through the *intentional* activities of teaching, that the educational conversation is made real. Of course I do not intend to say that only teachers talk in classrooms, and certainly not that only teachers *should* talk. Talking is merely one form that teaching sometimes takes; listening is another, probably more important, both efficaciously and morally. Rather, my point is that, whatever form a particular instance of teaching takes, the teacher is conveying a message and waiting for a response within a much larger conversation. Similarly, of course I do not mean that the content of this message is the responsibility of teachers alone. On the contrary, Ministry of Education guidelines talk, textbooks talk, standardized tests talk, college entrance requirements talk, etc., and what is said in these is, ideally at least, the outcome of the larger conversation among all of us. However, what should never be overlooked is that the teacher is necessarily in the moral middle of the educational conversation. The primary reason for this is that the focus of all this talk is on the students and what we want them to become, and teaching is the agency role through which educational messages pass.

What does this then mean within our general concern of moral education *for* multiculturalism? It means, first of all, that when we ask this question in the narrow sense of "moral education" we cannot afford to forget that *all* teachers are moral agents *qua* teachers. Cultural pluralism, *if* it is to be maintained, will *be* maintained through the activities of teachers, not in spite of them. If this is true, what it requires in terms of the organization of schools, the education of teachers, and the limits of teachers' professional freedom are all matters of further exploration and considerable importance. But, in addition, it also means that we can state more precisely one essential activity of teaching required by moral education in the narrow sense, *when we are concerned with the moral commitments that underlie and maintain multicultural education* as noted above. When I focused on the future needs of students in this context, I ended by emphasizing the formal aim of getting students on the inside of what I have called the performative understanding and use of moral discourse so that they will be able to work together on the problem of constructing the multicultural mosaic. The moral education teacher is the role most directly responsible for facilitating this outcome. By way of conclusion, I will briefly explain this in terms of the previously used metaphor of education as a conversation.

I have argued that education in general is a particular kind of moral instrument for the shaping of human persons. Moral education (in the narrow sense) is that area of this general endeavor in which we come clean and admit what we are doing! Moral education is that essential core of education where we must face up to the prescriptiveness of the differing visions of human personhood that permeate all educational activities—and face up to the fact that the people most directly affected by the prescriptions are persons still maturing. If education is likened to a long-range conversation about these differing visions, moral education is how we seek to treat as moral equals those most directly affected by both the outcome of the conversation and how it is conducted—by inviting and helping them join the conversation. It thus requires acknowledging the differences, problematizing the differences as prescriptive claims, conveying the need to maintain the common human conditions of dialogue as the foundation of dealing with the differences, and giving the students whatever language, skills, knowledge, and dispositional states necessary to their being equal participants and responsible partners in this conversation.

Moral education within an understanding of education as moral is then something alike a truth-in-advertising act. If I am right that the stance of all teachers must be seen within the performative attitude, it is doubly so for teachers of moral education. *They* must assume this stance while being overtly self-reflexive about how and why they have assumed it. It is only by problematizing what it means to make claims within this stance that they can leave room for students to assume it also—indeed, it is *through* this particular teaching activity that the possibility of future generations' continuing the educational conversation is realized. In short, if teachers in general are those who have the responsibility for doing the talking within the educational conversation, teachers of *moral* education are those who accept the obligation to teach the students to talk back. If students are to be encouraged to actively take the moral point of view necessary to construct the meaning within the multicultural mosaic, it will be in response to *this* orientation in teaching. In this sense, finally, the plural part of moral education—what everyone must share—can be found in the moral part of pluralism.

Notes

1. The potentially substantial impact of the entrenchment into law of a Charter of Rights and Freedoms in 1982 is now being experienced in many areas of Canadian society, and may change these relations.

2. Interestingly, the "mosaic" image seems to be seldom used in American literature on pluralism/multiculturalism, and when it *is*, it usually carries a connotation of something to be *avoided*. For example, Pratte (1980, 2) notes that Robert Park used it as early as 1928 in the American context but saw it as an image of segregation; Pratte apparently agrees when it is placed in a more contemporary context as well. A similar suggestion is made within Appleton's analysis (Appleton 1982, 154).

3. For statistics of distribution, see *Immigrant Landings to Canada 1971–1984*, Ethnocultural Data Office, Multicultural Program, Ontario Ministry of Citizenship and Culture, 1985.

4. Interestingly, the Report also claimed to have found, through its questionnaire, evidence to support the conclusion that "Students do not appear to be overly sensitive about or concerned with race and ethnic relations in their school" (p. vi). However, there were only three, rather ambiguous, questions asked on this topic, and a less sanguine interpretation could easily be given these limited data

5. This difference has recently come to the forefront to the extent that some insist on *contrasting* multicultural education and anti-racist education. For example, a well-known supporter of Ontario's "Heritage Languages" program, Jim Cummins, says, "What we need is not multicultural education but anti-racist education" (quoted in Ellwood 1989, 25).

6. I would like to note, however, that Ouellet himself has developed one of the most sophisticated programs of in-service teacher education that I have seen to promote this aim, though, oddly enough, he does not characterize the ingredients of his programs in moral terms. See Fernand Ouellet 1987.

7. A welcome exception, as I have clearly noted, is Kach and DeFaveri (1987).

8. Tom also differentiates education from other socially constructed phenomena in the following way:

> education differs from other categories of socially constructed phenomena in that it is a second-order construction, that is, our educational system is constructed in order to orient the young to such other social constructions as human institutions and the humanities, as well as to the natural world. (68)

Although I would also agree with this, I do not think it significantly affects the point I want to make here.

References

Appleton, N. 1982. "Democracy and Cultural Pluralism: Ideals in Conflict." *Philosophy of Education* 38: 151–158.

Banks, J. A. 1988. *Multiethnic Education: Theory and Practice*. 2nd ed. Boston: Allyn and Bacon.

Bullivant, B. M. 1984. *Pluralism: Cultural Maintenance and Evolution.* Clevedon, Eng.: Multilingual Matters.

Cheng, E. W. 1988. "A Survey of Students Attending a Culturally Diverse Secondary School." Lester B. Pearson C. I. Research Report of the Multicultural Committee, Scarborough Board of Education.

Crewe, N. 1987. "The Chair's Letter: A Letter from the Chair of the Toronto Board of Education on Some of the Current Developments in the Toronto School System," 105 (February).

Ellwood, W. 1989. "Learning by Root." *New Internationalist* (January 24–25).

Fernhout, H. 1989. "Moral Education as Grounded in Faith." *Journal of Moral Education*, 18 (3): 186–198.

Habermas, J. 1983. "Interpretive Social Science vs. Hermeneuticism." *Social Science as Moral Inquiry*, ed. N. Haan, R. B. Bellah, P. Rabinow, and W. M. Sullivan. New York: Columbia University Press.

Immigrant Landings to Canada 1971-1984. 1985. Ethnocultural Data Office, Multicultural Program, Ontario Ministry of Citizenship and Culture.

Kach, N., and I. DeFaveri. 1987. "What Every Teacher Should Know about Multiculturalism." *Contemporary Educational Issues: The Canadian Mosaic*, ed. L. L. Stewin and S. J. H. McCann. Toronto: Copp Clark Pitman.

Klein, J. Theodore. 1974. "Cultural Pluralism and Moral Education." *Monist* 58 (4): 683–693.

Malcolm, A. H. 1986. *The Canadians.* Toronto: Paper Jacks.

Mazurek, K., and N. Kach. 1986. "Culture and Power: Educational Ideologies in Multicultural Canada." In *Essays on Canadian Education*, ed. N. Kach, K. Mazurek, R. S. Patterson, and I. DeFaveri. Calgary: Detselig Enterprises.

McCarthy, T. 1978. *The Critical Theory of Jurgen Habermas.* Cambridge, Mass.: MIT Press.

McLeod, K. 1984. "Multiculturalism and Multicultural Education." In *Multiculturalism in Canada: Social and Educational Perspectives*, ed. Ronald J. Samuda, John W. Berry, and Michel Laferriere. Toronto: Allyn and Bacon.

———. (ed.). 1987. *Multicultural Education: A Partnership.* Toronto: Canadian Council for Multicultural and Intercultural Education.

Ouellet, F. 1987. "Intercultural Education: Teachers In-Service Training." In *Multicultural Education: A Partnership*, ed. K. McLeod. Toronto: Canadian Council for Multicultural and Intercultural Education.

Peters, R. S. 1966. *Ethics in Education.* London: George Allen and Unwin.

Pratte, R. 1972. "The Concept of Cultural Pluralism." In *Philosophy of Education 1972*, ed. Mary Anne Raywid. Edwardsville, Ill.: Philosophy of Education Society.

———. 1980. "Five Ideologies of Cultural Diversity and Their Curricular Ramifications." In *Philosophy of Education 1979* 35, ed. J. R. Coombs. Normal, Ill.: Philosophy of Education Society.

Taylor, J. J. 1986. Review Article. "'Education for All': Some Ethical Dimensions of the Swann Report." *Journal of Moral Education* 15 (1): 16–25.

Tom, A. R. 1984. *Teaching as a Moral Craft*. New York: Longman.

Troper, H. 1978. "Ethnic Populations and History of Education: Nationalism and the History Curriculum in Canada." *The History Teacher* 12: 11-27.

Yinger, J. M. 1986. "Intersecting Strands in the Theorisation of Race and Ethnic Relations." In *Theories of Race and Ethnic Relations*, ed. J. Rex and D. Mason. Cambridge: Cambridge University Press.

PLURALISM, VIRTUES, AND

THE POST-KOHLBERGIAN ERA

IN MORAL PSYCHOLOGY

Daniel K. Lapsley

On February 9, 1987, the following letter appeared in the "voice of the people" section of the *Chicago Tribune*, signed by a juvenile court judge:

American schools always have been...deliberately involved in the transmission of moral wisdom. By "moral wisdom" I mean eternal norms or standards of human behavior, beliefs about the rightness or wrongness of human conduct, recognized and affirmed over the generations. It is folly to suggest that one may educate without teaching morality. One may argue quite correctly that in a free society personal moral views may be submitted to the marketplace of ideas in adult society. However, it has never been seriously advocated that in public schools our children should be presented with an adult smorgasbord of morality options.... for many children in our society, the public school provides the only healthy indoctrination in practical human morality...before entering the rough and tumble world of adult pluralism.... Such "wisdom" is immutable; it does not change from age to age; it does not depend upon public opinion or practice for its efficacy. This "wisdom" is the foundation upon which cultures are built. When the foundation cracks, the lights flicker.... The lights are flickering, what shall we do? One thing we must not do is to compromise the integrity of our schools by asking them to teach...behavior inconsistent with wisdom. We must demand unequivocally that our children practice self-control and self-restraint in all areas of human temptation.... I for one vote no to dispensing contraceptive devices in our schools and would be very much opposed to any education not consistent with the ideals of personal purity and self-restraint in all areas of human passion.

This remarkable letter succinctly summarizes much of the anxiety that is evident among educators and theorists as they come to grips with what role, if any, values education should play in the public school curriculum. The author correctly notes, at least implicitly, that the very nature of instruction involves a commitment to certain values, even if the commitment is unrecognized or the values inarticulated. That morality options could be many among adults, that adult society is to be properly characterized as a veritable "smorgasbord of ideas," from which one could freely sample as in a "marketplace" so as to fashion a "personal morality," is not, in itself, recognized as an undesirable thing, but merely a healthy reflection of democratic pluralism, which is itself something to be respected (or at least tolerated as a necessary evil). Lurking among the pluralistic morality options, however, is an immutable wisdom that serves as the foundation of our culture, a wisdom that is impervious to the vagaries of conventional opinion, and so well-understood that it could "deliberately" be passed on to the next generation. The uses of this wisdom are to assist young people in making concrete moral decisions, such as whether to violate the immutable standards of purity and self-restraint by using contraceptives.

The following themes, then, emerge from a consideration of this letter: (1) Although value pluralism is a pervasive feature of American culture, there does exist, nonetheless, a certain foundational moral "wisdom" that is immutable, unchanging, and impervious to passing fashions and tastes. (2) Moral education, the transmission of moral wisdom, should be deliberate, and not left to happenstance, since not to attend to deliberate moral education is to abdicate our educational (and moral) responsibility toward the next generation, and to leave the "lights" of our society "flickering." (3) Finally, moral wisdom so imparted can be usefully deployed in order to *correctly* resolve practical moral dilemmas.

These very themes are a striking feature of Lawrence Kohlberg's approach to moral education, an approach that has simply dominated the field of moral psychology for the last several decades. Like our editorial writer, Kohlberg was concerned with how one might ground moral judging upon foundational moral principles that transcend conventional opinion and value pluralism. Like our editorial writer, Kohlberg was interested in how one might develop deliberate moral education strategies such that this sort of judging might be accessible to students, and thereby utilized in order to resolve moral dilemmas.

According to Kohlberg, the form or structure of reasoning that one brings to bear on moral dilemmas can be shown to undergo a series of developmental transformations as one moves through adolescence to adulthood. These transformations can be described in terms of six stages. Each succeeding stage in the sequence is said to allow one to better differentiate moral from conventional considerations in any given moral dilemma, a differentiation that is starkly conceived at the highest stages, where the deliberator is said to endorse a "moral ideal." The stage sequence possesses certain properties. For example, the sequence of stages is held to be universal, invariant, and descriptive of qualitative changes in moral thought. Further, developmental progression through the stages is said to reflect not only an advance in the use of sophisticated cognitive operations, but also an advance in the quality of moral reflection as well. That is, reasoning at the highest ("principled") stages (5 and 6) is said to be both psychologically sophisticated *and* morally adequate, with moral adequacy being judged by how well reasoning corresponds to philosophic criteria laid down in the formalist, Kantian tradition. By explicitly appealing to certain ethical principles (e.g., the Kantian categorical imperative), and by engaging in certain dilemma-solving methodologies (e.g., the Rawlsian "original position" or "moral musical chairs") one increases the likelihood that just solutions will be found for hard case dilemmas, solutions that will compel agreement because of their evident rationality and fairness. Indeed, at the highest stages one can expect universal agreement on the solution to moral dilemmas, since the press towards agreement is part of the moral ideal under which one operates, a claim that Kohlberg used as a foil against ethical (and cultural) relativism.

Although more will be said about this aspect of Kohlberg's theory, it is important to point out just how critical the issue of ethical relativism has been to Kohlberg's work. His entire project can be seen as an attempt to provide the psychological resources by which to combat relativism. Indeed, the extent to which any given theory in moral psychology can be seen to give aid or comfort to ethical relativism is to count as the chief mark against it, quite irrespective of whatever empirical evidence can be amassed in its favor. Any approach, for example, that emphasizes moral "socialization," either by manipulating reinforcers or by inculcating virtues, is to be rejected on the grounds that it implicitly reflects a commitment to ethical relativism. This commitment is evident in the behavioral tradition to the extent that ordinary moral language (e.g., good, right, ought) is reduced to value-neutral operational definitions ("positive reinforcement"). Insofar as societies possess different social contingencies for dispensing reinforcement, it follows that what gets called "good" may vary considerably across various cultures. That at least one culture thought it fit to reinforce the extermination of Jews is of some moment to Kohlberg. If what is "good" is a matter of social contingency, then one is hard pressed to provide a rational argument against Nazi morality.

The argument against the virtue tradition follows a similar form. Virtues are often seen as traits of character. Yet by one count there are at least 4,500 words in the English language that could refer to personality traits, and the number applying to specifically virtue traits must be correspondingly large. Consequently, any composition of a desirable list or "bag" of virtues must necessarily be arbitrary. Furthermore, and more to the point, Kohlberg argued that the meaning of virtue words is relative to conventional cultural standards, and is hence "ethically relative." He writes: "Labeling a set of behaviors displayed by a child with positive or negative trait terms does not signify that they are adaptive or of ethical importance. It represents an appeal to particular community conventions, since one person's 'integrity' is another person's 'stubbornness'" (Kohlberg & Mayer 1987). In Kohlberg's view, it was completely inappropriate for moral socialization theorists to pretend that what they described was simply an objective and empirical psychology of behavior, one that was "scientific" and therefore uncommitted to philosophical assumptions. Yet, by depriving moral behavior of motivational, cognitive, or interpretive elements, and by reducing ordinary moral language to putatively objective value-neutral descriptions of culturally specific patterns of habit-training, one could not help but find culturally relative moral values. In Kohlberg's view, moral socialization theorists take a stand on moral relativity without admitting it.

It should not be surprising that Kohlberg attempted to provide a psychological solution to the problem of ethical relativism in such a way that explicitly acknowledged the value-relevant nature of moral inquiry. Indeed, it remains one of Kohlberg's most significant achievements that his work encouraged a meaningful interpenetration of moral psychology and ethics (see Kohlberg 1981; Boyd 1986). This interpenetration can be described in a number of ways. First, Kohlberg extended the genetic epistemological project of Piaget (1970; see Kitchener 1986) to the moral domain in a more successful way than did Piaget (1932) himself. Thus, Kohlberg described his work as the "rational reconstruction of the ontogenesis of justice reasoning." As such, it was Kohlberg's aim to show that moral stage development yields an increasing appreciation of a "moral point of view," instantiated at Stage 6, that is normative, adequate, and justifiable in terms of relevant deontological theories of justice. In other words, "an adequate psychological theory of stages and stage movement presupposes a normative theory of justice," with the striking implication that "falsification of the empirical hypotheses of [the] psychological theory would...cast doubt on the validity of [the] normative theory" (Kohlberg, et al. 1983, 18). The normative theory of justice not only stakes out the psychological domain of inquiry, but also functions as one part of the developmental explanation for stage movement. "For instance, the normative theoretical claim that a higher stage is philosophically a better stage is one necessary part of a psychological explanation of sequential stage movement" (Kohlberg et al. 1983, 18). This entails, of course, that Kohlberg take a stand on the is-ought controversy (see Boyd 1986), and that he articulate the normative theory that grounds his conception of moral stage development (Kohlberg 1981). It also suggests a means by which ethical (and cultural) relativism is to be combated. Cultural relativity is transcended by locating culturally universal patterns of norms and elements that underlie, at some deep level of discourse and practice, all forms of moral judging and evaluating. These universal norms can be revealed only by sensitive hermeneutic inquiry. This inquiry would reveal, for example, that the seeming relativity of various cultural practices and customs is only apparent, reflecting mere "content" differences among societies, differences that are ultimately "structured" by a deep appreciation of universalizable and prescriptive moral norms. Hence, "the culturally variable customs of monogamy and polygamy are both compatible with the culturally-universal underlying moral norms of personal dignity, commitment, and trust in sexual relationships" (Kohlberg et al. 1983, 72).

Ethical relativity is combated by the natural developing tendency to seek the highest stage of development, at which point one could more easily differentiate the prescriptive and universalizable elements of a moral judgment from mere conventional considerations. When one reasons from the perspective of the moral ideal that Stage 6 describes, then one realizes that moral agreement is a necessary and desirable feature of moral discourse. Value pluralism, then, is something that is evident only to one still trapped in conventional forms of moral reasoning. Moral disagreement is endemic only among those who lack the cognitive developmental abilities to engage in sophisticated, dilemma-solving justice operations, operations that are at the disposal of the principled reasoner. The moral educational task, then, is to provide the contextual supports for motivating development to the highest stage where this sort of reasoning becomes possible.

The Kohlbergian response, then, to the problem of value pluralism is to argue that there are real possibilities for moral consensus if development is sufficiently motivated to the highest stages of moral development. Although there is pervasive empirical support for various aspects of Kohlberg's theory (e.g., Walker 1982; Walker, de Vries, & Bichard 1984) and for his approach to moral education (Power, Kohlberg, & Higgins 1989; Lapsley et al. 1989), it has become increasingly apparent that his entire approach to moral psychology may be unduly narrow, a narrowness that may, in turn, be based on two kinds of false moves. One of these, or so I will argue, is related to Kohlberg's antipathy for the importance of human virtues. The second regards the mechanics of principled reasoning itself. If Kohlberg has discovered a set of psychological facts about the course of moral development, and if these facts have implications for the validity of a normative theory of justice, then this state of affairs in moral psychology would undoubtedly be of singular importance to ethicists. Yet it is true to say that the facts of moral development, as understood by Kohlberg, have not penetrated very deeply into ethical discourse. I will suggest that the reason that this is the case has less to do with real or imagined deficiencies in moral psychology. Rather, it has more to do with the fact that the ideal Kohlbergian moral agent, adopting as she must the transcendental viewpoint of the (Rawlsian) original position, dislodged as she must then be from every social particularity, is an abstraction, an "epistemic subject," and not a *psychological* being at all. It is difficult to see how any set of psychological facts about human development could matter in an account of ideal rational agents who must become socially disembodied into impartiality and agreement. (And the fact that Kohlberg has never satisfactorily identified such a reasoner is of some importance.)

I should like to argue, then, that the Kohlbergian attempt to provide developmental arguments against ethical relativism is based on two mistakes, and that the project must, therefore, inevitably fail. Each will now be addressed in turn, then I will attempt to articulate what a "post-Kohlbergian era" in moral psychology might look like.

Stage 6 and the Transcendental Moral Agent

As I just implied there is currently no provision in the extant Kohlbergian interview and scoring procedures for identifying a Stage 6 moral reasoner (Colby, Kohlberg, et al. 1987). Yet the hypothetical nature of the final stage does not constitute sufficient grounds for simply jettisoning it from the theory. Indeed, the very coherence of the stage sequence, and the very force of the various moral psychological claims that the sequence entails, hinges on the requirement that the sequence be closed by a kind of reasoning that is denoted as Stage 6, even if this reasoning is nowhere descriptive of actual moral agents. Perhaps another way of stating this is to say that the genuinely interesting use of the theory as a foil against ethical relativism depends on Stage 6 being at least a theoretical possibility, even though no adequate procedure currently exists for identifying it' Why is this the case? One reason is related to the nature of developmental explanation in the structural developmental tradition out of which Kohlberg operated. Developmental stages, in this tradition, are imbued with teleological assumptions concerning the patterning and appropriate direction of change. Change is goal-directed towards a state of optimum complexity and adaptation, which is described as the final stage of development. If the developmental *telos* is to be attained, then certain intermediary stages are required. Developmental explanations, then, are not only teleological but functional. Hence, according to Kitchener (1983, 800), developmental explanations are "diachronic pattern explanations in which a part (a stage) is explained when one understands how it fits into the whole (sequence)—that is, how it fits into a temporal process directed towards a goal—and what contributing role (function) it played in the realization of this goal." The transition from earlier to later stages is given sense by understanding how the transitions function as a means for reaching the final stage.

Although Stage 5 involves the use of sophisticated cognitive operations, it is not the most "equilibrated" form of reasoning, and therefore cannot resolve certain problems in a way that is *most* adequate (in a psychological sense). Further, and given the complementarity that is said to exist between cognitive and moral operations, a Stage 5 reasoner cannot be expected to resolve certain moral dilemmas in a way that is either completely adequate, in a moral sense, or in a way that compels agreement, which is the main point of moral deliberation. And it is just this desire to describe how it is possible to generate agreement on rationally justifiable solutions to moral dilemmas that is at the heart of the Kohlbergian project, a project that clearly requires that Stage 6 be the *telos* of moral development, since it is here that the desire for rational agreement is satisfied.

Stage 6 moral reasoning is a thoroughly Kantian affair. The central point of moral reasoning is to bring about the correct solution to a moral quandary by linking the features of the dilemma to a covering law that is universally applicable, categorical, prescriptive, and rationally justified. Following Schneewind (1983) the covering law might be said to be a "classical first principle" to the extent that it (1) possesses generality and is hence context-free, (2) allows no exceptions, (3) is substantive, and not merely formal, in that concrete solutions to specific moral questions might be derived from it, and (4) is foundational, in the sense that the authority of the principle is "basic" and not therefore derived from any source extrinsic to reason itself. Hence, the moral law is authoritative, objective, and binding on all rational agents in virtue of their rationality. One is an autonomous moral agent to the extent that one takes on the moral law as one's own, and heteronomous to the extent that one acts for reasons other than what the demands of rationality require. It also matters for moral deliberation that the moral relevance of the situation be adequately identified, that moral and nonmoral considerations be carefully distinguished (Norton 1988), and that mechanisms be available for adjudicating appeals to competing moral rules (Solomon 1988), typically in light of the first principle.

Kant's "categorical imperative" is, of course, a vivid example of a classical first principle. It is also paradigmatic of Stage 6 reasoning (although Kohlberg sometimes allowed for other general ethical principles to ground moral problem solving). At this stage one reasons from the perspective of any rational, autonomous individual, in accordance with the "moral point of view," in terms that can be universalized (Meilaender 1984). The moral point of view gives form to Stage 6 deliberations in that it structures the kinds of principles that can be invoked. One takes the moral point of view if one is autonomous, impartial, willing to universalize, and informed about the relevant facts of the matter (Kohlberg et al. 1983).

A moral judgment is justified if it generates agreement by everyone who takes this view. "This means equal consideration of the claim or points of view of each person affected by the moral decision. This prescriptive role-taking is governed by procedures designed to insure fairness, impartiality, or reversibility in role-taking" (Kohlberg 1986, 497). These procedures are deliberately invoked at Stage 6 to serve as procedural justice checks on the validity of a moral judgment.

Kohlberg (1986) describes several of these procedures. One procedure is formalized in terms of Rawl's original position, where one must choose from the "original position" after donning the "veil of ignorance." Indeed, Stage 6 is described (as is Stage 5) in terms of a Rawlsian "prior-to-society" perspective of a rational moral agent who is aware of universalizable values and rights that any agent would choose to build into a society (Kohlberg 1986). Another formalized procedure is called "moral musical chairs," where one systematically determines if a candidate judgment is still acceptable when seen from the perspective of each claimant. One indication that a judgment is inadequate is just when it cannot be "reversed," i.e., when it cannot be consistently maintained from the perspective of other parties. In the famous Heinz dilemma, for example, where Heinz must choose between stealing a drug in order to save the life of his wife (and thereby violate the property rights of a druggist) or not to steal (and thereby violate the imperative to respect life), Kohlberg has determined that every Stage 6 reasoner who adopts the moral point of view will choose to steal the drug. This is so because the druggist would not insist on his property rights if *he* were in the position of Heinz's wife, i.e., his position could not be reversed from the perspective of the other party to the justice dispute. Similarly, Kohlberg has determined that no rational agent would endorse capital punishment from the original position, prior-to-society, since no agent could rationally choose death if it could be the case that it is the agent on death row. The judgment for capital punishment, then, is not reversible if seen from the perspective of the inmate. A fully reversible judgment, one that survives appraisal regardless of who is doing the appraising, will also therefore compel agreement, and will hence be universalizable. And just this perspective afforded by Stage 6 will allow one to transcend the plurality of moral options and the relativism that merely conventional reasoning is wont to breed.

A third formalization, one recently appended to the theory, emphasizes the dynamics of actual dialogue. Following Habermas, Kohlberg argued that disputants must take the "performative attitude" in actual moral dialogue, an attitude that is characterized as the active attempt to understand the point of view of others, and to coordinate this understanding with one' s own reasons in such a way that disputants will yield to convincing arguments. Dialogue of this sort is grounded by a number of presuppositions. Mutual respect, and the freedom and rationality of each disputant, are presupposed. Further, there are pragmatic considerations (understood as rules of argumentation) immanent in the very nature of rational discourse that commit disputants (at least intuitively) to presuppositions with normative content, and which therefore could function as a moral principle. According to Habermas, this principle is a formalization of Kantian intuitions, and assumes that every participant in moral dialogue must take into account the perspective of other disputants. "This principle can be stated in the following way: a valid norm has to satisfy the condition—that the consequences, intended or not, which will (probably) result from its *general* application for the interests of *every* individual affected would be consensually preferred by *all* of those involved" (Habermas, in Kohlberg 1986, 519). Can this principle be rationally justified? Is this a moral point of view that is valid for all cultures? Although Habermas intends this principle to function much like a principle of induction in theoretical discourse, he avoids the Popperian charge that such "first" principles are susceptible to infinite regress and to *apriorism* by claiming that all attempts to justify or refute this principle, by the very fact of entering into rational discourse, inescapably admit to pragmatic considerations governing dialogue that presuppose relevant aspects of the moral principle. Thus, he writes that

> everybody who attempts to refute the moral principle will be caught in a performative contradiction to the very pragmatic presuppositions which he cannot escape once he seriously

starts to argue at all. . . . The strategy of this form of argument is to accept the sceptical conclusion that these principles are not open to any proof, being presuppositions of reasoning rather than conclusions from it, but to go on to argue that commitment to them is rationally inescapable, because they must, logically, be assumed if one is to engage in a mode of thought essential to any rational human life. (Habermas, in Kohlberg 1986, 519)

Although Kohlberg formalizes Stage 6 in terms of the original position methodology, and in terms of moral musical chairs, and claims that these formalizations are consensus-seeking approaches to moral dilemmas, he has remarked that actual dialogue under the conditions of the performative attitude, as understood by Habermas, is the most advantageous means by which moral consensus is to be achieved (Kohlberg 1986, 527).

Our best hope, then, of reaching consensus on universal moral principles lies in achieving the moral point of view that is representative of Stage 6, and which is formalized in terms of the original position, moral musical chairs, and the ideal communication situation of actual moral dialogue. This is clearly a most sophisticated account of moral psychology, yet doubts remain concerning the adequacy of Stage 6. MacIntyre (1984, 23) noted that "A moral philosophy characteristically presupposes a sociology. . . . Thus it would generally be a decisive refutation of a moral philosophy to show that moral agency on its own account of the matter could never be socially embodied." I will press a similar claim against that aspect of Stage 6 which appeals to "ideal role-taking," whether it is expressed in terms of the original position or of moral musical chairs. Regarding the formalization of Stage 6 in terms of the performative attitude behind "legitimate speech acts," I will argue that this account of moral rationality is fundamentally incompatible with other formalizations of Stage 6, and whatever else may be said about Habermas's position, it cannot help Stage 6 in its task of transcending ethical relativism.

In his *After Virtue* MacIntyre (1984) argued that the eighteenth-century Enlightenment project of providing rational justification for objective and impersonal moral principles has failed. His account of this failure, and its consequence for contemporary moral philosophy, is relevant for my task here, for I shall argue that Kohlberg's project is just what one should expect in moral psychology if MacIntyre's thesis is true.

According to MacIntyre the search for foundational moral principles during the Enlightenment was motivated by the fact that the teleological understanding of moral injunctions and of their role in correcting untutored human nature was undermined by the rejection of Aristotelian teleological science and by the onslaught of secular Enlightenment thinking against theistic understandings of a Divine plan. The Enlightenment rejection of any notion of the *telos* of humankind (whether classical or theistic) therefore deprived moral injunctions of their justificatory force, insofar as the whole point of morality was to show how it was possible to bring human nature from how it *is* to how it could be if one were to realize one's *telos*. The categorical nature of moral judgments was lost, since the universal law that grounded such judgments could no longer be that which was commanded by God. The hypothetical nature of moral judgments was lost, since one could no longer justify those judgments regarding moral conduct in terms of what was required in order to reach one's true end. Moral judgments, then, lost any clear status, becoming inherited "linguistic survivals" divorced from a context which gave them force. In MacIntyre's view this was not necessarily seen as a lamentable state of affairs by those who had lived through this period. "Many of those who lived through this change in our predecessor culture saw it as a deliverance both from the burdens of traditional theism and the confusions of teleological thought. . . . The self had been liberated from all those outmoded forms of social organization which had imprisoned it simultaneously within a belief in a theistic and teleological world order and within those hierarchical structures which attempted to legitimate themselves as part of such a world order" (MacIntyre 1984, 60). The modern self, then, emerges emancipated, autonomous, and sovereign as a result of this collapse of classical theism.

Yet the ambiguous status of moral judgments which resulted from the "flight from authority" (Stout 1981) of the Enlightenment project presented modern moral philosophy with its characteristic problematic. According to MacIntyre (1984, 62):

> On the one hand the individual moral agent, freed from hierarchy and teleology, conceives of himself and is conceived of by moral philosophers as sovereign in his moral authority. On the other hand, the inherited, if partially transformed rules of morality have to be found some new status, deprived as they have been of their older teleological character and their even more ancient categorical character as expressions of an ultimately divine law. If such rules cannot be found a new status which will make appeal to them rational, appeal to them will indeed appear as a mere instrument of individual desire and will. Hence, there will be pressure to vindicate them either by devising some new teleology or by finding some new categorical status for them.

By grounding moral judgments on a psychological thesis (i.e, whether actions prescribed by a moral injunction increase happiness or pleasure), utilitarianism attempted to provide a "naturalistic" teleological foundation for morality. And it was the Kantian project that attempted to provide a new categorical status for moral judgments based on the requirements of practical reason. In MacIntyre's (1984) view, both projects failed, resulting in the modern predicament whereby we use moral speech to assert emotivist preferences, though cloaking our preferences behind the veneer of moral principles thought to provide objective "foundations" and "grounding."

Kohlberg's ideal moral agent, reasoning from the perspective of Stage 6, is ultimately an emotivist self as well. Whereas modern moral philosophy, according to MacIntyre (1984), attempts to vindicate the rationality and objectivity of moral judgments by finding some new teleological or categorical status for them, it is of interest to note that Kohlberg incorporates both strategies in his psychological theory. The categorical status is borrowed from the authority of the Kantian categorical imperative. The teleological foundation is found in the very nature of development itself. Recall that the very nature of functional developmental explanation assumes that development tends toward some goal or desired end state, e.g., the final stage. A sequence is explained when one can show how stage transition functions in such a way as to permit the attainment of the final stage. In the moral development theory the *telos* is realized when one talks like Kant when faced with moral dilemmas.

In traditional or classical polities the *telos* of human life was well understood. In the absence of community consensus on the proper ends of a good life, such as is the case in modern liberal societies, any proposed teleological formulation must necessarily be controversial, and therefore require justification. The choice of the Kantian imperative as a first principle of moral reasoning must remain unargued, however, on pain of infinite regress. In the Kantian scheme, "An agent can only justify a particular judgment by referring to some universal rule from which it may be logically derived, and can only justify that rule in turn by deriving it from some more general rule or principle; but on this view since every chain of reasoning must be finite, such a process of justificatory reasoning must always terminate with the assertion of some rule or principle for which no further reasons can be given" (MacIntyre 1984, 20). The choice of first principles, then, is to be left to the discretion of the moral agent, and has authority precisely because it is chosen.

It would then appear that Kohlberg's Stage 6 reasoner must also adopt unargued first principles and thereby fall prey to the state of affairs described by MacIntyre, whereby the language of impersonal, objective, and rational moral criteria is used to mask emotivist preferences. This perhaps explains the real import behind Kohlberg's desire to postulate the existence of a "soft" Stage 7, where one reflects on "the need to be moral in the first place," a reflection that might appropriately invoke religious or other appropriately cosmic considerations. It is one thing to use first principles in order to digest moral dilemmas, it is one thing to know *how* to be moral, quite another to justify *why* one should digest moral dilemmas in the first place, or *why* one should be moral. Stage 6 cannot tell us why morality is a desirable thing. To answer this question requires an appeal to extramoral considerations, and this is the business of Stage 7. Yet the need to postulate Stage 7 is symptomatic of the desire to provide at least some justification for the use of first principles other than to leave it to raw preference. That whatever Stage 7 reasons might be invoked would themselves require justification only pushes the infinite regress problem to another level, and would not, on this account, relieve the moral agent from ultimately choosing unargued moral allegiances for unargued Stage 7 considerations. Clearly, then, the elimination by the Enlightenment project of teleological considerations regarding proper and desirable ends of human life make the postulation of Stage 7 inevitable in moral psychology. The necessity for asking "open" or "limit" questions, which is the business of Stage 7, is only an interesting or necessary thing to do when moral judgments lack a clear teleological purpose.

It is also of interest to point out that to the extent that the Stage 6 reasoner might also be free to adopt first principles other than Kantian imperatives, such as the principle of utility or of benevolence (*agape*), it seems doubtful that dialogue on moral matters could be little more than the assertion of moral principles whose premises are incommensurable. It is just this incommensurability, the arguing from incompatible premises, that contributes to the interminability of moral debate, which is then dignified by the term "pluralism." As a result one would not be as sanguine as was Kohlberg that moral dialogue at Stage 6 could produce mere agreement, let alone agreement that was in some sense justified.

Indeed, it is notorious that other ethicists, presumably as skilled as was Kohlberg in using principled reasoning, could quarrel, with Kohlberg's favored solutions to hypothetical moral dilemmas (see, e.g., Locke 1986). One can see the justice, then, of MacIntyre's diagnosis of the predicament of modern moral philosophy, that for all the rhetoric of foundational moral principles there lurks instead the assertion of emotivist preferences, and this is as true in moral psychology as in ethics. It is not hard to see, for example, that our editorial writer, in touting the foundational importance of personal purity and self-restraint in sexual conduct, was doing little more that using the language of universal moral principles ("foundational wisdom") in order to mask an (emotivist) personal preference regarding the proper attitude one should

take towards contraception. Further, it may well be true that
monogamy and polygamy represent the identical allegiance
to universal principles of dignity and trust in relationships
(though what counts as dignity and trust begs for a historical analysis), but what is one to do when these values (or any
other) conflict in a practical moral conflict situation? It is little
wonder that Kohlberg (1986, 527) came to make a surprising
concession, that perhaps his theory is compatible with certain kinds of relativism ("perspectival" or "contextual") after
all, though not with "radical" relativism. This concession is
surprising since it robs Kohlberg's theory of much that made
it interesting, since clearly no appeal to psychological data is
needed to refute radical relativism.

There is still the formalization of Stage 6 in terms of "legitimate communication action" that needs to be considered.
One should first notice that the performative attitude underlying legitimate communication, and the implicit appeal to
normative pragmatic universals governing rational discourse,
applies equally well to dialogue about virtues as it does to the
kind of moral debates favored by Kohlberg. That universals
are presupposed in moral dialogue would entail that any rational discourse concerning, say, the status of "integrity" vs.
"stubbornness," would be enough to keep the moral skeptic
at bay, and deprive Kohlberg of any rationale for condemn-
ing virtues as necessarily "ethically relative."

Kohlberg (1986, 517) has written: "According to Habermas (1982), a Kantian respect for persons is a precondition for
argument or dialogue among philosophers and in this sense
justifies itself as the ultimate moral principle." He also approvingly cites McCarthy's (1982, 57) summary of Habermas's
theory:

> Philosophic hermeneutic stress that the interpreter of social
> phenomena is a member of a life-world, that the interpreter
> too occupies a specific historical, social, cultural position from
> which he or she tries to come to terms with the beliefs and
> practices of others. The understanding achieved is, as a result,
> inexorably situation-bound, an understanding from a point of
> view that is on the same level as what is understood. There
> are . . . no privileged positions outside of or above history from

which to view human life; there can be no interpreter without a language. . . .

Three comments are in order. First of all, Habermas does not take recourse to any ultimate foundations or ultimate principles (see, e.g., Habermas, in Kohlberg 1986, 531), or at least foundations that can be justified. Secondly, it is not at all clear that Habermas's challenge to the moral skeptic, appropriated by Kohlberg, can fend off anything more than a kind of radical "epistemological" relativism, which strikes one as a serious attenuation of the Kohlbergian project. As Carter (1986) pointed out, even if the validity claims underlying legitimate dialogue were fulfilled, this would not be sufficient to establish their universal and necessary validity. He writes that "even though analysis reveals what must be assumed for communication to be genuine, it is not clear exactly how we can establish an ideal-observer type objectivity for the content of those validity claims. We must assume that what we say is true, in order to communicate ideally, but this in no way shows that what we assume is, in fact, true, except from a perspective already within the circle of assumptions. [Hence], one's fundamental values, beliefs, methodology and even one's understanding of reason's place in the scheme of things, are taken by us to be true, and that they are *not* evidently universal or necessary, but only assumptive or traditional, or in some other way acceptable or even required by our point of view" (p. 14). On this point Kohlberg (1986) seems to agree, insofar as he now accepts the possibility that Stage 6 is helpless against "perspectival" relativism, a view that does not seem to leave the emotivist self far behind.

My third point is that whatever else can be said about the formalization of Stage 6 as a rational reconstruction of an ideal communication situation, it is incompatible with other formalizations of this stage. As noted above, Habermas does not assume that one must transcend social, cultural, or historical particularities, yet this is precisely what is required in order to reason "prior-to-society." Stage 6 is either a rational reconstruction of ideal and legitimate dialogue, or it is a prior-to-society perspective, but it cannot be both. The latter is assumed when Stage 6 is formalized in terms of the moral bargaining ("balancing perspectives") that takes place from the original position, after donning the veil of ignorance. One is to achieve impartiality by adopting a moral point of view of any rational individual, a view that represents a transcendental abstraction from one's own view, without knowing who one is. That one must become socially disembodied into impartiality, that one must stand outside of social structures, above history, and outside of time, that one must take the transcendental "perspective from eternity" (Stout 1981) in order to become the autonomous agent, is a view not only at odds with Habermas's assumptions, but one that is psychologically suspicious as well. One has no doubt that the kind of moral autonomy that Kohlberg seeks requires just this kind of social emasculation, but it pays the terrible price of yielding a transcendental self that is impoverished, fictive, and no self worth having. It is also worth noting that such a maneuver may not even achieve impartiality, since it has been argued that the autonomous moral bargainer actually reflects an implicit commitment to rational egoism (Stout 1981) and liberal individualism (MacIntyre 1988).

So the moral agent of Stage 6 is both an emotivist and transcendental self, which is to say no self at all. As MacIntyre noted (1984, 32), the emotivist "democratized" self "has no necessary social content, no necessary social identity, can assume any role or take any point of view, because it is, in and for itself, nothing." Yet Kohlberg is driven to this end because of his anxiety to provide a foundational moral psychology that can resolve disputes and counter ethical relativism. But the search for ultimate moral principles to serve foundational purposes in moral disputes is as reductionistic a strategy as any positivistic search for "basic" statements by which to resolve theoretical disputes in science (Stout 1981). The line of development in the philosophy of science beginning with Popper, and including Kuhn, Lakatos, and Laudan, among others, has shown how futile it is to expect any justificatory strategy to work in the rational appraisal of theories. Foundationalism in ethics fails just as surely as justificationism does in the philosophy of science, and for the same reasons. There is no "gap" between evaluative and descriptive statements, between fact and theory, between analytic and synthetic, between "is" and "ought."[1] There is no infallible basis that is to serve as the court of appeal in either theoretical or ethical disputes. And to say this is not to leave us helpless against the skeptic or the relativist. Historicist approaches do show how rational appraisal is possible, whether it be of ethical traditions (MacIntyre 1988; also, Stout 1981) or of scientific research programs (Lakatos 1978; see Serlin & Lapsley, 1990, in press, for the psychological case).

Kohlberg and Virtues

I have argued that Kohlberg, in attempting to provide psychological resources by which to combat relativism, and by which to transcend value pluralism, took the wrong turn into foundationalism, thereby yielding a fictive account of the emotivist, transcendental moral agent as a result. The second wrong turn concerns Kohlberg's treatment of virtues and of character education. Kohlberg objected to character education on two grounds. First, it is an arbitrary "bag of virtues" approach, and is therefore "ethically relative." Second, it does not seem to be the case, if the classic studies of Hartshorne and May (1928–1932) are to be believed, that virtue traits even exist, or cohere into something that could be called "character," since this research appeared to show that children do not consistently display such traits as honesty in various test-taking situations. It is unfortunate that so much weight has been given by Kohlbergians to the research by Hartshorne and May, since no one in the virtue ethics tradition could imagine that young children could have well-formed characters in the first place. This aside, I should want to argue, if only briefly, that a consideration of virtuous character must be prior to any consideration of how one goes about resolving hard case moral dilemmas.

The virtue ethics critique of deontological "quandary" ethics usually begins by noting just how constricted is its vision of the moral life (Norton 1988; Pincoffs 1983). For the quandarist the moral life is taken up with solving moral puzzles, in a juridical way, much like a critic or judge. The emphasis is on the problem, and allowable responses to the problem in light of the duties and obligations that are specified by general moral rules. In contrast, the virtue theorist is concerned with more than how one responds to borderline, hard case dilemmas, but rather with the problem of how to live well the life that is good for one to live. The emphasis is not so much on duty, but with the inculcation of those traits of character that permit one to live a virtuous life. The emphasis is on the formation of the agent, not with the solution to puzzles. Virtue theorists argue, correctly in my view, that the emphasis on forming the virtuous character must take priority over dilemma-solving as a moral educational task, since our ability to recognize or "see" a dilemma in the first place may well depend on who we are. As Meilaender (1984) points out, we would not be able to recognize hard cases, or determine what ought to be done, or what our duty was, or even whether the situation called for a moral response, unless we were a person of a certain sort. Again, what we see depends on who we are (see also, Dykstra 1981).

A splendid study by Donald R. C. Reed (1986) illustrates the difficulty that Kohlberg's rejection of character education has for his own moral educational project. The prototypic Kohlbergian moral education strategy has been called the "plus-one convention" (see Lapsley et al. 1989, for a review). The general plan is for students to discuss moral dilemmas, with the provision that counter-arguments be presented that reflect reasoning one stage above ("plus-one") the students' own. The discrepancy in views is said to induce "cognitive conflict," which then motivates development to the next highest stage. The plus-one convention was evidently inspired by the apparent success of the Socratic dialectic that was illustrated, for example, by the Socrates of the *Meno*. In this work one observes Socrates bringing a slave boy to an understanding of a principle of geometry through a dialectical ("Socratic") method. According to Reed (1986), however, what went apparently unnoticed by Kohlberg was the fact that Socrates could make little headway with Meno by the use of this method. Indeed, Reed (1986) argues that the purpose of the *Meno* was to illustrate just the limits of the Socratic dialectic. The dialectic will prove unavailing, the *Meno* illustrates, if the subject lacks sufficient character, and this apparently was the case with Meno (but not the slave boy). It was the Socrates of the *Republic*, a later work than the *Meno*, who described an educational regimen devoted to the task of inculcating those traits of character that would allow one to profit from the dialectic. Hence the two works must be read in tandem, according to Reed (1986). The *Meno* illustrates what can go wrong with the Socratic dialectic when a subject is lacking in character. The *Republic* illustrates how character is to be developed such that one could eventually profit from the dialectic. Although Kohlberg accepted the Socrates of the *Meno*, he rejected the Socrates of the *Republic* on the grounds that the latter was not "dialectical" education, but mere indoctrination. Yet not to see the connection between the *Meno* and the *Republic* is to miss the central Platonic point, that only those who are trained to do the good could be in a position to know the good. Consequently, as Meilaender (1984, 72) points out, "communities which seek simply to remain 'open' and do not inculcate virtuous habits of character will utterly fail at the task of moral education."

Towards the Post-Kohlbergian Era

I have argued that the Kohlbergian research program has been limited by two false moves. One was the desire to secure a foundation for moral judgments on psychological grounds in the interest of combating ethical relativism. The second was the rejection of virtues and character as the proper aim of moral education. The two false moves are not unrelated. Indeed, it is unremarkable that Kohlberg would eschew the development of virtuous character given his image of the Stage 6 moral agent, who must divest the self of social particularities and stand outside of culture and history for the sake of achieving impartiality. Who could be interested in character if moral rationality requires that it be transcended? Who could be interested in what "I" must do when the real question concerns what *any* (abstract, epistemic) individual must do? The twin moves also seem like quite natural efforts to extend the Piagetian genetic epistemological project into the moral domain, and only look like false moves from the contemporary vantage point, far after the authority of Piaget and the structural developmental movement has declined. But if my criticism of these twin features of Kohlberg's theory has force, then the post-Kohlbergian era in moral psychology is upon us.

What might this era look like? I can be little more than suggestive on this point, but a number of trends can be discerned already. It would appear that no grand theory of moral development, like Kohlberg's, is to be forthcoming in the post-Kohlbergian era. Indeed, moral psychology will undoubtedly go the way of intellectual development after the collapse of Piaget's theory. The study of intellectual development is now fragmented into numerous local and specific domains. These domains are typically understood by any number of mini-theories of limited generality, and most of these are inspired by the information-processing paradigm, a paradigm that does not have an obvious epistemological agenda. The fragmentation of the moral domain will continue apace and take a similar form. So, for example, developmental studies of moral emotions, forgiveness, prosocial reasoning, empathy, altruism, conceptions of social rules, equity, transgressions, authority, social justice, retribution, among others, will continue to be topics of great interest. Some areas, such as moral rule acquisition, especially of retributive and procedural justice rules, are already yielding to information-processing analyses (see Darley & Shultz 1990).

Although the empirical significance of these particular research domains is not to be doubted, it would not be unfair to say that their implications for moral education are not yet well developed. Even if they were, none would appear able to capitalize on the insight of the virtues ethics tradition that the development of character is the first task of moral education. One option that might seem obvious in light of this insight is that post-Kohlbergian research recover an interest in personological dispositions and traits of character. This suggestion undoubtedly sounds quixotic to those who are familiar with the unhappy status of traits in personality theory. Decades of research have simply failed to support the traditional assumptions underlying the notion of "global traits," e.g., that traits be readily detectable and show cross-situational consistency, stability, and temporal continuity (see Mischel 1968). It was precisely this notion of "trait" that was assumed by Hartshorne and May (1928–1932), whose results had such an important influence in leading Kohlberg to reject the study of virtue traits.

Yet there is no reason to be wedded to traditional assumptions about traits. Indeed, the conceptualization of personality dispositions has been undergoing remarkable development in recent years. According to Mischel (1990, 116–117) this conceptualization "called attention away from inferences about what broad traits a person *has* [in a context-free sense], to focus instead on what the person *does* in particular conditions in the coping process. Of course, what people do encompasses not just motor acts, but what they do cognitively and affectively, including the constructs they generate, the projects they plan and pursue, and the self-regulatory efforts they attempt in light of long-term goals." The contemporary study of "traits" now emphasizes "person-situation interactionism," and is subsumed under such research headings as competencies, personal constructs, and encoding strategies (schemes, scripts, prototypes, etc), expectancies, subjective values and goals, and self-regulatory systems (see Mischel 1990, for a review). These approaches to personality dispositions should prove useful to virtue theorists as they work out the parameters of character development.

Another promising line of research is being developed by Augusto Blasi (1984; 1985; 1989), in his work on moral identity and the moral personality. Blasi argues that the self is not a collection of traits or characteristics, but is rather an organization of self-related information. This information is ordered according to principles of psychological consistency (central-peripheral, important-unimportant, essential-unessential). To the extent that moral considerations (being good, just, virtuous) are judged to be central, important, and essential to one's self-understanding, and one is committed to living in such a way as to express what is central, important and essential about oneself, then one has a "moral identity." This suggests that one's identity may not include moral considerations, or may include them in degrees, suggesting further that moral identity, like the dispositional approach noted above, is a dimension of individual differences. Blasi's work also provides a perspective on moral action, which is seen to hinge on notions of fidelity and self-responsibility, i.e., a concern with being authentic or true-to-the-self in action. In his view, moral identity is that which motivates moral action. If moral considerations are self-defining, if they are a part of the "essential self" to the extent that self-integrity hinges on self-consistency in action, then not to act in accordance with one's identity is to risk losing the self.

Blasi's emphasis on identity is a particularly attractive aspect of his work, for it has important implications for our understanding of virtues. Identity, following Erikson, is an inherently "psychosocial" construct that is forged in communities. Identity is not mere self-definition but self-definition that is validated by society (or the communities in which we belong). It implies, among other things, an attempt to integrate and order the elements of our personality for the sake of living a meaningful life, one lived in fidelity to those projects, ideals, and choices that we commit to and "identify" with, and by which we are identified, in turn, by our community.

Virtues, too, make sense only in light of a community which seeks to develop people of a certain kind. The "life that is good for one to live" is social in nature and takes place in accordance with the specifications of community, such that some sort of "adaptation" to it is required in order to flourish (Wong 1988). The development of a virtuous character and of moral identity may not be two different kinds of development. Indeed, one might claim that the kinds of development that lead to the acquisition of moral identity is the minimal grounding of the virtuous character. That this may be so is suggested by the recent interest shown by virtue ethicists in certain "Eriksonian" identity themes (see, e.g., Rorty 1988; Kupperman 1988; Wong 1988). Insofar as a virtue ethic is concerned with the question of what it is to live a life well (i.e., to flourish), and with specifying those virtues the possession of which contributes to the realization of such a life, and to the extent that this specification must be grounded by the meanings and practices of a community, then a commitment to live this life is just what confers moral identity.

A recent work by John Kekes (1989) illustrates just how close is a meaningful dialogue between moral psychology and philosophy. Kekes argues that good judgment requires one to possess "breadth" and "depth," terms which describe different organizations of "moral idioms." Moral idioms can be described by the terms of approval and disapproval that are provided us by our social context. They are moral, specific, interpretive, and action-guiding, and they also describe character traits. One possesses breadth when one is aware that a range of competing interpretations of relevant idioms are possible when a complex moral situation is to be confronted. Indeed, to have breadth is just to know that a situation *is* morally complex, and that the actions specified by applicable idioms are contestable. Hence, "the important dimension of breadth is produced by awareness that even within one and the same moral tradition there are genuinely different moral idioms according to which moral situations can be objectively interpreted" (Kekes 1989, 139). No ideal, impartial judge can adjudicate the conflict of interpretations, since, even if all the facts are known, the weight given to the facts will vary as a function of the importance attributed them by participants. Breadth is just this sensitivity to the complexity of moral idiomatic interpretations that moral agents bring to problematic situations.

Insofar as good judgment can be paralyzed by this sensitivity, breadth needs to be complemented by moral depth. According to Kekes, depth is that which allows one to discern the right or appropriate response. It consists partly in the growing awareness that in spite of the diversity of possible moral responses there is an underlying unity that is captured by a particular idiom. "Through depth we can come to see that the unity of these superficially different forms of conduct is provided by steadfast adherence to one's conception of a good life in the face of adversity" (Kekes 1989, 141). To have depth also refers to our appreciation of the role that moral idioms play in our conception of a meaningful life. Kekes urges us to think of our idiomatic commitments as being of two kinds, those that are loose and conditional, and those that are unconditional and indefeasible. Depth is just the hierarchical ordering of these kinds of commitments, and such an ordering provides us with a moral perspective. To act contrary to our deepest indefeasible, unconditional commitments, to our moral perspective, is to risk psychological damage and the loss of characterological integrity. He writes "Unconditional commitments are the deepest, the most serious convictions we have; they define what we would not do, what we regard as outrageous and horrible; they are the fundamental conditions of being ourselves" (Kekes 1989, 167). Without these commitments, without depth, the integrity of our character is found wanting.

I mention this feature of Kekes's work in order to show just how similar it is to Blasi's psychological account of the moral personality. Where Kekes speaks of the structured organization of idioms, Blasi speaks of the organization of self-related information. Where Kekes describes this organization in terms of a continuum of self-commitment (conditional-unconditional, defeasible-indefeasible, surface-depth), Blasi describes it in terms of self-consistency (essential-unessential, central-peripheral, important-unimportant). Where Kekes says that our commitment to idioms of sufficient depth provides us with an action-guiding moral perspective, Blasi says that our commitment to the elements of the essential self provides us with action-guiding moral identity. Where Kekes describes this process as the development of a personal morality, Blasi describes it as the development of a moral personality.

Whether one is talking about a moral personality or a personal morality, one gets the sense that both authors would claim (especially Kekes) that essential selves with "deep" moral perspectives are well equipped to navigate their way through the morass of pluralistic conceptions of good lives, such that a life of personal integrity (being true to our commitments, or being true to-the-self-in-action) can be maintained. Kohlbergians might grant that this kind of "personal morality" (or "moral identity") might be action-guiding in the case of complex personal situations, where the question concerns "what am I to do such that my life can be lived with integrity, or that I might be true to my unconditional commitments," but deny that it can be of much help in resolving the kinds of pluralistic moral disputes that arise in the public sphere, in the domain of social morality. Here the task is to forge agreement, even though disputants may bring to the situation incommensurable moral premises. Yet hard cases are hard for everybody, and this difficulty does not call into question the priority of character education over "decision-ism." Being able to enter into legitimate moral dialogue may in fact presuppose deliberate adherence to the imperative to "respect persons," but the disposition to respect persons does not result from having sophisticated role-taking skills (since these skills could just as well be used for swindling or for sophistic ends), but rather from being a person of a certain kind. And, as Kekes points out, and as noted earlier, good judgment depends on correctly characterizing the situation (as one demanding a moral response), and this is seen to hinge on good character.

Conclusion

I noted much earlier that Kohlberg's theory took moral philosophy seriously. His embrace of the Kantian, deontological tradition was so complete that it is fair to say that his theory could not have been phrased absent these ethical considerations. I also noted, however, that although Kohlberg's appropriation of formalist ethics set the stage for dialogue with ethicists, his findings did not penetrate very deeply into ethical discourse. But there are grounds for thinking that the shoe is now on the other foot. I want to conclude by noting that to the extent that the nature of character traits is a critical feature of reflection in the virtue ethics tradition, then it would seem that the psychological study of personality and identity can hardly be neglected. Indeed, the parallelisms between Kekes and Blasi, the "Eriksonian" themes that show up in recent writings in virtue ethics, are testimony to the common project that is set before psychologists and ethicists. One could even point to the converging interest in "narrative" as a concept for understanding ethical traditions (MacIntyre 1977) and virtue education (Hauerwas 1980), on the one hand, and for understanding self (Gergen & Gergen 1988) and personality (McAdams 1985) development, on the other. As a result of these converging interests there is now real cause for optimism that dialogue among ethicists and psychologists will bring mutual benefits to either discipline, and vindicate Kohlberg's belief in their ultimate penetrability.[2]

Notes

1. I am endorsing a point made by Stout (1981) that the positing by prescriptivists of an unbridgeable chasm between "is" and "ought" is a product of a discredited foundationalist epistemology. See Hampshire (1983) for more doubts on the putative is-ought gap. For more on the similarity between ethics and the philosophy of science, see Schneewind (1983). For an alternative view, see B. Williams (1985, esp. chap. 8).

2. I am grateful for the comments provided by Owen Flanagan, Donald R. C. Reed, Paul Warren, Albert Howsepian and Augusto Blasi on a draft of this essay.

References

Blasi, A. 1984. "Moral Identity: Its Role in Moral Functioning." In *Morality, Moral Behavior, and Moral Development*, ed. W. Kurtines and J. Gewirtz. New York: Wiley.

———. 1985. "The Moral Personality." In *Moral Education: Theory and Application*, ed. M. Berkowitz and F. Oser. Hillsdale, N.J.: Erlbaum.

———. 1989. "The Integration of Morality in Personality." In *Perspectivas acerca de cambio moral: Posibles intervenciones educativas*, ed. I. E. Bilbao. San Sebastiano: Servicio Editorial Universidad del Pais Vasco.

Boyd, D. 1986. "The Ought of Is: Kohlberg at the Interface between Moral Philosophy and Developmental Psychology." In *Lawrence Kohlberg: Consensus and Controversy*, ed. S. Modgil and C. Modgil. Philadelphia: Falmer.

Carter, R. 1986. "Does Kohlberg Avoid Relativism?" In *Lawrence Kohlberg: Consensus and Controversy*, ed. S. Modgil and C. Modgil. Philadelphia: Falmer.

Colby, A., L. Kohlberg, et al. 1990. *The Measurement of Moral Judgment*. Vol. 2. Cambridge: Cambridge University Press.

Darley, J., and T. Shultz. 1990. "Moral Rules: Their Content and Acquisition." *Annual Review of Psychology* 41: 525–556.

Dykstra, C. 1981. *Vision and Character*. New York: Macmillan.

Gergen, K. J., and M. M. Gergen. 1988. "Narrative and the Self as Relationship." In *Advances in Experimental Social Psychology*, vol. 21, ed. L. Berkowitz. San Diego, Calif.: Academic Press.

Habermas, J. 1982. "A Universal Ethic of Communication and Problems of Ethical Relativity and Skepticism." Paper presented at the International Symposium on Moral Education, Fribourg University, Switzerland.

Hampshire, S. 1983. "Fallacies in Moral Philosophy." In *Revisions: Changing Perspectives in Moral Philosophy*, ed. A. MacIntyre and S. Hauerwas. Notre Dame, Ind.: University of Notre Dame Press.

Hartshorne, H., and M. May. 1928–1932. *Studies in the Nature of Character*. New York: Macmillan.

Hauerwas, S. 1980. "Character, Narrative, and Growth in the Christian Life." In *Toward Moral and Religious Maturity*, ed. C. Brusselmans. Morristown, N.J.: Silver Burdett.

Kekes, J. 1989. *Moral Tradition and Individuality*. Princeton, N.J.: Princeton University Press.

Kitchener, R. 1983. "Developmental Explanations." *Review of Metaphysics* 36: 791–818.

———. 1986. *Piaget's Theory of Knowledge: Genetic Epistemology and Scientific Reason*. New Haven, Conn.: Yale University Press.

Kohlberg, L. 1981. *The Philosophy of Moral Development*. San Francisco: Harper & Row.

———. 1986. "A Current Statement on Some Theoretical Issues." In *Lawrence Kohlberg: Consensus and Controversy*, ed. S. Modgil and C. Modgil. Philadelphia: Falmer.

Kohlberg, L., C. Levine, and A. Hewer. 1983. *Moral Stages: A Current Formulation and a Response to Critics*. Basel: Karger.

Kohlberg, L., and R. Mayer. 1987. "Development as the Aim of Education." In *Child Psychology and Childhood Education: A Cognitive-Developmental View*. New York: Longman.

Kupperman, J. 1988. "Character and Ethical Theory." *Midwest Studies in Philosophy* 13: 115–125.

Lakatos, I. 1978. "Falsification and the Methodology of Scientific Research Programmes." In *The Methodology of Scientific Research Programs*, vol. 1, *Imre Lakatos Philosophical Papers*, ed. J. Worrall and G. Currie. Cambridge: Cambridge University Press.

Lapsley, D., R. Enright, and R. Serlin. 1989. "Moral and Social Education." In *The Adolescent as Decision-Maker*, ed. F. Danner and J. Worral. Orlando: Academic Press.

Locke, D. 1986. "A Psychologist among the Philosophers: Philosophical Aspects of Kohlberg's Theories." In *Lawrence Kohlberg: Consensus and Controversy*, ed. S. Modgil and C. Modgil. Philadelphia: Falmer.

MacIntyre, A. 1977. "Epistemological Crises, Dramatic Narrative, and the Philosophy of Science." *Monist* 6: 453–472.

———. 1984. *After Virtue*. Notre Dame, Ind.: University of Notre Dame Press.

———. 1988. *Whose Justice? Which Rationality?* Notre Dame, Ind.: University of Notre Dame Press.

McAdams, D. 1985. *Power, Intimacy, and the Life Story: Personological Inquiries into Identity*. Homewood, Ill.: Dorsey.

McCarthy, T. 1982. "Rationality and Relativism." In *Habermas: Critical Debates*, ed. J. Thompson and D. Held. Cambridge, Mass.: MIT Press.

Meilaender, G. 1984. *The Theory and Practice of Virtue*. Notre Dame, Ind.: University of Notre Dame Press.

Mischel, W. 1968. *Personality and Assessment*. New York: Wiley.

————. 1990. "Personality Dispositions Revisited and Revised: A View after Three Decades." In *Handbook of Personality Theory and Research*, ed. L. Pervin. New York: Guilford.

Norton, D. 1988. "Moral Minimalism and the Development of Moral Character." *Midwest Studies in Philosophy* 13: 180–195.

Piaget, J. 1932. *The Moral Judgment of the Child*. New York: Free Press.

————. 1970. *Genetic Epistemology*. New York: Norton.

Pincoffs, S. 1983. "Quandary Ethics." In *Revisions: Changing Perspectives in Moral Philosophy*, ed. A. MacIntyre and S. Hauerwas. Notre Dame, Ind.: University of Notre Dame Press.

Power, F. C., L. Kohlberg, and A. Higgins. 1989. *Lawrence Kohlberg's Theory of Moral Education*. New York: Columbia University Press.

Reed, D. R. C. 1986. "Socratic Moral Education: Kohlberg and Plato." Unpublished doctoral dissertation, Vanderbilt University.

Rorty, A. 1988. "Virtues and Their Vicissitudes." *Midwest Studies in Philosophy* 13: 136–148.

Schneewind, J. B. 1983. "Moral Knowledge and Moral Principles." In *Revisions: Changing Perspectives in Moral Philosophy*, ed. A. MacIntyre and S. Hauerwas. Notre Dame, Ind,: University of Notre Dame Press.

Serlin, R., and D. Lapsley. 1990. "Meehl on Theory Appraisal." *Psychological Inquiry* 1: 169–172.

————. Forthcoming. "Rational Theory Appraisal in Psychological Research and the Good-Enough Principle." In *Statistical and Methodological Issues in Psychological and Social Science Research*, vol. 2, ed. G. Keren. Hillsdale, N.J.: Erlbaum.

Solomon, D. 1988. "Internal Objections to Virtue Ethics." *Midwest Studies in Philosophy* 13: 428–441.

Stout, J. 1981. *The Flight from Authority: Religion, Morality and the Quest for Autonomy*. Notre Dame, Ind.: University of Notre Dame Press.

Walker, L. 1982. "The Sequentiality of Kohlberg's Stages of Moral Development." *Child Development* 53: 1330–1336.

Walker, L., B. de Vries, and S. Bichard. 1984. "The Hierarchical Nature of Stages of Moral Development." *Developmental Psychology* 20: 960–966.

Williams, B. 1985. *Ethics and the Limits of Philosophy*. Cambridge, Mass.: Harvard University Press.

Wong, D. 1988. "On Flourishing and Finding One's Identity in Community." *Midwest Studies in Philosophy* 13: 342–351.

WHAT HAPPENS WHEN AN ETHICS OF CARE FACES PLURALISM: SOME IMPLICATIONS FOR EDUCATION

Ann Diller

The favored term is "differences," the issue is pluralism: a pluralism that reveals itself as the silences of women are being broken.[1] At first we seemed to be hearing a single new plurality of gender, namely a woman's voice *qua* "woman." Now we are discovering the differences among women, as we hear from particular women, diverse and complex, as well as gendered.

Issues of "difference" among women have emerged, in part, from the increasingly conscious practice of an ethics of care—the ethics which has been identified as the moral voice of women. The ethics of care advocates the practice of caring attentiveness as the central moral act. As women have started to direct this attentiveness toward each other, we have discovered not only our commonalities but also our differences.

This recognition of differences among us then initiates the search for a viable approach to plurality that can still remain true to the precepts of an ethics of care. After a brief review of the central tenets in an ethics of care, I take up this search.

First we will consider two standard forms of pluralism from an ethics of care perspective. I then introduce two additional forms of pluralism that I take to be at work in recent dialogues among women and in the ethics of care itself. With all four of these in mind, we will turn to questions of education where I suggest specific applications for teaching and learning.

1. The Ethics of Care

Four distinctive features structure the ethics of care: (1) a rational ontology—the nature of being human is being in relation; (2) a relational ideal; (3) a methodology of caring attentiveness; and (4) an insistence upon knowledge of the particular.[2]

For an ethics of care, a relational ontology reminds us that being human means to be in relation. We humans are connected creatures——none of us would be here now without the connections of human relationships of care, nurturance, and interdependence. Furthermore this being-in-relation is given to us in quite specific forms and shapes. When we are born we do not choose whether or not to be related—we just are related; neither do we choose our family, our race, our nationality, ethnicity, class, or century.

Confronted with these relational givens, ethical traditions construct a variety of ideals. For some the ideal is a transcendence that aims to free us from this network of relationships, to transcend our human attachments and bonds. But for an ethics of care the ideal is to improve our relationships, not to transcend them. We become morally mature not by achieving transcendence or independence but rather by participating responsibly in caring relations.

The quality of our relations is then an issue for moral practice, a question of ethical achievement. To improve the quality of our relations requires moral labor. To create, maintain, and enhance caring relationships among ourselves constitutes the central moral task. The question is how to do this, what method to use.

Sara Ruddick calls it "attentive love." Nel Noddings chooses the term "engrossment"; she talks also of "receptivity." Marilyn Frye used the image of the "loving eye" and contrasts it to the "arrogant eye." Sara Hoagland simply advocates "attending." Simon Weil (1951, 114) tells us:

> In the first legend of the Grail, it is said that the Grail . . .
> belongs to the first comer who asks the guardian of the vessel,
> a king three-quarters paralyzed by the most painful wound,

"What are you going through?" The love of our neighbor in all its fullness simply means being able to say to him: "What are you going through?"...Only he who is capable of attention can do this.

Although these authors diverge in other ways, their conceptions of attentiveness show a remarkable convergence. They all agree that when we attend to each other in this special way we must temporarily suspend our own projects, set aside our own agendas, and bracket our *a priori* expectations; we do this in order to apprehend another's reality on its own terms. Noddings observes that it is as if we "become a duality" when we find ourselves able to "see and feel with the other" (Noddings 1984, 30).

Furthermore, as Noddings (1984, 30) makes clear, we are talking about "reception" not about projection. The task is not to analyze, not to imagine what I would feel in someone else's situation: "I do not 'put myself in the others shoes' so to speak...asking 'How would I feel in such a situation'." In fact, it is not an "I" question at all; my own feelings are not, at present, the issue. My entire attention is taken up with what the other person is feeling.

In addition to distinguishing "receptive" attending from other ways of attending, such as projection, these authors, as well as Carol Gilligan and other advocates of an ethics of care, would agree with Iris Murdoch (1970, 34) when she says that to undertake such attentiveness constitutes a distinctively moral act:

> I have used the word "attention," which I borrow from Simone Weil, to express the idea of a just and loving gaze directed upon an individual reality. I believe this to be the characteristic and proper mark of the active moral agent.

For Nel Noddings this receptive attention is the basic move in her Ethics of Care: "At bottom, all caring involves engrossment. The engrossment need not be intense nor need it be pervasive...but it must occur" (Noddings 1984, 17).

While the attentiveness of "engrossment"[3] provides the moral methodology for an ethics of care, what one attends to are particular persons in specific situations. Acquaintance with the particular constitutes the primary form of moral knowledge and carries a commitment to respect the singular character of each person in their own context.

This conjunction of engrossment-attention with an insistence on giving primacy to the particular has helped to foster women's mutual attending and to support personal articulation. Such efforts have, in turn, generated open expressions of difference and divergence among women. We have begun to hear the voices of aged women, women of color, spiritual women, non-spiritual women, lesbian women, heterosexual women, bi-sexual women, women as mothers, women as non-biological mothers, women as non-mothers, and so forth (cf., Delpit 1988; Lugones and Spelman 1983; Riley 1988; Spelman 1988).

These revelations of differences, of women's pluralities have been exciting. But they have also raised new questions; for example, the pressing political problems of how women can make coherent political demands, or present a unified political front, amid such a welter of diversity. And it raises moral questions for those who would embrace almost any variation on an ethics of care.

Once we recognize that we are "many," that the differences may run deep, and are, as yet, only partially revealed, how does an ethics of care maintain relational connections, while, at the same time, accepting and supporting differences?

One thing is clear, we do need the structures of plurality. Maria Lugones knows very well that as Hispana and as woman she is looking for an explicit pluralism, and needs the structures of pluralism:

> When I do not see plurality stressed in the very structure of a theory, I know that I will have to do lots of acrobatics—of the contortionist and the walk-on-the-tightrope kind—to have this theory speak to me without allowing the theory to distort me in my complexity. (Quoted by Spelman 1988, 80)

But the question remains of what moral stance to take toward these pluralities.

2. Two Standard Forms of Pluralism

What forms of pluralism can an ethics of care envision? Let us first consider two familiar forms: (1) a pluralism of co-existence; and (2) a pluralism of cooperation.

2.1 Pluralism of Coexistence

A pluralism of coexistence requires basic non-interference, combined with mutual tolerance, and, ideally, mutual respect for those who differ from us. A pluralism of coexistence is by no means easy to achieve or to maintain, and there is much to be said in its favor. William James (1899, 169) sums up its features and appeal:

> It is negative in one sense, but positive in another. It absolutely forbids us to be forward in pronouncing on the meaninglessness of forms of existence other than our own; and it commands us to tolerate, respect, and indulge those whom we see harmlessly interested and happy in their ways, however unintelligible these may be to us. Hands off. . .

James's "hands off" point recurs in a recent statement by a woman of color speaking to white women about the contrast between obligation and friendship; "obligation" resembles "hands off":

> Out of obligation you should stay out of our way, respect us and our distance, and forego the use of whatever power you have over us—for example, the power to use your language in our meetings, the power to overwhelm us with your education, the power to intrude in our communities in order to research us and to record the supposed dying of our cultures, the power to engrain in us a sense that we are members of dying cultures and are doomed to assimilate, the power to keep us in a defensive posture with respect to our own cultures. (Lugones and Spelman 1983, 30).

2.2 Pluralism of Cooperation

However attractive "hands off" may be, life in our contemporary world is so interdependent that we can rarely have coexistence without some encroachment from demands for cooperation. Whether we think of Plato's *Republic* or of modern multi-national corporations, specialization pervades our lives and enmeshes us in pluralisms of cooperation.

With a pluralism of cooperation our common interest leads us to work together in order to achieve complex ends that would be virtually impossible for any of us to accomplish alone. In the pluralism of cooperative specialization differences can become constructive, or even essential, for handling complexities inherent in the common enterprise, while less constructive differences are set side, or ignored, so everyone can "get the job done."

What happens when we look at these pluralisms of co-existence and cooperation from an ethics of care perspective? I think we must conclude that while each helps us to regulate, to negotiate, and to profit from our human differences, they are not sufficient for the relational tasks of human communities. For example, a pluralism of coexistence can provide necessary conditions, basic ground rules, to enable other more demanding forms of pluralism to flourish. But for the rearing of children, the care of the sick and the elderly, the enhancement of personal relations, the endeavors of friendship and affection, a pluralism of coexistence is simply not enough (cf., Baier 1987).

Similarly, a pluralism of cooperation or collaboration, while crucial for survival and for facilitating constructive forms of interdependency is also insufficient to meet the concerns of an ethics of care. For one thing the relations among persons need not be taken as end-in-themselves but can be merely instrumental. Whatever our skills and differences are, these can be treated as no more than means to our common ends. There is still no intrinsic reason to care for each other. This does not mean such caring cannot arise or is not often part of a cooperative endeavor, it simply means caring is not essential, or constitutive, and thus may be absent or avoided. A pluralism of cooperation can function on a purely task-oriented level. If our engagement in furthering common enterprises is suspended or superseded, the grounds for a moral pluralism may also disappear.

Thus neither a pluralism of co-existence nor one of cooperation is sufficient for an ethics of care even though both are important and necessary. What then might be a pluralism

for an ethics of care? At least two additional forms of pluralism seem to me to be at work in recent dialogues among
women, and in the practices of the ethics itself: a pluralism
of co-explorers, and a pluralism of co-enjoyment.

3. Pluralism of Co-Explorers

As women start to articulate what has been masked, dis-
torted, or denied, the experience resembles an expedition into
new, unexplored territory. We become explorers, adventurers
into unfamiliar territory, the territory of hidden experiences.
Using the methods of caring attentiveness, of engrossment,
we search for new understanding.

Once we begin practicing engrossment, transformations
occur. Nel Noddings describes the transformation in her own
personal experience that occurred with a colleague for whom
she had "never had much regard" and "little professional
respect":

> Somewhere in the light banter of lunch talk, he begins to talk
> about an experience in the wartime navy and the feelings he
> had under a particular treatment. He talks about how these
> feelings impelled him to become a teacher. His expressions
> are unusually lucid, defenseless. I am touched—not only by
> sentiment—but by something else. It is as though his eyes
> and mine have combined to look at the scene he describes. I
> know that I would have behaved differently in the situation,
> but this is in itself a matter of indifference. I feel what he
> says he felt. I have been invaded by this other. Quite simply,
> I shall never again be completely without regard for him. My
> professional opinion has not changed, but I am now prepared
> to care whereas previously I was not. (Noddings 1984, 30–31)

Noddings's account is apropos in that it makes explicit both
the changed perception and the fact of continuing differences.
The recognition of plurality has not diminished; indeed it may
be heightened by additional specificity, but the relationship
between the persons has changed. A new understanding alters the landscape; it lessens the power of differences to build
barriers and to maintain fences of disregard.

But what Noddings recounts is only a one-way, unidirectional understanding. She gives no indication that there has been mutual understanding, or even a reciprocal effort at engrossment. In order to do *co*-exploring all the parties must engage in engrossment practices.

For an unmistakable example of co-explorers, I want to turn to an often cited dialogue between Maria Lugones, Hispana, and Vicky Spelman, white/Anglo woman, entitled: "Have We Got a Theory for You! Feminist Theory, Cultural Imperialism and the Demand for 'The Woman's Voice'" (1983). Sometimes each of the co-authors speaks singly in her own voice while at other times they speak jointly. This published Lugones-Spelman dialogue gives us a printed example of the co-exploring process. It addresses both the procedures and the substantive issues for pluralistic exploration. The following quotation is found near the end of the dialogue, spoken "Problematically in the voice of a woman of color":

> If you enter the task out of friendship with us, then you will be moved to attain the appropriate reciprocity of care for your and our well-being as whole beings, you will have a stake in us and in our world, you will be moved to satisfy the need for reciprocity of understanding that will enable you to follow us in our experiences as we are able to follow you in yours. (Lugones and Spelman 1983, 30)

It is this emphasis on a "reciprocity of understanding," a mutual attentiveness, that marks a caring pluralism.

In addition to its clear call, both by precept and example, for a reciprocity of understanding, the Lugones-Spelman dialogue brings out some further aspects for serious co-explorers to consider. For one thing we have to confront the personal discomfort that arises when we try to follow another person into their own culture and life experiences. An honest recognition of the demands and discomforts leads to the question of why undertake such an expedition. Maria Lugones speaks, in "an Hispana voice," to these issues:

> The only motive that makes sense to me for your joining us in this investigation is the motive of friendship, out of friendship. . . . I see the "out of friendship" as the only sensical motivation for this following because the task at hand for

you is one of extraordinary difficulty. . . . this is not to suggest that . . . you should try to befriend us for the purpose of making theory with us. The latter would be a perversion of friendship. Rather, from within friendship you may be moved by friendship to undergo the very difficult task of understanding the text of our cultures by understanding our lives in our communities. The learning calls for circumspection, for questioning of yourselves and your roles in your own culture. . . . This learning is then extremely hard. . . . (Lugones and Spelman 1983, 23, 30)

Lugones identifies here not only the difficulty of "understanding the text of our cultures" but also one reason why we may be hesitant and unsuccessful in our efforts to do so—namely the requirement that we must question ourselves and our roles in our own culture, an uncomfortable procedure that can endanger one's established sense of self. Why then would anyone do this? Maria Lugones answers: "out of friendship" or "from within friendship you may be moved by friendship."

When she identifies friendship as the appropriate moving force, Lugones points us toward the recursive effects of reciprocal understanding. A transformation of the sort which Nel Noddings describes in her encounter with her colleague may cultivate the grounds for friendship and affection. But for this recursive effect to occur the process must get going in the first place. How does it start? Lugones explicitly says we should *not* "try to befriend" each other "for the purpose of making theory."

4. Pluralism of Co-Enjoyment

What can give genuine friendship a chance to develop in the first place? To answer this question we need to return to the issue of particularity, to the insistence that moral knowledge consists of specific knowledge about particular persons. But which specific knowledge do we need to attend to? When we ask Simone Weil's question "What are you going through?" we tend to hear about suffering, sorrows, grief, or pain. All of which do constitute an integral part of our lives. But only a part.

In his essay "On a Certain Blindness in Human Beings," William James calls upon an extended quotation from Robert Louis Stevenson's "The Lantern-bearers," in which Stevenson describes the details, and the essential glory, of those nights when children with a tin bull's-eye lantern under their top-coat "asked for nothing more." Stevenson first takes his readers inside the rich fantasies of these "lantern-bearers on the links" and he then gives us the contrast of their outward appearance:

> To the eye of the observer they *are* wet and cold and drearily surrounded; but ask themselves, and they are in the heaven of a recondite pleasure, the ground of which is an ill-smelling lantern. . . . The observer (poor soul, with his documents!) is all abroad. . . . For to miss the joy is to miss all. In the joy of the actors lies the sense of any action. That is the explanation, that the excuse. To one who has not the secret of the lanterns the scene upon the links is meaningless. (James 1899, 154–155)

Here we have, as James the Pluralist well knew, the clue for a crucial refinement on our claims about knowledge of the particular, namely which particulars it is that give us the fullest, the most essential, knowledge of someone: "to miss the joy is to miss all."

As we reveal to each other not only our complaints, anger, suffering, and fears, but also our joys, pleasures, and vital interests, we become more "alive" to one another. We have all had the experience of trying to "make conversation" with someone who seems a mute dullard until we hit upon their area of real interest, and suddenly they transform themselves before our eyes into an animated, vital, even fascinating being.

If, furthermore, we stop to ask when each of us finds ourself most alive, feels the most like ourselves, surely it is not limited to those times when we are in the midst of sorrow or pain. In fact, do we not think of times when we are happily engaged in doing what we like best, whether it be a strenuous challenge or a comfortable pleasure? Can anyone really know us who knows nothing of our personal joys?

It is not enough, then, to have moved from the general to the particular—to concrete specific knowledge of persons-in-situations, unless we have also begun to understand what "really matters" to this particular person. And here is where "to miss the joy" is at least to miss a great deal, if not all.

To return to Lugones's emphasis on friendship, part of what friendship is about is a delight in each other's joys—a co-enjoyment. In advocating a pluralism of co-enjoyment, I want to suggest that co-enjoyment serves an ethical pluralism in a number of ways. Co-enjoyment can work as a moving force to encourage and sustain efforts at mutual caring attention. Co-enjoyment also functions as an ideal, a goal or desirable aim; and it rewards us along the way.

In our relations with friends and lovers, as well as with our own children, whom we do sometimes experience as "strangers" inhabiting an alien culture, is it not the case of mutual enjoyment in each other's presence, a delight in each person's particularity, the remembrance of this, the knowledge of its possibility, that sustains our commitment, that keeps us working at the tasks of reciprocal understanding which enable us to stay open, attentive, and sensitive to each other? And is it not also such loving attentiveness that supplies the conditions for releasing this knowledge of the person that in turn sparks the vital, quickening "meetings" where joy in each other arises? But to supply the right conditions to release this knowledge is itself a matter of knowledge. Our joys can be quite fickle about revealing themselves. In a delightful passage written decades before talk of our "fragmented selves" was in vogue, Virginia Woolf captures the conditional, often whimsical, nature of our personal pluralities:

> these selves of which we are built up, one on top of another, as plates are piled on a waiter's hand, have attachments elsewhere, sympathies, little constitutions and rights of their own, call them what you will . . . so that one will only come if it is raining, another in a room with green curtains, another when Mrs. Jones is not there, another if you can promise it a glass of wine—and so on; for everybody can multiply from his own experience the different terms which his different selves have

made with him—and some are too wildly ridiculous to be mentioned in print at all. (Woolf 1928, 308–309)

True self-disclosure, our telling joys do have their own "terms," do require certain conditions to be present, otherwise they remain concealed so that one's existence and encounters with others proceed as if "Life is Elsewhere" (Rimbaud, quoted by Kundera 1974, v). And it does seem that life is elsewhere for persons and students who are perceived as "different." If we take the pluralisms of co-enjoyment and co-explorers seriously, what does this mean for education, for the conditions we find and create in educational settings?

5. Education and the Four Pluralisms

A relational ontology reminds us that as persons-in-relation students' selves are constructed not only by internal school and classroom configurations but also by powerful connections within families, neighborhoods, and other personal networks. These connections help to constitute the "fragmented" selves who walk into school settings, some bearing, as Virginia Woolf reminds us, their own "wildly ridiculous" terms, others willing to accept more modest terms for an honest engagement in serious discourse. If we bracket the "wildly ridiculous," for the moment anyway, what conditions might we strive for to create a modest and moral pluralism?

I believe we need a set of conditions that can create educational spaces which are both safe and expansive: (a) safe psychologically, as well as physically, so that exchanges of particular, and relevant, moral knowledge become possible; and (b) expansive enough that co-exploring occurs as a standard practice, while occasions of co-enjoyment do happen.

But when an educational situation has in place, at best, only a tenuous pluralism of co-existence, what do we do?

First of all, I think we should not discount the significance of both co-existence and cooperation for educational practice. The basic requirements for a pluralism of co-existence are crucial structures that must at least be enforced, if they cannot be taught and learned in more effective ways. As relatively manageable, delineated units, educational institutions (in contrast to nation-states or other large political configurations) are in a position to enforce and implement a pluralism of co-existence. One can expect that members of an educational institution will refrain from harming one another and shall exhibit outward tolerance as well as being respectful, even "polite," regardless of their inward feelings or attitudes.

In the second place, a judicious, able use of the pluralism of cooperation is an effective as well as appropriate educational practice; effective in part because of its indirectness. A cooperative effort often elicits mutual understanding, camaraderie, and bonding. Eliot Wigginton's work, including his students' nationally known "Foxfire" project, seems to me an excellent example. Wigginton himself says:

> Too often we fail to see any common bonds between ourselves. Maybe if we set about with our kids creating some fertile ground for those bonds, we'll find how close our interests and our instincts and our needs as human beings really are. And maybe we'll find again the rich wisdom in that sense of shared responsibility and love that once existed. (Wigginton 1975, 130)

Third, I think we should, at times, aim straight for the pluralism of co-enjoyment not only as a long-term, distant possibility but also as an everyday "happening" consciously structured into our teaching-and-learning lives. Again Eliot Wigginton's work with students exemplifies this practice and reflects his own commitment to co-enjoyment in education:

> I am convinced that we, as adults must constantly cling to, affirm, and celebrate with our kids those things we love: sunsets, laughter, the taste of a good meal, the warmth of a hickory fire shared by real friends, the joy of discovery and accomplishment, empathy with the Aunt Aries and their triumphs and sorrows, the constant surprises of life. . . . (Wigginton 1975, 130)

In many instances, however, the demands of conventional education may inhibit or constrain the occasions available for co-enjoyment. This is where a pluralism of co-explorers fits most readily into standard educational practices; it is, after all, a form of inquiry. And, as we shall see in the next section, co-exploring lends itself directly to explicit educational methodology.

In sum, the groundwork for a moral pluralism, the necessary conditions, the fallback position, whether it be in education or in the world must be a pluralism of co-existence, which in itself is no mean achievement. In addition a pluralism of cooperation is not only an ideal of participatory democracy, it is also needed for the sheer business of living our interdependent lives, for the effective pursuit of common enterprises, including education. And a pluralism of co-enjoyment can inspire us, reward us, and move us toward increased understanding of each other. But for an educational methodology where the explicit practices are to be both moral and plural we must turn to the pluralism of co-explorers.

6. Co-Exploring in Education

One of the best examples of co-exploring in education that I have run across is found in Peter Elbow's practice of what he calls "methodological belief." Although Elbow's terminology differs from an ethics of care's 'engrossment' or 'caring attentiveness,' the central moves are strikingly similar. Furthermore, it is avowedly a matter of "teaching." As Elbow himself observes, methodological belief

> is only a small extension (if that) of what most good teachers or leaders naturally make happen: getting the others to try to see the truth in a point of view which at first they find alien, absurd, or repellent. (Elbow 1986, 274)

In his account entitled "Stumbling Onto Methodological Belief" Elbow describes the following incident from his own teaching experiences. Students are commenting on each other's writing. One student sees another student's piece as angry while for everyone else including the writer this interpretation seems "obviously false." But no one can object because of Elbow's "rule not to object." Then later on the author of the piece exclaims: "Wait a minute. Now that you make me look at it this way, I remember that I *was* angry when I was writing. And I can see now that I *did* express some of that anger in this innocent little story" (Elbow 1986, 259).

Elbow's incident illustrates key conditions for creating and maintaining a safe, expansive educational space. Psychological safety has been explicitly structured into the proceedings by the teacher. In Elbow's case these conditions are created by his "methodological belief rule":

> When a reader is telling what she sees in a text or what happened to her in reading, the writer and the other readers must not just shut up, they must actively try as hard as they can to believe her—see and experience the text as she does. (Elbow 1986, 259)

Notice that while we need safe conditions to express ourselves, to be heard, to hear each other, we also need these conditions in order to hear ourselves, to hear our own "angry" writing, our taboo emotions, our "demons" that we so easily project onto "the other" if we fail to accept them in ourselves.

In addition to meeting our safe space requirement, Elbow's rule also encourages expansiveness. While the structure is relatively safe, it is not stagnant, but rather is safe enough to encourage students to take risks both in speaking and hearing. The educational setting allows for serious honest articulation of unconventional, even seemingly bizarre interpretations, trusting that at least others must "shut up," and they may be trying in good faith to imagine what it would be like to believe what is being said.

To enter sincerely into Elbow's believing game is to undertake a practice similar to the moral methodology advocated by an ethics of care. We meet another person via engrossment; we temporarily suspend our own projects and reality in order to "feel with" and "believe with" the other. But to make this effort of methodological belief is not a simple matter.

As we noted in our discussion of co-exploring, to follow another person into their reality can be uncomfortable and threatening. Lisa Delpit describes the problem when she talks about how difficult it is to get white educators to listen to what parents and teachers of color say about their own children, how hard it is to hear each other across cultural, racial, ethnic, and economic barriers:

> To do so takes a very special kind of listening, listening that requires not only open eyes and ears, but open hearts and minds. We do not really see through our eyes or hear through our ears, but through our beliefs. To put our beliefs on hold is to cease to exist as ourselves for a moment—and that is not easy. It is painful as well, because it means turning yourself inside out, giving up your sense of who you are, and being willing to see yourself in the unflattering light of another's angry gaze. It is not easy, but it is the only way to learn what it might feel like to be someone else and the only way to start the dialogue. (Delpit 1988, 297)

This feeling of discomfort, and its accompanying resistance, can arise not only when someone seems to be attacking or criticizing us, but also when someone else simply differs from us in strange, unfamiliar ways.

One fear that blocks us from full engagement in Peter Elbow's believing game or in Noddings's engrossment or in listening and hearing another culture on its own terms is the fear that the "rightness" of our own position may be undermined, that our grip of certainty on our own beliefs may be loosened. So long as we divide our beliefs and perceptions into either right or wrong, we are caught in this fear—in the apprehension that sooner or later we shall have to play the right vs. wrong game. But what if we changed the game? That is what Elbow tries to do with his "believing game": "What makes this process different from most academic inquiry is that we are not trying to construct or defend an argument but rather to transmit an experience, enlarge a vision" (Elbow 1986, 261).

Changing the game is also, in a sense, what an ethics of care does. It changes the game of moral inquiry, changes what we take to be the moral problem.

In his fascinating book on creativity, D. N. Perkins tells this story of a changed problem:

> Early on in the space race, NASA spent much time and effort seeking a metal robust enough to withstand the heat of reentry and protect the astronauts. The endeavor failed. At some point, a clever person changed the problem. The *real* problem was to protect the astronauts, and perhaps this could

be done without a material that could withstand reentry. The solution, the ablative heat shield, had characteristics just opposite to those originally sought. Rather than withstanding the heat, it slowly burnt away and carried the heat away from the vehicle. (D.N. Perkins 1981, 217)

From an ethics of care perspective, to persist in trying to determine who is "right," and by implication who is "wrong," resembles the NASA search for a metal to withstand the heat of reentry. We need instead to solve the *real* problem which is how to improve our relationships with each other. And, as with the NASA heat shield, the characteristics most appropriate for this task may be just the opposite of those that lead us to insist on and defend our "rightness."

Foucault's description of "the polemicist"[4] in pursuit of "the triumph of the just cause he has been manifestly upholding from the beginning" details the moral, or rather immoral, parallel with the NASA search for a heatproof metal:

> One gesticulates: anathemas, excommunications, condemnations, battles, victories, and defeats...the sterilizing effects: Has anyone ever seen a new idea come out of a polemic? And how could it be otherwise, given that here the interlocutors are incited, not to advance, not to take more and more risks in what they say, but to fall back continually on the rights that they claim, on their legitimacy, which they must defend...one mimics war, battles, annihilations, or unconditional surrenders, putting forward as much of one's killer instinct as possible. But it is really dangerous to make anyone believe that he can gain access to the truth by such paths, and thus to validate, even if in a merely symbolic form, the real political practices that could be warranted by it. (Foucault 1984, 383)

Foucault's contrast between the polemicist style and that of "an equal discussion" or "a shared investigation" was for him also an issue of morality: "I insist on this difference as something essential: a whole morality is at stake, the morality that concerns the search for the truth and the relation to the other" (Foucault 1984, 381).

Nel Noddings similarly rejects the pursuit of justification and contrasts it to an ethics of care:

As one-caring, I am not seeking justification for my action; I am not standing alone before some tribunal. What I seek is completion in the other—the sense of being cared-for and, I hope, the renewed commitment of the cared-for to turn about and act as one-caring. . . . (Noddings 1984, 95)

Thus an ethics of care changes the problem from one of trying to determine who is right to a problem of how to create and maintain caring relationships.

One might say that the framework shifts from a monistic search for The Right to a pluralistic search for better relationships for all of us; relationships in which co-explorers work together to achieve reciprocal understanding, to pursue complex truths via shared inquiry, attentive to each person's account of the terrain as they travel it. In these very efforts themselves, and in some measure of successful outcome for our relations, lies the morality of the enterprise, not in withstanding or winning the heated battles of justification.

What does this changed problem mean for education *per se*? What if the question does become how to improve relations for all of us? Of course, the only adequate answer is that we shall have to find out by engaging in honest efforts of co-exploration in educational settings. Nonetheless let us look at one example chosen from the safe subject of animal fables.

In her research on children's moral orientations, D. Kay Johnston uses the fable of the moles and the porcupine. A porcupine in search of a winter home is taken in by a family of moles. But then the moles run into difficulties with the porcupine's size and quills. The children are asked what the moles should do.

After the children have given their own initial, spontaneous answers, the interviewer then asks what is, for our present purposes, the first key question: "Is there another way to solve the problem?" (Johnston 1988, 55). This question does not yet "change the problem" but it does already move away from the presumption that there is one and only one "right" solution. It sets up the possibility of a pluralistic approach to solutions; it allows for but does not require changing the problem.

Then as the interview continues, if the child has answered according to what Johnston terms "the rights orientation" and is not able to "switch orientations," the next question becomes: "Is there a way to solve the dilemma so that all of the animals will be satisfied?" This second question does change the problem for children whose own spontaneous solutions were answers such as: "The porcupine has to go definitely. It's the mole's house." or "It's their ownership and nobody else has the right to it."

Here we teachers and educators are on old familiar ground, namely that of Socratic, or maieutic, questioning. Assuming that our structures now provide the conditions for safe, expansive co-exploration, asking such questions as "Is there a way to solve the dilemma so that everyone will be satisfied?" can turn attention away from the search for impossible heat shields of impenetrable rightness to the "real problems" of living creatures and their relationships with one another.

Here are some of the children's answers to the changed problem:

> Wrap the porcupine in a towel.
> There'd be times that the moles would leave or the porcupine would stand still or they'd take turns doing stuff—eating and stuff and not moving.
> The both of them should try to get together and make the hole bigger.
> They (moles) should help the porcupine find a new house. (Johnston 1988, 53)

Wrapping the porcupine in a towel is not the same as taking turns moving around in the burrow or helping her to find a new home, but neither are they mutually exclusive; and they are all preferable certainly to homicidal plots against the porcupine. These different approaches point neither to one right answer nor to an infinity of possibilities with no way to choose among them.

Notice that any or all four of our forms of pluralism can come into play now. For example, they may engage in a pluralism of co-explorers in order to reach the realization that ultimately a pluralism of co-existence would be best, and the way to get there would be a pluralism of cooperation in helping the porcupine to find, or to dig out, a new burrow of its own. Meanwhile, as they dig together, they may become friends and learn to enjoy each other's company. Or they may discover, via co-exploration, that moles and porcupines are fascinating company for one another so long as the moles can be protected from being quilled. So they plan an expanded living-dining area, plus large separate quarters for the porcupine, remembering to specify a rule that the porcupine must wear a towel around herself when she works in the kitchen with the moles.

What then is the moral of the fable for us? Not simply that it is a safe, rather fanciful tale. What matters is that it can initiate expansion of our perceptions about moral possibilities. Being safe is only the launching pad, the starting point, the beginning of an expedition that should take us into new possible moral worlds, where we leave behind our fortresses of rightness, where we even stop searching for a better version of rightness, and we set out instead to explore together a new terrain, a new territory where the dominant vision is one of enjoyable relationships for us all.

If our educational efforts are successful, monistic frameworks will have altered, broken apart, expanded, so that plurality becomes part of our moral universe; and all four forms of pluralism—co-existence, cooperation, co-exploration, and co-enjoyment—are now live possibilities for us.

If we pursue these pluralisms with a moral methodology of careful attentiveness, if we make serious efforts to attain reciprocal understanding of each other's worlds, it will not mean that differences and misunderstandings cease to exist. Quite the contrary. In fact, we shall take differences for granted as the nature of the terrain, and shall accept misunderstandings as one of the inevitable hardships of the expedition. But it will mean that we face these hardships together, that we stay with the expedition, and continue as co-explorers, always ready to delight in an occasion for co-enjoyment.[5]

Notes

1. I will not stop to analyze the concept of 'pluralism' since I agree with the position taken by Dwight Boyd (this volume). I am also in agreement with the thesis of Boyd's essay. In fact, my section on educational practices could be seen as an extended discussion of ways to "invite and help" students "to join the conversation" that Boyd describes.

2. The most widely discussed proponents of what I am calling "An Ethics of Care" are Carol Gilligan (1982, 1986, 1987, 1988), Nel Noddings (1984, 1986) and Sara Ruddick (1980, 1989). There are important differences among them; for example, Sara Ruddick seems more sensitive to the influence the social political culture has on the expression of a nurturant ethics and on the ways in which it can go wrong. But I think it is fair to say that these writers all share the features I have distilled as central to the ethics of care. There is now a voluminous body of literature on the topic of women's morality; and much of it is concerned with the ethics of care, including important critical analyses by feminist thinkers and others. Such analysis is beyond the scope of this essay, but I have addressed these issues elsewhere (see Diller 1988; Houston and Diller 1987); and there are now a number of collections that contain key papers and relevant critical discussions (see Baier 1985, 1986, 1987; Brabeck 1989; Code, Overall and Mullett 1988; Friedman 1987; Frye 1983; Grimshaw 1986; Hanen and Nielsen 1987; Kittay and Meyers 1987; Martin 1985; and Pearsall 1986). For additional references, as well as a suggestive overview of the potential relations between ethical relativism and feminist thought, see Morgan 1990.

3. Noddings's term 'engrossment' does sound ungainly, but it has the advantages that Charles Sanders Pierce noted for his 'pragmaticism'—it is not likely to be stolen, misused, romanticized, or misunderstood; it does, therefore, suit our present purposes.

4. Janice Moulton (1983) critiques what she terms 'The Adversary Method' used in philosophic discourse along lines similar to those of Foucault's characterization of "the polemicist."

5. My thinking on the questions in this essay, and on related philosophical issues, has been helped and furthered over the years by regular, ongoing discussions characterized by both co-exploration and co-enjoyment with Barbara Houston, Jane Roland Martin, Beatrice Nelson, Jennifer Radden, Janet Farrell Smith, Susan Franzosa, Susan Laird, and Kathryn Morgan. And my final drafts have been improved by Carol Hochstedler's editorial assistance. I thank them all.

References

Baier, Annette C. 1985. "What Do Woman Want in a Moral Theory?" *Nous* 19 (no. 1, March): 53-63.

———— 1986. "Trust and Antitrust." *Ethics* 96 (January): 231–260.

———— 1987. "The Need for More Than Justice." In *Science, Morality, and Feminist Theory*, ed. Marsha Hanen and Kai Nielsen. Calgary: University of Calgary Press.

Belenky, Mary Field, Blythe McVicker Clinch, Nancy Rule Goldberger, Jill Mattuck Tarule. 1986. *Women's Ways of Knowing: The Development of Self, Voice, and Mind.* New York: Basic Books.

Boyd, Dwight. 1991. "The Moral Part of Pluralism as the Plural Part of Moral Education." This volume.

Brabeck, Mary M. (ed.). 1989. *Who Cares: Theory, Research, and Implications of the Ethic of Care.* New York: Praeger.

Code, Lorraine, Christine Overall, and Sheila Mullett (eds.). 1988. *Feminist Perspectives: Philosophical Essays on Method and Morals.* Toronto: University of Toronto Press.

Delpit, Lisa C. 1988. "The Silenced Dialogue: Power and Pedagogy in Educating Other People's Children." *Harvard Educational Review* 58 (no. 3, August): 280–298.

Diller, Ann. 1988. "The Ethics of Care and Education: A New Paradigm, Its Critics, and Its Educational Significance." *Curriculum Inquiry* 18 (no. 3): 325–342.

Elbow, Peter. 1986. *Embracing Contraries: Explorations in Learning and Teaching.* Oxford: Oxford University Press.

Foucault, Michel. 1983. "Politics and Ethics: An Interview." In *The Foucault Reader*, ed. Paul Rabinow. New York: Pantheon.

Friedman, Marilyn. 1987. "Beyond Caring: The De-Moralization of Gender." In *Science, Morality, and Feminist Theory*, ed. Marsha Hanen and Kai Nielsen. Calgary: University of Calgary Press.

Frye, Marilyn. 1983. *The Politics of Reality: Essays in Feminist Theory.* Trumansburg, N.Y.: Crossing Press.

Gilligan, Carol. 1982. *In a Different Voice.* Cambridge, Mass.: Harvard University Press.

———— 1986. "In a Different Voice: Women's Concepts of Self and of Morality." In *Women and Values*, ed. Marilyn Pearsall. Belmont, Calif.: Wadsworth.

———— 1987. "Moral Orientation and Moral Development." In *Women and Moral Theory*, ed. Eva Feder Kittay and Diana Meyers. Totowa, N.J.: Rowman and Littlefield.

———— 1988. "Remapping the Moral Domain: New Images Self in Relationship." In *Mapping the Moral Domain*, ed. Carol Gilligan, Janie Victoria Ward, and Jill McLean Taylor. Cambridge, Mass.: Center for the Study of Gender Education and Human Development.

Gilligan, Carol, Janie Victoria Ward, and Jill McLean Taylor (eds.). 1988. *Mapping the Moral Domain: A Contribution of Women's Thinking to Psychological Theory and Education.* Cambridge, Mass.: Center for the Study of Gender Education and Human Development.

Grimshaw, Jean. 1986. *Philosophy and Feminist Thinking.* Minneapolis, Minn.: University of Minnesota Press.

Hanen, Marsha, and Kai Nielsen (eds.). *Science. Morality, and Feminist Theory*, supp. vol. 13, *Canadian Journal of Philosophy*. Calgary, University of Calgary Press.

Hahn, Thich Nhat. (1989). "Seeding the Unconscious: New Views on Buddhism and Psychotherapy." *Common Boundary* (November-December): 14–21.

Harding, Sandra, and M. Hintikka. 1983. *Discovering Reality: Feminist Perspectives on Epistemology, Metaphysics, Methodology, and Philosophy of Science*. Dordrecht: Reidel.

Held, Virgina. 1987. "Non-Contractual Society." In *Science, Morality, and Feminist Theory*, ed. Marsha Hanen and Kai Nielsen. Calgary: University of Calgary Press.

Hoagland, Sarah Lucia. 1988. *Lesbian Ethics*. Palo Alto, Calif.: Institute of Lesbian Studies.

Houston, Barbara. 1987. "Rescuing Womanly Virtues: Some Dangers of Moral Reclamation." In *Science, Morality, and Feminist Theory*. ed. Marsha Hanen and Kai Nielsen. Calgary: University of Calgary Press.

Houston, Barbara, and Ann Diller. 1987. "Trusting Ourselves To Care." *Women and Philosophy*, special issue, *Resources for Feminist Research*, vol. 16 (no. 3).

James, William. 1899. *Talks to Teachers on Psychology: And to Students on Some of Life's Ideals*. New York: Norton Library Edition (1958).

Johnston, D. Kay. 1988. "Adolescents' Solutions to Dilemmas in Fables: Two Moral Orientations—Two Problem Solving Strategies." In *Mapping the Moral Domain*, ed. Carol Gilligan and Janie Victoria Ward, and Jill McLean Taylor. Cambridge, Mass.: Center for the Study of Gender Education and Human Development.

Kittay, Eva Feder, and Diana Meyers (eds.). 1987. *Women and Moral Theory*. Totowa, N.J.: Rowman and Littlefield.

Kundera, Milan. 1974. *Life Is Elsewhere*. Trans. Peter Kussi. New York: Penguin Books.

Lugones, Maria C., and Elizabeth V. Spelman. 1983. "Have We Got a Theory for You! Feminist Theory, Cultural Imperialism and the Demand for 'The Woman's Voice'." *Women's Studies International Forum* 6 (no. 6); reprinted in *Women and Values*, ed. Marilyn Pearsall. Belmont, Calif.: Wadsworth, 1986.

Martin, Jane Rowland. 1985. *Reclaiming a Conversation: The Ideal of the Educated Woman*. New Haven, Conn.: Yale University Press.

Morgan, Kathryn Pauly. 1990. "Strangers in a Strange Land: Feminists vs Relativists." Forthcoming.

Moulton, Janice. 1983. "A Paradigm of Philosophy: The Adversary Method." In *Discovering Reality*, ed. Sandra Harding and M. Hintikka. Dordrecht: Reidel.

Mullett, Sheila. 1987. "Only Connect: The Place of Self-Knowledge in Ethics." In *Science, Morality, and Feminist Theory*, ed. Marsha Hanen and Kai Nielsen. Calgary: University of Calgary Press.

——— 1988. "Shifting Perspective: A New Approach to Ethics." In *Feminist Perspectives*. ed. Lorraine Code, Christine Overall, and Sheila Mullett. Toronto: University of Toronto Press.

Murdoch, Iris. 1970. *The Sovereignty of Good*. London: Routledge and Kegan Paul.

Noddings, Nel. 1984. *Caring: A Feminine Approach to Ethics and Moral Education*. Berkeley, Calif.: University of California Press.

——— 1986. "Fidelity in Teaching, Teacher Education, and Research Teaching." *Harvard Educational Review* 56 (no. 4, November).

Pearsall, Marilyn (ed.). 1986. *Women and Values: Readings in Recent Feminist Philosophy*. Belmont, Calif.: Wadsworth.

Perkins, D. N. 1981. *The Mind's Best Work*. Cambridge, Mass.: Harvard University Press.

Rabinow, Paul (ed.). 1984. *The Foucault Reader*. New York: Pantheon Books.

Rich, Adrienne. 1978. *The Dream of a Common Language: Poems 1974–1977*. New York: W. W. Norton.

Riley, Denise. 1988. *"Am I That Name?": Feminism and the Category of "Women" in History*. Minneapolis, Minn.: University of Minnesota Press.

Ruddick, Sara. 1980. "Maternal Thinking." *Feminist Studies* 6 (no.2, summer); condensed and reprinted in *Mothering*, ed. Joyce Treblicot. Totowa, N.J.: Rowman and Allanheld.

——— 1989. *Maternal Thinking: Towards a Politics of Peace*. Boston: Beacon Press.

Spelman, Elizabeth V. 1988. *Inessential Woman: Problems of Exclusion in Feminist Thought*. Boston: Beacon Press.

Treblicot, Joyce (ed.). 1984. *Mothering: Essays in Feminist Theory*. Totowa, N.J.: Rowman and Allanheld.

Weil, Simone. 1951. "Reflections of the Right Use of School Studies with a View to the Love of God." In *Waiting for God*. New York: G. Putnam's.

Wiggington, Eliot. 1975. *Moments: The Foxfire Experience*. Washington, D.C.: IDEAS.

——— 1986. *Sometimes a Shining Moment*. New York: Anchor Books.

Woolf, Virginia. 1928. *Orlando*. New York: Harcourt Brace Jovanovich.

CHARACTER, CONSCIENCE, AND
THE EDUCATION OF THE PUBLIC

James W. Fowler

This essay investigates three fresh angles of approach to the challenge of reconstituting a *paideia* in American public education. Here is how I will proceed: First we will examine the critique of "formalism" in American education marshalled by E. D. Hirsch, Jr., in his recent book *Cultural Literacy: What Every American Needs To Know*.[1] In this connection I will also reflect on Edward McClellan's work in the history of moral education in the United States in the twentieth century. Second, we will explore a critique of this society's privatization of dialogue regarding normative perspectives on what are worthy ends for human lives. Here I will draw upon work by Robin Lovin. Third, I will direct attention to Thomas F. Green's proposal that a recovered concept of *conscience* become an organizing center for character education.[2] In conclusion I will present and discuss a model for interdisciplinary understanding of moral education which I hope will point a way toward the reconstitution of a *paideia* for the pluralistic context of the United States to the end of this century and for the next. My overall aim is to help us see that any educational approach to character formation that can help us must combine both *substantive* attention to narratives and the formation of moral attitudes and skills, on the one hand, with attention to stimulating the supporting *formally describable* capacities for social perspective taking and moral reasoning, on the other.

225

Progressivism and Formalism
in American Moral Education

E. D. Hirsch, Jr., and the sources upon which he has drawn in *Cultural Literacy*, point to a period at the turn of the present century as the time in which a transformation of fundamental importance in thinking about the conduct of public education occurred. One might say that the public signal of the coming ascendancy of Progressivism in public education was given with the 1918 document entitled, *Cardinal Principles of Secondary Education*.[3] This report was the work of a commission on the reorganization of secondary education appointed by the National Education Association. It consciously aimed to replace and supersede the influential 1893 *Report of the Committee of Ten*, the product of a prestigious panel chaired by President Charles W. Eliot of Harvard University.[4] This earlier committee had undertaken its task in the 1890s in the midst of new pressures to diversify secondary education, opening it to wider populations and making it responsive to the need for vocational training to meet the more complex demands of an urbanizing industrial society. In summarizing the position of the Eliot committee, Hirsch writes:

> The earlier report assumed that all students would take the same humanistic subjects and recommended giving a new emphasis to natural sciences. It took for granted that secondary school offerings would continue to consist of just the traditional areas that its subcommittees had been formed to consider— Latin, Greek, English, other modern languages, mathematics, physics, chemistry and astronomy, natural history, botany, zoology, physiology, history, civil government, economy and geography.[5]

In important ways the Eliot committee resisted the turn to formalism in education.[6] It explicitly rejected the teaching of English composition as a skill to be pursued in isolation from other subject matter. It held out for requiring of all secondary students an encounter with the substantive contents of the subjects included in the curriculum, even as it insisted upon the importance of integrating the contents of the various subject areas. Only a hint of formalism appeared in its justification for including the study of ancient languages and of geography in the curriculum. "It subscribed to the claim that studying Latin and Greek 'trains the mind' and that studying geography enhances '(1) the power of observation, (2) the powers of scientific imagination, and (3) the powers of reasoning'."[7]

The 1918 *Cardinal Principles of Secondary Education* went directly contrary to the emphasis on subject-matter and content of the 1893 report. "Instead," says Hirsch, "it stressed the seven fundamental aims of education in a democracy: '1. Health. 2. Command for fundamental processes. 3. Worthy home membership. 4. Vocation. 5. Citizenship. 6. Worthy use of leisure. 7. Ethical character.'" He continues,

> The shift from subject matter to social adjustment was a deliberate challenge to the 1893 report and to conservative school practices generally. American education should take a new direction. Henceforth, it should stress utility and the direct application of knowledge, with the goal of producing good, productive, and happy citizens.[8]

Hirsch's book recounts the dramatic victories which progressive ideas and approaches, relying more and more extensively on formalistic methods, won over the older ideals of a substantive, coherent, and uniform curriculum. Hirsch recognizes strong reasons for the emergence of formalism and for the deemphasis of substantive consensus. He points, however, to the democratic commitments involved in having a range of documents and knowledge that all students are required to know. He says: "Certainly the idea that everyone can and should start out from the same educational foundation was an admirable democratic ideal that needs to be renewed."[9] And, commenting on the excesses of the romantic effort to center the curriculum in the experiences and unique needs of the child, he says, "Indeed, if traditional facts were to be presented unimaginatively or taught ignorantly or regarded as ends in themselves, we would have much to deplore in a return to traditional education. But dry incompetence is not the necessary alternative to lively ignorance."[10]

Now let us look at the history of efforts at moral education from the 1920s to the present. Here we will also see striking developments in the direction of *formalism*. It is interesting to note the parallels between the decline in emphasis on character education from the 1920s and 1930s and the deemphasis upon common standards and established fields of required subject matter in school curricula. In a history of character education in America, B. Edward McClellen discusses the Character Education Movement, which had a fragmentary time of ascendancy in the Midwest and West from about 1880 to 1935. This movement, McClellan suggests, was always more programmatic than theoretical. It was "built not so much on a thorough and coherent analysis of social change as on a vague sense that modern specialization threatened the wholeness of both the society and its individuals."[11] During the first decade of this century the character education movement proposed specific courses in ethics or morals and sought a place in the curriculum for issues that seemed to be neglected elsewhere in the school program. By the middle of the second decade, however—when the *Cardinal Principles* report was written—the character development proponents

> had lost their faith in the adequacy of specific courses and began instead to try to suffuse the whole program of the school with the goals of character education. Now their hope was to encourage all teachers to emphasize the ethical dimensions of their subjects, to exploit the educational value of the student codes of conduct, and to suffuse extracurricular activities with moral purpose.[12]

Such coherence as the Character Education Movement's proposals had came from the use of "morality codes," which amounted to lists of desirable traits of character and behavior. Such lists are what Lawrence Kohlberg, forty years later, would refer to scornfully as "bags of virtues." The list proposed by William Hutchins in 1917 is representative. It outlined "ten laws of right living": self-control, good health, kindness, sportsmanship, self-reliance, duty, reliability, truth, good workmanship, and teamwork.[13] Although such lists exerted considerable influence and came to provide the basis for district and statewide emphases in character education, they remained vague and were subject to a wide variety of interpretations.

Progressivism's growing insistence on professionaliza-
tion and specialization in teacher education led to a deemphasis on the nineteenth-century commitment of teachers to use
every means available to them to ingrain good moral habits
in their students. The publication in 1928–30 of the now famous studies by Hugh Hartshorne and Mark A. May raised
serious scientific questions about the effectiveness of teachers'
use of heavily didactic approaches to moral education. Such
perspectives, McClellen observes, "gave the critics powerful
ammunition and put the character education movement in a
defensive posture that it was never able to abandon."[14]

Though the emphasis upon character education continued on well into the 1950s, it was the principles of progressivism which shaped the most influential thinking about
moral education between the 1930s and 1980s. The same formalistic tendencies which Hirsch and others have criticized in
progressivism generally can be clearly seen in its approaches
to moral education. Impressed by "modernism," progressivism
expressed an impatience with tradition and convention. Over
against ideals of consistency and dependability in character,
it called for recognition of the need for flexibility in moral
judgment and action. Impressed by the differentiation of
spheres of action in modern society, it taught the relativity
of contexts and norms. Progressivism gave rise to the concept
of "values"—portable attitudes centering in commitments to
excellence and to the worth and uniqueness of each individual
which could be "applied" insightfully in many different and
unprecedented situations.[15] McClellan writes:

> Rejecting the notion that the school should teach specific moral
> precepts or encourage particular traits, progressive educa-
> tors hoped to cultivate in students both a quality of open-
> mindedness and a general ability to make moral judgments.
> Their model for ethical behavior was the disinterested expert,
> the professional who brought both a spirit of inquiry and a
> high level of competence to the solution of problems. What
> worked in the world of science and technology, they believed,
> would work as well in the solution of other human problems, if
> only students could be taught moral imagination, "the ability
> to picture vividly the good or evil consequences to self and to
> others of any type of behavior."[16]

Progressivist approaches to moral education placed heavy burdens upon teachers. They expected, without being very clear or specific about how to do these things, that teachers would use the full range of curricular resources as contexts for consistent raising and addressing of moral issues. With its emphasis upon rational analysis of moral problems, and upon the need for technical knowledge, it is not surprising that moral education, under progressivist influences, shifted its attention from the elementary years to the high schools as the principal locus of concern. Influenced by positivism in science and by an optimist confidence in the scientific method, progressivists brought the distinction between facts and values. Many of them were not able to see the ideological biases that informed their own precommitments regarding moral education. McClellan helpfully points to some of these:

> Their values were the values of elite professionals, and their approach to moral education encouraged a strong deference to expertise and a relatively uncritical acceptance of scientific method. Their politics tended toward collectivism of various shades, but their cosmopolitanism sometimes kept them from appreciating the potential value of such primary associations as the family, the parish, the community, and the ethnic neighborhood.[17]

Marked by vagueness, unable to identify specific virtues which it wanted to teach, disenchanted with traditions and conventions, progressivist moral education depended upon good will, certain abstract ideals, and, unconsciously, upon the diminishing capital of traditions of character education and religious teachings for its substance. In trying to assess its pre–World War II impact McClellan writes, "In the end, progressive theorists may have done more to destroy conventional approaches to moral education than to provide a compelling modern alternative. So it is."[18]

Between 1945 and the early 1960s there was little direct attention given to moral education in the public schools. McClellan cites three reasons for the shift away from character education in the post–World War II era: (1) The heavy emphasis upon developing technical and scientific skills, associated with the revolutions in electronics, physics, and medicine coming out of the war. (2) The obsession with countering the threat of communism as an ideological alternative to western democracy, which turned the teaching of civics and moral education in the direction of arming American youth for international competition in an ideologically divided world. (3) The growing tendency of Americans to draw sharp distinctions between the private and public realms in their lives, and to establish different behavioral norms in each sphere.[19]

When efforts were made to return to an explicit agenda of moral education in the public schools in the 1960s and 1970s the two dominant models that emerged seemed to signal the complete victory of formalistic approaches over character education or the teaching of virtue. "Values Clarification" canonized values relativisim as the fundamental truth about the moral domain. It also served to confirm that morality and values were domains where emotions and subjectivity prevail, thus furthering the privatization of ethical considerations. The second approach which emerged in the 1970s was the cognitive developmental approach to moral reasoning of Lawrence Kohlberg. At first blush Kohlberg's work seemed to partake of the same formalism that had begotten concern with "values" and "values clarification." Orienting to "justice" as a unitary virtue, Kohlberg's Kantian and Rawlsian project seemed to stay in the realm of the formal, with its deontological and procedural characterization of justice. Nonetheless, it aimed strong blows at the emotivism and the relativism upon which the values clarification approach rested, affirming in robust ways that moral deciding and acting have strong rational foundations and that public forms of reasoning can and must be used in moral adjudication and persuasion. We will return to a discussion of what needs to be conserved from Kohlberg's important project at a later point in this essay.

From Covenant to Social Contract:
Privatized Moral Reasoning

In an astute article published in 1986[20] Robin W. Lovin has suggested that the tendency for Americans to separate the public and private domains of their lives, and to restrict moral concerns to the latter, has a long history. He points to fundamental changes occurring in English political and economic thought between the 1630s and the 1780s as a primary source of the relegation of the discussion of the substantive ends and standards for human living to the realm of the private and the religious.

As a benchmark for his argument Lovin offers us a fresh characterization of the meaning and power of the idea of a convenant society—the primary informing political and social vision for the New England colonies:

> A covenant idea of society emerges when people are not content to see their relations to one another simply in terms of natural ties such as kinship, marriage relations, or the accidents of being born in the same village, or speaking the same language, or living under the same ruler. A covenant society is one in which the members are bound together by choice, by mutual commitment, more than by chance. A covenant society is one in which the members see their moral obligations as growing out of this commitment, so that they not only hold their neighbors to a higher standard of conduct than they might if they were just thrown together at random; they expect more of themselves and they acknowledge that others who share in the covenant have a right to examine and criticize their behavior. Above all, the covenant creates this sense of mutual accountability not only to one another, but before God. It is not the moral health of each individual which is under scrutiny, but the righteousness or waywardness of the whole society. This sense that there is a common good, a well-being of the whole society that cannot be measured just by summing up the achievements and faults of all the individuals in it, is crucial to the covenant idea.[21]

Within the framework of the idea of covenant the need for public discourse about matters affecting the common good was understood and expected. Because of the structure of accountability to each other and to God it was reasonable to debate and try to persuade one another regarding the meaning of scripture or tradition as guides for the community's responding to specific situations of challenge or policy choice. Moreover, it was reasonable to argue out the possible implications of legislation or policy for the collective and personal virtues of the population. Law was understood to be an organ of moral education as well as social order.

For a variety of reasons, however, seventeenth- and eighteenth-century political philosophy, in the hands of Thomas Hobbes, John Locke, Adam Smith, and others, began to formulate rationales for government which increasingly undermined the basis for public dialogue about virtue, the question of worthy ends for human living, and substantive conceptions of the common good. Instead, their approaches brought forward an awareness of the multiplicity of human desires and ends, and stressed the individuality and irrationality of each person's subjective notions of the good. In an irony not lost on Lovin, these philosophers of an "age of reason" presided over the dethronement of reason as a central participant in the establishing and confirming of substantively normative visions of the ends or purposes of human life and community.

By the time of the Constitutional Convention of 1789 the idea of the covenant community had become somewhat strange and distant. The conception of a community where people acknowledged an accountability to each other for their personal and corporate actions did not fit well with the assumption that each person's goals or ends were established by factors of subjective impulsion or desire, and were not susceptible to alteration through rational persuasion. Reason itself, on the way to becoming restricted to the establishment and investigation of matters of fact, no longer seemed available for forming or reforming agreements regarding the ends and goals of human life. Increasingly the role of reason envisioned in the new political theory was instrumental: It functioned personally and corporately to protect and/or further the individual interests and ends of persons. This view led to a conceiving of the role of government in terms of the rational relinquishment of a measure of personal autonomy for the sake of establishing a central authority. This central authority—of which Hobbes's *Leviathan* is one symbol— would insist upon that degree of fairness and respect for the rights of each of the members of the society, compatible with the equal respect for all others, to pursue their personal conceptions of the good. These are the essential foundations of the replacement of the idea of a covenant with the concept, in its several forms, of the social contract.

Harking back to our previous discussion of formalism in education in general, and in moral education in particular, we are reminded by Lovin's analysis that these twentieth-century emergences have had strong antecedents that span the decades back to the late eighteenth century. It is ironic that contemporary interpreters of democracy who call themselves "conservative" should be such articulate spokesmen for eighteenth-century liberalism, with its stress upon individual rights and the sovereign subjectivity of individual notions of the good.[22] Lovin's summary of the implications of that tradition for our concern with *paideia* is important:

> Public life is no longer thought of as a place to learn and practice virtue. Virtues, if we are to have them at all, must be inculcated in the home, or the church, or perhaps in the understandings that provide a code of decent professional conduct for lawyers, scholars, bankers, and so forth. Public life does not so much require virtue as it requires the restraint of vice.[23]

Lovin makes a strong case for retrieving and reconstituting an understanding of reason that recognizes its power to illumine questions of the worthy and just ends of persons and societies. As a step toward such retrieval of reason, especially in the moral domain, let us turn now to a proposal in moral education that has as one of its animating concerns that moral education should be, from the outset, *civic* education.

The Formation of Conscience
for Participation in Public Life

Thomas F. Green's John Dewey Lecture for 1984 is entitled, "The Formation of Conscience in an Age of Technology."[24] Green's goal is to reclaim a more comprehensive understanding of the *moral* in moral development than either the cognitive developmentalists or the Durkheimian sociologists have employed. In choosing the concept *conscience* as his unifying and inclusive term for that aspect of human knowing and being that needs to be formed in moral education he knows that he is taking a unique tack in the present discussion. His principal thesis is that moral education has to do with the forming of attitudes and virtues, which, in the light of the liberal political and ethical theories we discussed above, would be regarded as "non-moral" or "pre-moral" virtues. Green wants to show the ways in which conscience both permeates and draws from such qualities as our manners of doing our work and conducting the business of everyday life, our loyalty and fidelity as members of groups and associations, our sense of identity and rootedness in a place and with people, and our capacity for imagining and keeping solidarity with generations yet unborn. Conscience involves all these dimensions, Green says, as well as that more usual understanding of the term which refers to the imperativeness of doing what is one's duty, even when it requires the sacrifice of one's pleasure or going against the sense of one's own best interest. He says:

> It is a simple fact that each of us has the capacity to judge our own conduct and even to stand in judgment on what we discern to be the composition of our own affections. The point I want to stress about this experience is not that it involves judgment of moral approval or disapproval, but simply that it is judgment that *each of us makes in our own case.* In short, it is reflexive judgment. Furthermore, it is judgment always accompanied by certain emotions which, if not exactly the same, are nevertheless like moral emotions. I can feel guilt, shame or embarrassment at a job poorly done and these are the same feelings I have when viewing some moral failure of mine. This capacity of ours to be judge, each in our own case, is all that I mean by conscience. Conscience, as St. Thomas put it, is simply reason commenting upon conduct. And this capacity, please note, extends far beyond the capacity to comment merely upon matters of morality narrowly conceived. It can extend to self-judgment even in such matters as washing the car, planting the garden, getting dressed, or crafting a good sentence. These are all activities that can be done well or badly in our own eyes. They are all activities subject to the commentary of conscience.[25]

While Green understands conscience in this unitary and comprehensive way, he points out that it speaks to us in different voices. He identifies and discusses five such voices.

They include the following: (1) the conscience of *craft*; (2) the conscience of *membership*; (3) the conscience of *responsibility*; (4) the conscience of *memory*; and (5) the conscience of *imagination*. Let me try to characterize each of the voices briefly.

The conscience of craft. At the most obvious level Green is proposing that conscience involves making habitual an attitude of doing the things one undertakes thoroughly and well. This means acquiring a sense of the standards for excellence in the domains of one's activity. It also means conscientious work at the acquisition and practice of the requisite *skills* involved. "Developing a sense of craft is not all there is to the formation of conscience," says Green, "Still it is an important part. . . . We make a serious mistake if we fail to recognize the conscience of craft and to acknowledge that *it may be in the acquisition of a 'sense of craft' that the formation of conscience takes place most clearly.*"[26] Following the Greeks, Green invites us to see that forming the conscience of craft is part of the larger task of learning to live well. The principle sin for the Greeks, Green says, was not, as is commonly thought, *hubris*, the inflation or pride that "goeth before a fall." Rather, he suggests, the cardinal sin is properly *homartia*—the missing of the mark or the target, as in archery or in art. In *homartia* one fails to live well, in some comprehensive sense, through repeated carelessness, inattentiveness, or through a stubborn refusal or inability to learn.[27]

The conscience of membership. Green observes that most discussions and approaches to moral education focus upon conscience and the development of judgment as primarily individual matters. Only after attending to the qualities needed in the management of one's individual life do we ask about one's fitness for public life or service. He proposes an arresting counterpoint: "[A] conscience formed for conduct in the skills of public life is more likely to be a conscience suited to private life than a conscience formed merely for private life is likely to be suited for public life."[28] This thesis represents a strong claim that the community is prior to the individual. We should note, in passing, that this thesis runs directly counter to the assumption underlying social contract theory. The person is indelibly social and the formation of the person occurs in the context of the relations, meanings, rules, laws and culture of

the community. Moral development as the formation of conscience means forming a set of bonds—of attachment—to the
community. It means forming the moral emotions which are
appropriate toward the norms which give permanence, legitimacy and stability to the community's *praxis*—its way of living and being. If we take this priority of community over the
individual seriously, Green says, it significantly alters our
approach to moral education:

> By such a thesis, civic education can no longer be viewed as a
> mere addendum, a mere footnote, to moral education, some-
> thing that comes after the main business has been accom-
> plished. On the contrary, education for a public life would
> have to be viewed as the central problem which, being under-
> stood, then allows us to understand the formation of private
> conscience.[29]

Green points to two essential sets of skills required for
effective exercise of the conscience of membership. The first
skill he points to involves learning that whenever one is asked
whether a given policy or proposal is a good thing for *us* (the
group) to do, it is never sufficient merely to answer "No." "It
is necessary," Green says, "to go on and add some proposal
for improvement." After trying to exercise this skill one may
decide that though the present proposal is less than ideal, it
is the best possible now. Or one may decide that one must
develop more skill in order to be able to propose an improvement. In either case one has entered more deeply into the
proposal, the situation, the minds of one's fellows, and into
one's own responsibilities and possibilities for growth.

The second set of skills required for the conscience of
membership involves a self-critical use of empathy. "Whenever it is asked whether X is a good way for us to do Y, then
if you answer 'no' and offer a better way, or if you answer 'yes,'
you are obliged to confront three more questions. (1) Whose
interests are you expressing? (2) Whose interests are you *not*
expressing? and (3) How does your proposal balance the goods
being sought (from these *several* perspectives)?" Green goes
on to say,

> Indeed, the very act of *stating* the interests of others, *as oth-
> ers see them*, and stating them out loud and, if possible in the

actual presence of those others—that is often in itself a powerful exercise in empathy, an exercise by which the interests of
others are allowed to actually enter into our own.... Such a
lesson requires the actual *employment* of empathy and at the
same time promotes its *acquisition*.[30]

In his critique and rejection of the work of Lawrence
Kohlberg, Green seems to be unable to recognize just how
central to Kohlberg's developmental theory and his practice
of the "Just Community School" this kind of disciplined
empathy—social perspective taking, Kohlberg calls it—really
is. Nor does Green seem to see or acknowledge that Kohlberg's
explicit goal in moral education is to provide for the practical
acquisition of the skills, understanding, and commitment to
the common good which Green himself calls for. Green's impatience with Kohlberg stems, in part, from his concern with
other aspects of the conscience of membership, which have
to do with entering into and taking upon one's own identity
the stories and myths, the morals and the meanings of the
community. These factors Kohlberg does neglect. We will give
more attention to them when we speak of the conscience of
memory, a bit farther on.

The conscience of responsibility.[31] By this Green refers
to the conscience of duty and obligation. In a manner that
reminds of us W. D. Ross's justly famous discussion of *prima
facie* duties,[32] Green wants to impress upon his readers that
"there are certain moral practices of almost daily experience
with which the voice of conscience as duty speaks clearly. I
have in mind the keeping of promises, as well as the keeping
of contracts and confidences, which are like promises. When I
say, 'I promise,' the future becomes firmly fixed. By pronounc-
ing those words I declare that whatever may be my prudential
interests at some future time, I shall lay them aside. Instead,
I shall perform the promised act."[33]

The final two voices of conscience which Green identifies can be understood as closely related to the voice of the
conscience of membership. They are the *conscience of memory*
and the *conscience of imagination*. By reference to the conscience of memory Green affirms the importance of narrative
—especially the myths and stories that link us to the past

and meanings of our peoples and place—in the formation of our characters and our sense of "rootedness." By rootedness he means the deep sense of identification with and assent to the distinctive sources of strength (mixed always with some weaknesses or limits) which form the soils that have nurtured us toward personhood, language, meanings, myth, and aspiration.

> What I am here attempting to point to as rootedness is often called for in the modern world as commitment.... But the word 'commitment' is inadequate and misleading. It rings with overtones of will, as though I am free to choose what I am not free to choose.... We are not free to choose it, but we can reach a point where we possess as our own what already we have been given. And...[w]e might attain that point where we learn to work not only within but *upon* our inheritance. That is rootedness, and it is hard to suppose that there can be any education complete without it or any *moral* education at all without it.[34]

The conscience of memory means keeping faith with those persons and traditions who have formed us. It means claiming as our own the legacy of value and worth they sacrificed for; it means endeavoring with all we are to be as faithful and generative in our time with the inheritance as they were in theirs.

The conscience of imagination. It is the lure and pull and corrective power of the conscience of imagination which, while faithful to the past, allows us to engage it critically and transformatively. This is the imaginative faithfulness by which persons claim solidarity with and ethical responsibility for generations yet unborn. For Green, this is that aspect of conscience formed by prophets, poets, and visionaries. The critical and visionary imagination of the prophetic conscience is rooted in the conscience of membership and memory. It seeks always to radically enlarge the inclusiveness of membership, however, and it looks for those sources and promises in the memory which guide the community toward its most humane calling. It also attends to the "dangerous memories," the repressed, denied, and shameful past, which is the source of distortions in the present, and a resource for identification with those who are afflicted and oppressed by our ways of being.[35]

Responsible Selfhood: A Model

Let us examine the chart entitled "Responsible Selfhood: A Model for Character Development." The chart shows the interrelated components of character formation as we have identified them. It seeks to convey that the components, while separably identifiable, work in interaction with each other and in a more or less comprehensive and coherent unity in person and in communities. There is no suggestion that one or another of the components precedes the other in development, or that there is a necessary sequence in which they emerge. Rather, development of certain sorts is built into the model, as we will see more clearly in a moment. There is, however, a kind of cumulative richness intended in the spatial representation of these components which results in or constitutes character and the virtues. Crudely, it might be put this way: The provision of rich normative *Stories*, plus the forming of *Moral Attitudes*, plus the stimulation and support of *Developmental Abilities*, plus the systematic provision of *Information and Knowledge*, taken all together in environments where students are known and experience care and accountability, maximize the possibility of the formation and nurture of *Virtues and Strengths of Character*. The value of such a model is that it clarifies how each subject matter area in the curriculum, each curricular or extra-curricular activity, as well as the leadership approaches of teachers and administrators and the ethos of the school as community, can contribute to one or more of the aspects of character education. Theoretically and practically the cumulative flow of the model also helps us begin to appreciate, in contemporary terms, the remarkable multi-dimensional range of meanings which the classical concept of the virtues comprehends.

Now let us look at each component of the model in a bit more depth.

Stories. Our discussion of Green's work on the conscience of membership and the conscience of memory sets the stage

Responsible Selfhood:
A Model for Character Development

Stories

—Belonging and Inclusion
    Family   Religion
    Nation   Global
    Friends   Workmates
—Suffering and Heroism
—Virtue and Vice
—The Meaning of Community(s)
—The Nature of Reality (God)

Developmental Abilities   *Moral Attitudes*

—Cognitive Development   —Voices of Conscience
    —Of Craft
—Social Perspective Taking   —Of Sacrifice
    —Of Membership
—Moral Reasoning and Judgment   —Of Memory
    —Of Imagination

Information and Knowledge

Strengths of Character: Virtues

—Prudence: Good Judgment, Dialogue, Discernment,
    Seeing Things Whole
—Justice: Fairness, Equity, Network of Care, Inclusion
—Courage: Resoluteness, Resourcefulness, Loyalty,
    Determination, Sacrificial Commitment
—Temperance: Self-Management, Discipline, Balance and
    Proportion

[Theological Virtues]

—Faith   —Hope   —Love

for our consideration of the fundamental importance of *narrative* in the development of character. Of course there is, in our time, a growing body of literature in the so-called "ethics of character" which compellingly delineates the ways in which certain kinds of stories provide us with indispensable moral orientation, motivation, and identifications.[36] As the chart suggests, normative stories of belonging and inclusion (Green's conscience of membership and memory) come to us from our families, our nation, our religious traditions, our colleagues, and friends. Increasingly in our time we are receiving stories that invite us to membership in the global community (Green's conscience of imagination). Such narratives help to establish our sense of rootedness. They provide important sources of identity and identifications. They establish the moral horizons in which we construe present situations requiring moral initiatives or responses, as well as giving us a repertoire of the previous initiatives and responses of others. Narratives portray vivid examples of the virtues and of vice. They conserve and convey the sacred history and meanings of our communities. And some narratives—our religious "classics"—bring to expression our community's memories of the disclosure-transformation events which reveal the character and being of the transcendent.[37]

For purposes of character education in the public schools the stories of the school itself, its mission and character, are important, as are the "myths" that teams or classes within the school create as they live and work together. Helping children and youth reclaim some of their family, racial, or ethnic stories can provide important dimensions of identification and membership, as the tremendous influence and energy generated by Alex Haley's book and television series *Roots* so powerfully demonstrated. Moreover, the history of the nation and of states or regions must be taught in such ways that it provides opportunities to glean from the narratives and biographies identifications with instances of suffering and heroism, fidelity and compassion, oppression and liberation.[38] Most of all, the story of this nation must be compellingly told in such a way that it makes vivid and accessible the vision of covenant solidarity and accountability, as well as the dedication to equality, freedom, and the inalienable rights of each person to life, liberty, and the pursuit of happiness. It must be told as an inclusive "story of our stories," and must include accounts of the "dangerous memories" which require that we continue to widen the bounds of membership and stay responsive to prophetic criticism and visions.[39]

Developmental Abilities. There is an important place in character and civic education for the contributions of cognitive developmental theories and approaches to moral education. As our discussion of civic education in Green's perspective suggested, the cognitive ability and willingness to grow in the disciplined empathy of social perspective taking contributes to a crucial set of skills that are integral to character development. As the work of Lawrence Kohlberg and his associates has shown, social perspective taking is constitutive for moral and ethical reasoning. They have demonstrated that there is a developmental sequence of stages in the acquisition and exercise of these cognitive functions. While Kohlberg's theory and research is less helpful in accounting for the role of moral emotions in disciplined empathy, to include the Kohlberg perspective in a more comprehensive account of character, as we are doing here, helps us to make that connection.

Part of the strength of a model like this is that it begins to suggest linkages between developmental abilities and both the components of story and moral attitudes. Developmental capacities also affect students' appropriations of the component of *Information and Knowledge*, about which we have not yet spoken, but which Hirsch's concern with the necessary contents for cultural literacy highlights. Such developmental abilities can be nurtured in engagement with each and every subject-matter area of the curriculum. The skills of perspective taking can of course be cultivated in classroom activities and interactions and in extracurricular community involvements. But they can also be augmented through the study of literature, through the engagement with conflicts in science or social studies, and through historical and biographical studies. The different forms of moral reasoning can be taught, not as abstract theories, but as frameworks of analysis for understanding and evaluating critical moments in the nation's past (Lincoln's decision to write the Emancipation Proclamation) or in any particular figure's biography (Daniel

Ellsworth's decision to release the *Pentagon Papers*). When actual issues arise in the life of the school or community, the preparation made by utilizing and understanding these different modes of ethical reasoning and the skills of disciplined empathy can be crucial resources in civic education.

Moral attitudes. After having read and digested Green's writing on the voices of conscience I found his imagery and account of the moral emotions to be the most adequate characterization I have found for the attitudes we seek to inculcate in the Responsible Selfhood approach. The voices of conscience he has identified hold together the cognitive operations accounted for in our developmental abilities component and the normative perspectives deriving from our stories component. While highlighting the moral emotions, Green's discussion suggests their interpretation with the other aspects of character and civic interaction.

Because I have discussed the voices of conscience in an earlier part of this essay it is not necessary to examine them again here. Let me merely offer a few thoughts about how schools, as communities, can nurture these voices and the moral attitudes they bring into focus. We must acknowledge at the outset that family and home, and perhaps religious contexts, provide the first and perhaps most influential early influences on the formation of the voices of conscience. However, as day care and nursery school childcare programs expand there is both increased possibility and responsibility for influencing the development of these moral attitudes. Clearly the conscience of craft represents an area in which schools and schooling can make great contributions. The provision of materials and contexts, the teaching of techniques and modes of approach, the offering of supports, and the teaching of standards can occur at every level of education in ways that nurture conscientiousness, confidence, and competence. As regards the conscience of membership, schools can provide vitally important and formative experiences of belonging, and they can foster the skills and attitudes of effective and loyal membership. Through the stories they make accessible to their students, and through the way community and order are administered, students can form deeper respect for duty and for the importance of truth-telling and promise-keeping, for honesty and respect for property, and for loyalty in friendship and fidelity in confidences. They can come to understand the point of rules and laws, and develop in their capacities to discern what fairness and justice require. In all these ways schools can help to form the conscience of responsibility. From my previous discussions in this essay, the reader can see how a similar accounting of the school's potential for nurturing the voices of memory and imagination can be spelled out.

Information and knowledge. Hirsch's work on cultural literacy, with which we began this chapter, has the effect of jarring us out of an unreflective repetition of the notion that what is "basic" in education is learning "Readin', Writin' and 'Rithmatic." He and his sources show how real literacy involves having information enough at our disposal, and practice enough at ordering it into cognitive maps, that we can process, evaluate, select, understand, digest, and utilize the overwhelming amounts of information that are accessible to us in print and other media. What one of his sources calls "world knowledge" Hirsch calls "cultural literacy," by this he means,

> the network of information that all competent readers possess. It is the background information, stored in their mind, that enables them to take up a newspaper and read it with an adequate level of comprehension, getting the point, grasping the implications, relating what they read to the unstated context which alone gives meaning to what they read. In describing the contents of this neglected domain of background information, I try to direct attention to a new opening that can help our schools make the significant improvement in education that has so far eluded us. The achievement of high universal literacy is the key to all other fundamental improvements in American education.[40]

Without laboring the obvious, it becomes clear how interrelated the acquisition of information and knowledge is with each of the other components of the Responsible Selfhood approach to character education.

Strengths of Character: Virtues. In the introduction to the Responsible Selfhood model I indicated that cumulatively the components of character that it depicts flow together to form and fund the strengths of personhood which have traditionally been called "virtues." Reading an account of the classic Greek virtues like that of Joseph Pieper[41] makes one aware of just how rich a range of interrelated and interdependent qualities those concepts integrated. One of the revelations for me connected with our work on the Responsible Selfhood approach has been the recognition that virtues are dynamic qualities of person constituted by the convergence of *at least* as many aspects of moral personality as this model seeks to depict. In this concluding section neither space nor my expertise will allow anything like a full-orbed consideration of the virtues toward which we aim in an American *paideia* based on this model. For the time being, therefore, I take this traditional listing and offer brief explications of a contemporary reinterpretation of the virtues, based on what has gone before in this essay. To make these meanings truly contemporary, however, care must be taken not to let these old names bring with them the legacy of sexual and ethnic or racial exclusivism and class privilege which citizenship connoted in the Greek *polis*.

Prudence. In this redrawing of the virtues prudence becomes the composite term for "good judgment." Good judgment involves, of course, having sufficient knowledge of the relevant circumstances in any situation requiring response or initiative. But, following Hirsch, it also means having the cognitive ordering or mapping of that knowledge so as to illumine in relevant ways the complexities and subtleties of the situation. Moreover, prudence involves skills of consultation, dialogue and discernment with others. Informed by moral attitudes and conscience, and by stories that offer both motivation and models of effective concern for the common good, prudence, as good judgment, reaches decisions—or contributes to group decision-making—on the basis of a deliberate effort at seeing things whole.

Justice. Traditionally justice means "giving to each his or her due." We cannot here rehearse Aristotle's rich account of the different modes of justice. In this contemporary reconstitution of the virtues justice includes such capacities as the commitment and competence to establish fairness. It includes equity and even-handedness, both in interpersonal relations and in social policy and the treatment of groups. It means consideration and care for the networks of care and interdependence that make being and well-being possible. And it embraces the imperative to keep open and expanding the membership of those entitled to regard and treatment with full humanity and humaneness.

Courage. For the Greeks courage was the quality of emotional and intellectual fortitude sufficient to carry out what prudence and justice determined to be the proper course of action in any situation. It is hard to improve upon that conception of this composite set of qualities. However, informed by the conscience of imagination, courage, in the service of the common good in a convenantally based society, must have a forward looking component—the nerve and resoluteness to hold in view the future dangers and threats to the common good, and to insist upon engaging them. Courage also exhibits resourcefulness, a determined readiness to find means to do what justice and prudence require. Finally, courage involves the strengths of loyalty and fidelity to those causes, persons, and institutions for which one has covenant responsibility.

Temperance. In contemporary terms the traditional concept of temperance becomes "self-management" or "discipline." It is related to the conscience of membership and memory and grows out of self-knowledge and clarity about what constitutes worthy man- or womanhood. Temperance is also grounded in the conscience of craft in the sense of learning to live well and being a kind of artist with one's life. Involving balance and proportion, temperance is proficiency in the ability consistently to discern and "hit the mark."

On the chart that depicts the Responsible Selfhood approach I have also listed the traditional "theological virtues" of faith, hope, and love. This is not the place to try to demonstrate that these virtues do not depend, for their validity and imperativeness, upon their biblical rootage. Suffice it to say that without love, commitment to the other virtues we have discussed tends to deteriorate and fall too much into the self-regarding use of virtues to establish one's own worth. Similarly, without hope—hope in the responsiveness and fidelity of others, hope for a future in which to be virtuous and committed to the common good, the virtues tend to lose their point. Finally, the whole setting of the virtues, as conceived here, is one of covenant commitment to a commonweal, a common good. And without faith—a trust in the loyalty to that covenant community, and the body of story and myth that gives it its determinate character and corporate vocation—concern with the virtues can deteriorate to a kind of individualistic manicuring of one's own soul. Faith, hope, and love, therefore, are not dispensable in the Responsible Selfhood approach, though in order to be constitutional in contexts of public education, their inclusion cannot depend upon or be justified solely upon the basis of their formulation in the New Testament.

Notes

1. E. D. Hirsch, Jr., *Cultural Literacy: What Every American Needs to Know* (Boston: Houghton Mifflin Company, 1987).

2. Thomas F. Green, *The Formation of Conscience in an Age of Technology*, John Dewey Lecture, 1984 (Syracuse, N.Y.: Syracuse University, 1984).

3. C. D. Kingsley, ed., *Cardinal Principles of Secondary Education: A Report of the Commission on the Reorganization of Secondary Education, Appointed by the National Education Association* (Bulletin, 1981, no. 35. Washington, D.C.: Department of the Interior, Bureau of Education, Government Printing Office, 1918). (Cited in Hirsch, *Cultural Literacy*, 235.)

4. National Education Association, *Report of the Committee of Ten on Secondary School Studies* (Washington, D.C.: Government Printing Office, 1893). Hereafter cited as Eliot, report of the Committee of Ten. (Cited in Hirsch, *Cultural Literacy*, 235).

5. Hirsch, *Cultural Literacy*, 117.

6. By "formalism" I mean the identification of certain operations of knowing and understanding as requisite for full adult participation in society and its enterprises of science, business, government, family life, and the like. As the subject matter of the particular disciplines began to grow exponentially in the early twentieth century, educators began to see the futility of hoping that everyone could master the requisite *contents* of the several fields of inquiry. Moreover, that content rapidly became obsolete. The important thing became "learning to learn" and developing the requisite intellectual capacities to enable one to operate effectively in a complex society. Formalism is the subordination of particular subject matter disciplines and their "canons" of required information to the task—using whatever such matter is at hand—of evoking and strengthening the formally describable capacities of intellectual inquiry.

7. Hirsch, *Cultural Literacy*, 117.

8. Ibid., 118.

9. Ibid., 121.

10. Ibid., 125.

11. B. Edward McClellan, "A History of Character Education in America" (unpublished paper for Conference on Moral Education and Character, United States Office of Education, September 1987), 9.

12. Ibid., 10.

13. Ibid.

14. Ibid., 13.

15. Thomas F. Green writes, "It would not be too much to say that until about the third decade of this century nobody had values. They had beliefs, virtues, expectations, hopes, sometimes good fortune, luck, and even a bit of happiness. What they *did* was to *value* (verb) certain things, some more than others, because they believed those *things* were of greater or less *value* (predicate) or had greater or less *worth*" ("Teaching and the Formation of Character" unpublished paper, Conference on Moral Education and Character, United States Office of Education, September 1987).

16. McClellan, "History of Character Education," 16.

17. Ibid., 18.

18. Ibid., 19.

19. Ibid., 22–24.

20. Robin W. Lovin, "Social Contract or a Public Covenant?" in *Religion and American Public Life* (New York: Paulist Press, 1986), 132–145.

21. Ibid., 135.

22. The best example is Michael Novak, *The Spirit of Democratic Capitalism* (New York: Simon and Schuster [Touchstone], 1982).

23. Lovin, "Social Contract or a Public Covenant?" 139.

24. Published as a small monograph, *The Formation of Conscience in an Age of Technology* (Syracuse, New York: Syracuse University, 1984).

25. Green, *Formation of Conscience*, 2–3.

26. Ibid., 12.

27. Ibid., 6.

28. Ibid., 7.

29. Ibid.

30. Ibid., 13–14.

31. The term Green uses for this is the conscience of *sacrifice*. The use of the term *sacrifice* in ethical thought has become, rightfully, a red flag for those doing ethics in ways that try to include and address women's experience. In my interpretation the use of the term *sacrifice* is not intrinsic to the meaning Green is trying to convey. Though he clearly wants to imply that one should do one's duty, and that one should sacrifice one's desire to pursue other pleasures when duty conflicts with that desire, it is clear that Green sees duty as arising out of promises freely made and not out of assuming and docilely fulfilling traditional roles that may have institutionalized patterns of dominance and subordination.

32. W. D. Ross, *The Right and the Good* (London: Oxford University Press, 1930), esp. chap. 2.

33. Green, *Formation of Conscience*, 19–20.

34. Ibid., 21-22.

35. See Johannes Metz, *Faith in History and Society* (New York: Crossroad/Seabury Press, 1980), esp. chap. 5 and following.

36. See Steven Crites, "The Narrative Quality of Experience," *Journal of the American Academy of Religion* 39 (no. 3, September 1971): 291–311; James Wm. McClendon, *Biography as Theology* (Nashville, Tenn.: Abingdon Press, 1974); Stanley Hauerwas, *Vision and Virtue* (Notre Dame, Ind.: University of Notre Dame Press, 1974), *Truthfulness and Tragedy* (Notre Dame, Ind.: University of Notre Dame Press, 1977), *A Community of Character* (Notre Dame, Ind.: University of Notre Dame Press, 1981); and Craig R. Dykstra, *Vision and Character* (New York: Paulist Press, 1981). For important background sources for these perspectives see H. Richard Neibuhr, *The Meaning of Revelation* (New York: Macmillan, 1941) and James G. Gustafson, *Christian Ethics and the Community* (Philadelphia: Pilgrim Press, 1971).

37. For the idea of the "classic" see David Tracy, *The Analogical Imagination* (New York: Crossroad Press, 1981), esp. chaps. 3–5.

38. For an important discussion of the teaching of history in such ways that it contributes to character development see Charles Strickland, "Curricular Approaches to Character Education: History and Biography," Emory University (unpublished paper prepared for Conference on Moral Education and Character, United States Office of Education, September 1987).

39. This essay begs one very central, very important question: There must be a "cultural canon" of normative stories and information pertinent to formation in civic education. Such stories must indeed be part of a rich, inclusive "story of our stories." In the project on ethics and public education we are addressing this question, but are not yet prepared to offer such a canon or criteria for establishing it. Unlike biblical canon, the civic canon should not be closed-ended, though there certainly will be certain non-negotiable "classics" that must be included in any listing. For efforts at establishing such a canon, see Horace M. Kallen, *Cultural Pluralism and the American Idea: An Essay in Social Philosophy* (Philadelphia: University of Pennsylvania Press, 1956); and Hirsch, *Cultural Literacy*, chap. 4.

40. Hirsch, *Cultural Literacy*, 2.

41. Joseph Pieper, *The Four Cardinal Virtues* (Notre Dame, Ind.: University of Notre Dame Press, 1966).

IS PLURALISM POSSIBLE IN
AMERICAN PUBLIC EDUCATION?

Michael R. Olneck

Celebrants of pluralism pronounce the ethnic "unmeltable" (Novak 1971), and proclaim that "we are no longer an American melting-pot, nor do we want to be" (Lee and Oldham, n.d.). There is, the American Association of Colleges of Teacher Education enunciates, "No One Model American" (Commission on Multicultural Education 1973, 264). In response to the demands of mobilized minority groups, federal, state, and local resources are allocated to bilingual education, ethnic studies, and multicultural education.

In response, perceiving and fearing a "new communalism" (Janowitz 1983) or "new particularism" (Higham 1975), critics see in such rhetoric and such practices evidence that, as Philip Gleason has written, "the traditional Americanist position has not only been placed on the defensive, it has been left virtually undefended" (1980, 56). R. Freeman Butts, for example, sees "civism" (i.e., "principles of good citizenship in a republic") as having been supplanted by particularistic loyalties (1977), while Abigail Thernstrom concludes that "the public school no longer functions to transmit a common culture" (1980, 4). Nathan Glazer argues that we have abandoned the "consensus" of the mid-1960s, which extended to African-Americans the embrace of a distinctive American ethnic pattern characterized by public neutrality and private freedom, and have instead made a commitment to facilitating the maintenance of ethnic heritage and requiring school authorities to take into account ethnic and linguistic differences in education (1975; 1983).

I will argue here that however ambitious the aspirations of pluralists, and however acute the anxieties of their critics, pluralism, properly defined, does not characterize the practices, organization, or ideology of the American public schools, nor is it likely to in the foreseeable future. Belief that it does, or that it can, stems, in part, from a confusion between the meaning of diversity and the meaning of pluralism.

Pluralism, if it is to have any distinctive meaning, must pertain to the multiplicity of communities or collectivities which comprise a society, and not merely to manifested differences among individuals in background, heritage, values, and styles. While pluralism need not require juridical autonomy as implied in the prerogatives of Quebec Province to elevate and protect the French language, or as implied, more modestly, in demands of the 1960s for African-American community control of schools in New York City and elsewhere, authentic pluralism must in some fashion recognize the identities and claims of groups *as groups*, must facilitate or at least symbolically represent and legitimate the collective institutional and cultural lives of groups, and must enhance the salience of group membership as a basis for participation in society, though not necessarily as a basis for distributive outcomes or life chances. Authentic pluralism in schooling also requires, to the extent that valued cultural differences among groups are real, that pedagogy, curricular form and content, and modes of assessment be congruent with and preserve those differences, so long as the groups in question wish this to be so.

Examination of the policies, practices, and materials which define so-called "pluralism" in American public schools shows that, whether for good or for ill, our schools fall far short of realizing these ends. While some would suggest that the multiculturalism and bilingualism of the 1970s and 1980s represent a historic repudiation of state neutrality in matters of ethnic identity and presage "national" or "minority" rights in a manner previously unknown in the United States, I would argue, as I do in my current work (see e.g., Olneck 1989a; 1989b), that there is, instead, a historical continuity that links aspects of the Americanization movement of the 1910–1925 period, the intercultural education movement of the 1930s and 1940s, the intergroup education movement of the early 1950s, and the practices, if not the aspirations, of multicultural and bilingual education in the 1970s and 1980s. While the community control movement of the 1960s must be exempted from this conclusion, the most noteworthy aspect of the community control movement from the point of view of my argument is its failure to attain widespread legitimacy or implementation.

I reach the conclusion of historical continuity across ostensibly contradictory movements primarily by subordinating the question of how educational practice recognizes and constructs ethnic cultural differences to the question of how educational practice recognizes and constructs ethnic collectivity. I argue that hegemony of the paradigm of individual differences links the pedagogical practices and curricular content of movements that apparently contrast with one another and highly circumscribes the institutional, pedagogical, and curricular recognition of the legitimacy of ethnic collectivity.

Moreover, institutionalization and routinization of pedagogical practices and curricular content ostensibly favorable to pluralism transmute, despite the original intentions of committed pluralists, oppositional and transformatory impulses into historically dominant assimilative configurations of practice and ideology.

In reaching these conclusions, I do not ignore the fact that recent educational movements are more sympathetic to cultural diversity than were pre–World War II movements. Nor do I neglect the significance of conflicts over pluralism in the schools as occasions for reordering and redefining status and power relationships between ethnic minorities and dominant groups. Nevertheless, I believe it valid to conclude that pluralism as practiced in American public schools confirms rather than transforms dominant understandings of the legitimate relationship between ethnicity and polity, and reinforces rather than fragments the "common cultures."

Here, rather than use limited space to argue for the validity of the contention of fundamental ideological continuity across eight decades, I will instead argue for the descriptive validity of my characterizations as they pertain to contemporary multicultural and bilingual education. I will conclude with some brief reflections on the prospects for authentic pluralism in American public education.

Multicultural Education

Multicultural education of all varieties rhetorically celebrates differences and lauds the preservation of distinctive cultural identities. Some prominent multicultural theorists call for the cultural diversification of pedagogy and curriculum, both to overcome discontinuities between schooling and students' social identities and cultural practices, and to advance parity of recognition and power to heretofore subordinated and marginalized groups. Multiculturalism could, in principle, eliminate the privileged position enjoyed by white-Anglo culture and perspectives and could reconfigure the symbolic order, in which, as Joseph Gusfield (1963; 1981), Clifford Geertz (1973), Murray Edelman (1971; 1977), and others have demonstrated, status is conferred, norms sanctioned, and social phenomena are authoritatively defined and interpreted, so as to accord parity to minorities in constructing what is authentically and validly American, and in defining legitimate criteria of academic achievement and success.

Multicultural theorists anticipate and embrace the enduring public salience of distinctive cultural identities, and some seek to harmonize relationships among groups not, as their intercultural education precursors did, by rendering differences irrelevant, but by cultivating cross-cultural competencies which permit the recognition and affirmation of ethnic identity in contexts of multigroup interaction.

Multiculturalists, in contrast to the Americanizers of the early part of the century, and in contrast even to interculturalists of the inter-war and World War II periods, do not symbolically privilege an all-embracing, shared, unitary national community and identity. While they represent shared democratic ideals and values, and widely distributed "mainstream" cultural characteristics as factors for national cohesion, these are not centered as primary objects of devotion or celebration. Rather, the national culture is depicted as a synthesis emerging through mutual acculturation, out of the interaction among members and nation's constituent groups.

Despite these ostensibly "pluralistic" features of much multicultural education rhetoric and theory, multiculturalism, in its more prevalent forms, fails, as noted above, to articulate an authentic ideology of pluralism, is fundamentally integrative and incorporative, and is possibly reproductive of prevailing relations of power and control.[1]

This is because the more prevalent forms of multicultural education are symbolically infused with the construct "individual differences," and do little to explicitly represent, legitimate, recognize, or institutionalize the claims and experiences of ethnic collectivities. Moreover, multicultural education commonly isolates, individualizes, homogenizes, depoliticizes, and fragments culture, and like its precursor, intercultural education, aims often to do little more than harmonize relationships among culturally diverse individuals by cultivating attitudes of empathy, appreciation, and understanding. These may well be laudable purposes, but they should not be confused with pluralism.

Multiculturalism tends to subsume ethnicity into an ideology of differences and concerns itself with the diversity or variation among individuals. At the center of multiculturalism's symbolic structure is the unique individual whose varying cultural inheritances, multiple affiliations, and autonomous preferences determine personal identity and style.

In the paradigm of the "unique individual," ethnicity is first and foremost an expression of individual personal identity, rather than a dimension of American social structure or a dynamic organizing bounded, stratified, and competing or conflicting collective entities. While some multiculturalists assert the value of multicultural education for preparing individuals for participation in the groups of which they are members (see, for example, Banks 1987; 1988), the practices and symbolism of much multicultural education give little evidence of serving this purpose, if only because individuals are rarely represented in the contexts of group membership, obligation, or participation. Instead, as Hazel Carby has observed in her critique of British multiculturalism, the school is assumed to be an institution which "can isolate the individual from serving as a member of a social group and give priority to individual experience" (1980a, 8).

In multicultural curricular materials, ethnicity as personal identity is represented in such activities as inquiring into students' "backgrounds" or "heritages" (see, for example, Lee and Oldham, n.d.; Redford 1977), and providing opportunities for students to answer questionnaires with titles like "Ethnicity in My Life" (Smith and Otero 1977) and "How Important is Ethnicity to Me?" (King 1977). Such activities, particularly when undertaken in ethnically heterogenous classrooms, focus attention on the characteristics of individual or familial behavior that differentiate students from one another. While individual identification with the practices of a group is a necessary aspect of participation in a community or collectivity, the form in which such identification is constructed and represented in the practices of multicultural education emphasizes individuation, rather than group consociation.

Multiculturalists also render ethnicity consistent with the core American norms of individual expression (Varenne 1977; Bellah et al. 1985; Beeman 1986) by representing ethnic identity as an option or voluntary choice. James MacDonald (1974, 168), for example, characterizes the goal of multicultural education as encouraging diversity "not as separation by group but as intentional choice of life style by all individuals." "Students," James Banks (1988, 280) writes, "should be helped to understand that, ideally, all individuals should have the right to select the manner and degree of identifying or not identifying with their ethnic groups."

For some multiculturalists, an individual's range of choice extends even beyond that of identifying with his or her own ethnic inheritance to that of adopting and participating in the cultures of other groups. Banks, for example, writes, "[s]tudents need to learn that there are cultural and ethnic alternatives within our society that they can freely embrace" (1987, 12; see also Banks 1974; 1988). Multicultural education, according to the Association of Supervisors and Curriculum Developers, includes efforts to "help students avail themselves of as many models, alternatives, and opportunities as possible from the full spectrum of our cultures" (ASDC 1977, 3; see also Baker 1983). When it encourages cultural eclecticism and voluntarism, multicultural education undermines the commitments that would sustain the ethnic boundary maintenance that is a prerequisite for genuine pluralism (on ethnic boundary maintenance, see Barth 1969).

By affirming and centering the autonomous individual whose cultural identity is a matter of relatively unconstrained choice, multicultural education locates ethnicity well within the established symbolic and conceptual order through which Americans perceive and interpret society and polity (see Varenne 1977; Olneck 1989a). Multicultural education of this variety premises no significant reformulation in the principles and structures of American institutions and is especially incongruent with the collective claims and communal identities of historically anomalous (and exploited and subjugated) groups whose self-definitions and historical relationships with society cannot be readily comprehended through the lenses of liberal individualism (see Rizvi 1986; Bullivant 1981b; and Masemann 1981).

Despite having emerged out of demands by mobilized, subordinated ethnic groups, multiculturalism has both expanded the dimensions of differentiation with which it is concerned to include age, gender, social class, handicapped status, and even drug use (Baker 1983; G. Grant 1977; Sleeter and Grant 1987), and focused almost exclusive attention on the content of cultural practices, rather than on the social organizations of and structured relationships among racially and ethnically defined groups. The result, as Cameron McCarthy has recently observed, is to amalgamate minority "differences" into the plurality of differences that percolates throughout the educational system (1988, 268), thereby diminishing the distinctive import of racism in the United States (Berlowitz 1984; Banks 1986), and of race and ethnicity as distinctive dynamics of social structure.

The confusion of pluralism, which anticipates bounded (though interacting) communities of identity and interest with diversity is, despite important exceptions (see e.g., Lee 1972), pervasive within multicultural education. Some multiculturalists explicitly equate the condition of cultural diversity with pluralism (see, for example, Garcia 1982, 7; Tiedt and Tiedt 1979, 117). Like the intercultural educators of an earlier period, many multicultural educators concern themselves with the manifestation of differences per se and endeavor to cultivate appreciation and tolerance for diversity as such. The imagery of diverse family configurations and assertions of the need to learn that there is "no one kind of family" (G. Grant 1977, 67–68), for example, are ubiquitous. Young children are also oriented to the ubiquity and acceptability of individual differences by investigating differences in such attributes as taste buds, earlobes (Pasternak 1977), skin, hair, and eye color (King 1977), fingerprints (Tiedt and Tiedt 1979), animal habitats and behavior patterns (Baker 1983), and in names, words, and proverbs across cultures and languages (Tiedt and Tiedt 1979).

In much of the material intended for classroom use in multicultural education, especially that for younger pupils, study and activity is centered on the content of discrete cultural practices. Culture is conceived of as having "components" (e.g., visual arts, music and dance, food, recreation, holiday celebrations, literature, folklore, and oral traditions, clothing, language, ways of life) which can be learned about, imitated, and "shared" (see, for example, Tiedt and Tiedt 1979; Pasternak 1979; King 1977; Lee and Oldham, n.d.; Seattle Public School District No. 1, 1975, 1979). Cultural practices are construed in multicultural education as expressive characteristics of members of particular cultural groups, not as interrelated practices which organize bounded collectivities and serve to help articulate (in both senses of the word) political and economic relationships among groups (see Carby 1980b, 1982; Moodley 1983; Bullivant 1981a).

A particularly striking example of the political and historical myopia characteristic of some multicultural materials is to be found in Seattle's *Rainbow Activities* (1975). An exercise entitled "Friends and Neighbors" treats Seattle's Native American "neighbors." Students learn that "some of our Native American neighbors live in cultural groups called tribes in areas called reservations. . . . There are only 300 separate tribes left in America of the more than 1,000 that existed before . . ." (p. 82). Students are then asked to consider the things we might like to know about Native Americans, including American Indians' special interests, special days, foods, clothing, musical instruments, and so on. While a sophisticated analysis of white-Indian history might well be inappropriate for young children, immature cognitive development among primary grade pupils cannot explain the absence of such questions from these materials as "why don't we have any Native American friends?" "Why do Native Americans live on reservations?" and "What happened to the other 700 tribes?"

Multiculturalism, as represented here, neglects sources of cultural differentiation in relations of power, dominance, and subordination (Carby 1982), neglects noncultural sources of ethnic stratification (Rizvi 1986; Bullivant 1981a, 1981b, 1984), and by erecting a division between private cultural and public political domains (Bullivant 1981a, 1981b, 1984; Rizvi 1986; Carby 1982), blunts the potential for multicultural education to advance the instrumental ends of disadvantaged and subordinated ethnic groups, and to reduce ethnic inequalities (Bullivant 1981a, 1981b; Kallen 1983; Carby 1980a, 1982; Moodley 1983).

The discourse of multiculturalism is, as Hazel Carby has so emphatically observed, not the voice of ethnic and racial minorities speaking for themselves. It is, rather, often the voice of white middle-class education professionals speaking about "problem" groups (1980a; Aoki et al. 1984) and about the solutions to the problems posed by "diversity." Despite the intentions of some multiculturalists to challenge dominant standards of assessment, definitions of legitimate knowledge, acceptable pedagogical perspectives, and Anglocentric cultural and historical perspectives, multicultural education as ordinarily practiced tends to merely "insert" minorities into the dominant cultural frame of reference (Aoki et al. 1984), to be transmitted within dominant cultural forms (MacDonald 1977; Masemann 1981) and to leave obscured and intact existing cultural hierarchies and criteria of stratification (Carby 1980a; Masemann 1981; Moodley 1983; Bullivant 1981a, 1984; Aoki et al. 1984). Ironically, multicultural education reinterprets and re-presents minority culture and minority identity in the idioms of, from the perspectives of, and within constraints imposed by dominant cultural forms (Aoki et al. 1984; Carby 1982; Moodley 1986), while at the same time failing to provide support for collective cultural maintenance or revitalization (Kallen 1983), or for autonomous ethnic institutions which define and represent groups' identities and interests (Bullivant 1984; 1986).[2]

Hegemony of the dominant cultural frame of reference in multicultural education may be seen in particular in the emphasis placed on teaching students to "appreciate" the "contributions" of specific ethnic groups to American culture, society, and history. Intended to foster "respect" for the contributions of others, and "pride" in the contributions of one's own group, the metaphorical device of "contributions" symbolically appropriates, transforms, and integrates particularistic experiences and traditions into a common symbolic order. The idea of contributions presupposes fundamentally equivalent contributors (cf. Errington 1987) with outward and other-regarding orientations, and is inherently hostile to sources of meaning, identity, and affiliation that are autonomous from the common culture.

Moreover, the symbolism of "contributions" obscures and mystifies possibly conflict-attended processes of culture "transfer." Tiedt and Tiedt, for example, tell students that in studying "pockets of people who share a unique background and culture," they "will discover a variety of interesting ideas, living patterns, and contributions" (1979, 144). The Pennsylvania Dutch, for example, the authors continue, have "developed an attractive and distinctive style of art. They *share* such folk songs as the following with us" (ibid., 144, emphasis added). In studying Indians, Tiedt and Tiedt tell students, they will learn about "the many things we *gained* from the Indians" (ibid., 161, emphasis added).

One might offer a similar interpretation of the symbolic construct "heritage," also prominent in multicultural rhetoric and texts. The idea of "heritage," even as it permits continuity through cultural "preservation," highlights the contrast between, on the one hand, past identities and "origin," and, on the other, present identities and commitments. At the same time, it contrasts a small terrain of cultural "carryover" and limited occasions of commemoration or remembrance with the more encompassing areas and occasions of common practice and participation (on such "symbolic ethnicity," see Gans

1979). "Heritage" signifies a personal possession or characteristic, not a community of participation or obligation.

It is, of course, possible to attribute too much autonomous power to a symbol per se. The meanings attaching to and the social actions responding to a symbol depend upon institutional and historical context, audience, authority displaying the symbol, and so on. The meaning of "contributions" may be very different in the rhetoric and texts of Americanizers during the period of World War I, of parochial schools during the 1920s, of African-American community schools during the 1960s, and of multicultural classrooms in American public schools of the 1970s and 1980s. But, because it is a device that emphasizes the simultaneous and equivalent participation and significance of *all* groups in American history and society, and because it is a symbol which conjures harmony and cooperation, I would contend that the meaning of "contributions" in the symbolic universe of multicultural education is closer to that in the symbolic universe of the Americanizers than it is to that of African-American community schools.

While my analysis of multicultural education may be conceded, it may be objected that multicultural education is insufficiently coherent and insufficiently widespread and well organized (see Sleeter and Grant 1987) to warrant resting my analysis on it alone. Rather, because bilingual education has for twenty years enjoyed a degree of official sanction, it, not multicultural education, may be the movement and practice which is most instructive of the limits and possibilities for pluralism in American public schools.

Bilingual Education

While my analysis here of bilingual education is more limited than my analysis of multicultural education, my interpretation of bilingual education is not, however, dissimilar from my interpretation of multicultural education.

Bilingual education in the United States is publicly legitimized through the rhetoric of equal opportunity ideology (Masemann 1979), with the effect of blunting the pluralist potential which is inherent in bilingual education and which the most committed bilingual education advocates wish fulfilled. This is not because equal opportunity ideology inherently renders bilingual education remedial or compensatory, though it does so in practice. It is, rather, because equal opportunity ideology recognizes only the rights of individuals to be free of exclusionary discrimination, and the needs of individuals to acquire the competencies requisite for participation in the mainstream. It provides no sanction for the affirmative claims of collectivities or, even, for the claims of individuals to be granted the curricular means of realizing their ethnic identities.

Judicial and executive sanction for bilingual education derive from a civil rights interpretation of the disproportionate academic failure and dropout rates of linguistic minorities as the consequences of practices resulting in statutorily impermissible "exclusion" of those minorities from "full participation" in or from "enjoyment of benefits" of their schooling. Congressional provision for bilingual education derives from a similar concern to eliminate the "barriers" or "handicaps" precluding satisfactory educational progress. Official policy defines the need to be rectified as the "limited English proficiency" of language minority students.

The construction of bilingual education as a remedy to the heretofore neglected limitations in English proficiency experienced by language minority students circumscribes the population for whom bilingual education is regarded as legitimate. It is only for students who "need" it as a means by which to acquire English proficiency and to maintain progress in school subjects. Moreover, under this construction, bilingual education is to be provided for only so long as it is "needed." While the questions of who needs bilingual education and of what the necessary duration of participation is are heatedly debated, the critical point is that equal opportunity ideology implies limited eligibility for and limited duration of bilingual education. Proponents of more inclusive and more extensive measures are compelled to argue within terms set by others that such measures are "necessary."

Further, under the construction of bilingual education as a remedy for limited English proficiency, the proponents of bilingual education are thrown on the defensive by evaluation studies whose results cast doubt on claims that bilingual education "works," and they must contend with claims that other approaches (e.g., English as a Second Language, immersion) may be more "effective." They must contend as well with claims that the educational failure experienced by language minority students derives from low socioeconomic status, not from linguistic differences per se. The implication of the last claim is taken to be that such students are in need of conventional compensatory education measures, not bilingual education. Bilingual education, then, must be argued for and defended in terms that are indifferent to, and sometimes even hostile to pluralistic purposes.

Equal opportunity ideology does, however, provide some openings for pluralist claims, and the terms of the ideology are somewhat elastic. For example, the U.S. Commission on Civil Rights in one report expanded the definition of exclusionary practices beyond failure to remedy limited English language proficiency (United States Civil Rights Commission 1972). The Commission interpreted a school's failure to utilize students' home cultures in its pedagogy as a denial of pride that fosters alienation and withdrawal. Proponents of more inclusive and more extensive forms of bilingual education use the argument that generating and sustaining self-esteem and attachment to school among language minority students require programs that are fully bicultural as well as bilingual, and also programs which strive for home language retention, as well as for English language acquisition and subject matter mastery. It is important to note, however, that such claims have not proven persuasive to Congressional majorities, that they, too, are logically susceptible to empirical refutation, and that they, too, are predicated on the paradigm of individual student needs. They do not, therefore, provide a secure warrant for language pluralism in American schools.

The practice of bilingual education in the United States operates, therefore, under strong political, ideological, and programmatic constraints. While opponents of bilingual education deplore the inclusion in programs of students whom they deem able to function in English-only classrooms, empirical studies establish that most programs are, in fact, transitional, include large components of English, and are limited to bona fide Limited English Proficiency students (Hakuta 1986). One ethnographic study found that even when a bilingual education program is designated "developmental" (i.e., maintenance), it fails to generate spontaneous use of Spanish on the part of Latino children (Masemann 1983; see also Masemann 1978). Indeed, Joshua Fishman, the preeminent sociolinguist studying bilingualism, ethnicity, and language policy, argues that bilingual education may, under some circumstances, even accelerate the shift from home language to the societally dominant language (Fishman 1977).

Ethnographic study shows further that the organization of symbols, time, space, and pedagogy in even maintenance programs can replicate dominant cultural forms, emphasize individualization, and fail to cultivate the expression of ethnic identity (Masemann 1983; see also Masemann 1978). As Fishman (1977) has observed, bilingual education can readily trivialize biculturalism, rendering language and culture "things" to be appreciated, respected, and remembered, but failing to sustain the collective beliefs, identifications, behaviors (including language use) and sensibilities necessary for constructing group life. *Even* maintenance bilingual education for language-minority students, while it may provide resources for socioeconomic advancement in "broker" work and accelerate acculturation, is unlikely to foster communal solidarity or cultural continuity unless *interethnic* communication is bilingual (Hernandez-Chavez 1978).

Bilingual education as constructed by official policy and practice, I conclude, instructs us more in the limits than in the possibilities for pluralism in American schools.

Conclusion

Robert Bellah and his colleagues, in *Habits of the Heart*, recently observed that Americans hold their values as "personal preferences," and do not identify them with a "social or cultural base that could give them broader meaning" (Bellah et al. 1985, 7). "For most Americans," Bellah et al. write, "the only real social bonds are those based on the free choice of authentic selves" (ibid., 107). The individual in American society is, in the authors' terminology, most likely to see herself or himself as an "unencumbered" self, rather than as a "constituted" self who is related to a "community of memory," and who is engaged in "practices of commitment" which "define the community way of life . . . [and] the patterns of loyalty and obligation that keep the community alive" (ibid., 152–155).

Bellah et al. also observe that "Americans . . . feel most comfortable in thinking about politics in terms of a consensual community of autonomous, but essentially similar, individuals. . . . For all the lip service given to respect for cultural differences, Americans seem to lack the resources to think about the relationship between groups that are culturally, socially, or economically quite different" (ibid., 206).

In somewhat similar mood, Peter Berger and Richard John Neuhaus, in *To Empower People*, critique our society's "megastructures" (among which we may count at least some of our public schools), which they say are "typically alienating" insofar as "they are not helpful in providing meaning and identity for individual existence" (Berger and Neuhaus 1977, 2). Berger and Neuhaus argue for the vitalization of "mediating structures" as "value-generating and value-maintaining agencies" (ibid., 6).

Reflecting on the problems of alienation and social cohesion, Berger and Neuhaus observe the paradox "that wholeness is experienced through affirmation of the part in which one participates" (ibid., 41). Rejecting the idea that mere diversity constitutes pluralism, Berger and Neuhaus argue that particularism is the essence of pluralism, and venture that "[t]he goal of public policy in a pluralistic society is to sustain as many particularities as possible in the hope that most people will, accept, discover, or devise one that fits" (ibid., 44).

There is currently little in the discourse, symbols, or curricular and pedagogical practices of education for pluralism in American schools that is likely to cultivate Bellah's "constituted self," nor to advance "practices of commitment" related to "communities of memory." Nor are the discursive, symbolic, or curricular and pedagogical resources for nourishing and sustaining the particularities which Berger and Neuhaus contend are the essence of pluralism readily apparent.

To advance such ends in our public institution would require sociological and political preconditions, ideological transformations, and Constitutional reformulations that seem unlikely. In brief, ethnicity per se, and not religion, would have to be a primary category of identification, yet all data on language attrition, intermarriage, residential dispersion, occupational mobility and differentiation, ethnic self-identification, and participation in ethnic communal life, suggest that Richard Alba's term "the twilight of ethnicity" is, for whites, at least, entirely apt (Alba 1985).[3]

If religion must provide the matrix for pluralism among whites, then pluralism in the public sphere would require reversal of standing Supreme Court decisions defining the wall of separation between church and state, or imaginative innovations, like Minnesota's provision for education tax credits for *all* students, that evade the prohibitions of those decisions.

With respect to non-whites, authentic pluralism may well require recognition of collective "minority rights" (as distinct from the rights of individual minority group members) for which there is little precedent. Neither of the Supreme Court cases of the 1920s which overturned, in one instance, an Oregon law compelling attendance at public schools, and, in another instance, a Nebraska law prohibiting the teaching of foreign languages, recognized the claims of communal entities. And even decisions upholding affirmative action measures are cast within the framework of vindicating violations of individual rights, not conferring group entitlements. Only the successful remobilization of aggrieved minority groups is likely to compel the state to concede measures which approximate the recognition of minority rights. While the occurrence and outcomes of future struggles cannot be confidently predicted, defense of the modest gains made by minorities during the 1960s and early 1970s is today sufficiently problematic (see Omi and Winant 1986) that forecasting the expansion of minority rights in the foreseeable future would seem unwarranted.

Finally, to achieve an authentic pluralism, we would have to redefine our conception of "public" so that what is "common" and "universal" is understood to be realized through what is "particular," rather than through transcending, superseding, or setting aside what is, in the terms of prevailing civic ideology, "parochial."

Failing these preconditions, transformations, and reformulations, it will continue to fall to nonpublic institutions to nourish the pluralism from which public institutions are constrained. And because these institutions are overwhelmingly religious in sponsorship, it is difficult to see how they can serve to define the racial, ethnic, and linguistic pluralism upon which parity of power and equality of life chances for people of color and other minorities may ultimately prove to depend.

Notes

Funding for the research on which this essay draws came from the Spencer Foundation, the Graduate School of the University of Wisconsin-Madison, and from the Wisconsin Center for Educational Research, under a grant from the National Institute of Education, Grant Number NIE-G-84-0008. Opinions expressed herein do not necessarily reflect the position, policy, or endorsement of any of the funding sources.

1. In this essay, I only argue for the validity of this interpretation. I do not provide an account of *why* multicultural education takes the forms it does. An adequate account would have to identify the constraints and the mediating mechanisms which determine curricular and pedagogical forms. On no account should this interpretation be read as an attack on multicultural education, which has, from its inception, had to struggle to secure legitimacy and place. That "strong" versions of multicultural education do not prevail is not for want of such vision within the field. Rather, multicultural education, like all movements which seek to redress inequalities of status and power, must contend with the ideological and material resources of opposing dominant groups and institutions (see Sleeter, 1989).

2. Most of the sources cited in this paragraph pertain to Great Britain, Australia, and Canada. I cite them to indicate that others have advanced interpretations similar to my own and to credit others for insights that I judge applicable to the United States. The contexts and histories of multiculturalism differ to some extent from society to society, and characterizations pertaining to multiculturalism in one setting cannot automatically be applied to multiculturalism in another setting (Sleeter, 1989). Nevertheless, there are common features to multiculturalism as it has developed in a number of countries sharing a dominant English-speaking history, as well as in other Western nations (see Masemann 1981).

3. Ethnicity here refers to specific national ancestry. Ethnic group formation processes, including the linguistic construction of the majority

group by people of color and other minorities, could in theory prove Alba's contention erroneous. The term "Euro-American," currently in use among some minority activists, could, for example, come to denote the majority group, and such a group could acquire cultural definition and identity.

References

Alba, R. 1985. "The Twilight of Ethnicity among Americans of European Ancestry: The Case of Italians." In *Ethnicity and Race in the U.S.A.: Toward the Twenty-First Century*, ed. R. Alba. New York: Routledge.

Aoki, T., W. Werner, J. Dahlie, and B. Connors. 1984. "Whose Culture? Whose Heritage? Ethnicity Within Canadian Social Studies Curricula." In *Cultural Diversity and Canadian Education*, ed. J. Mallea and J. C. Young. Ottawa: Carleton University Press.

ASCD Multicultural Education Commission. 1977. "Encouraging Multicultural Education." In *Multicultural Education: Commitments, Issues, and Applications*, ed. C. Grant. Washington, D.C.: Association for Supervision and Curriculum Development.

Baker, G. C. 1983. *Planning and Organizing for Multicultural Instruction*. Reading, Mass.: Addison-Wesley.

Banks, J. A. 1974. "Cultural Pluralism and the Schools." *Educational Leadership* 32: 163–166.

———. 1986. "Race, Ethnicity and Schooling in the United States: Past, Present and Future." In *Multicultural Education in Western Societies*, ed. J. Banks and J. Lynch. New York: Praeger.

———. 1987. *Teaching Strategies for Ethnic Studies*. Boston: Allyn and Bacon.

———. 1988. *Multiethnic Education: Theory and Practice*. Boston: Allyn and Bacon.

Barth, F. 1969. *Ethnic Groups and Boundaries: The Social Organization of Culture Difference*. Boston: Little, Brown and Company.

Beeman, W. 1986. "Freedom to Choose: Symbols and Values in American Advertising." In *Symbolizing America*, ed. H. Varenne. Lincoln, Neb.: University of Nebraska Press.

Bellah, R., R. Madsen, W. Sullivan, A. Swidler, and S. Tipton. 1985. *Habits of the Heart: Individualism and Commitment in American Life*. Berkeley: University of California Press.

Berger, P., and R. Neuhaus. 1977. *To Empower People: The Role of Mediating Structures in Public Policy*. Washington, D.C.: American Enterprise Institute for Public Policy Research.

Berlowitz, M. 1984. Multicultural Education: Fallacies and Alternatives. In *Racism and the Denial of Human Rights: Beyond Ethnicity*, ed. M. Berlowitz and R. Edari. Minneapolis: Marxist Educational Press.

Bullivant, B. M. (1981a). Multiculturalism-Pluralist Orthodoxy or Ethnic Hegemony. *Canadian Ethnic Studies* 13: 1–22.

————. 1981b. *The Pluralist Dilemmas in Education: Six Case Studies*. Sydney: George Allen and Unwin.

————. 1984. *Pluralism: Cultural Maintenance and Evolution*. Clevedon, England: Multilingual Matters.

————. 1986. "Towards Radical Multiculturalism: Resolving Tensions in Curriculum and Educational Planning. In *Multicultural Education: The Interminable Debate*, ed. S. Modgil, G. K. Verman, K. Mallick, and C. Modgil. London: Falmer Press.

Butts, R. F. 1977. "The Public School as Moral Authority." In *The School's Role as Moral Authority*, ed. R. F. Butts, D. H. Peckenpaugh, and H. Kirschenbaum. Washington, D.C.: Association for Supervision and Curriculum Development.

Carby, H. V. 1980a. "Multicultural Fictions." Stenciled Occasional Paper, Race Series: SP No. 58, Centre for Contemporary Cultural Studies, University of Birmingham, Birmingham, England.

————. 1980b. "Multi-Culture." *Screen Education* 34: 62–70.

————. 1982. "Schooling in Babylon." In *The Empire Strikes Back: Race and Racism in 70s Britain*, Center for Contemporary Cultural Studies. London: Hutchinson.

Commission on Multicultural Education of the American Association of Colleges of Teacher Education. 1973. "No One Model American." *Journal of Teacher Education* 24: 264–265.

Edelman, M. 1971. *Politics as Symbolic Action: Mass Arousal and Quiescence*. Chicago: Markham.

————. 1977. *Political Language: Words That Succeed and Policies That Fail*. New York: Academic Press.

Errington, F. 1987. "Reflexivity Deflected: The Festival of Nations as an American Cultural Performance." *American Ethnologist* 14: 654–667.

Fishman, J. 1977. "The Social Science Perspective." *Social Science*, vol. 1, *Bilingual Education: Current Perspectives*. Arlington, Va.: Center for Applied Linguistics.

Gans, H. 1979. "Symbolic Ethnicity: The Future of Ethnic Groups and Cultures in America." *Ethnic and Racial Studies* 2: 1–20.

Garcia, R. L. 1982. *Teaching in a Pluralist Society: Concepts, Models, Strategies*. New York: Harper and Row.

Geertz, C. 1973. *The Interpretation of Cultures*. New York: Basic Books.

Glazer, N. 1975. *Affirmative Discrimination: Ethnic Inequality and Public Policy*. New York: Basic Books.

————. 1983. *Ethnic Dilemmas 1964–1982*. Cambridge, Mass.: Harvard University Press.

Gleason, P. 1980. "American Identity and Americanization." In *Harvard Encyclopedia of American Ethnic Groups*, ed. S. Ternstrom, 31–58. Cambridge, Mass.: Harvard University Press.

Grant, G. 1977. *In Praise of Diversity: Multicultural Classroom Applications*. Omaha, Neb.: Center for Urban Education, University of Nebraska at Omaha.

Gusfield, J. R. 1963. *Symbolic Crusade: Status Politics and the American Temperance Movement*. Urbana, Ill.: University of Illinois Press.

―――. 1981. *The Culture of Public Problems: Drinking-driving and the Symbolic Order*. Chicago: University of Chicago Press.

Hakuta, K. 1986. *Mirror of Language: The Debate on Bilingualism*. New York: Basic Books.

Hernandez-Chavez, E. 1978. Language Maintenance, Bilingual Education, and Philosophies of Bilingualism in the United States. In *International Dimensions of Bilingual Education*, ed. J. Alatis. Washington, D.C.: Georgetown University Press.

Hingham, J. 1975. *Send These To Me: Jews and Other Immigrants in Urban America*. New York: Atheneum.

Janowitz, M. 1983. *The Reconstructing of Patriotism: Education for Civic Consciousness*. Chicago: University of Chicago Press.

Kallen, E. 1983. "The Semantics of Multiculturalism." In *Consciousness and Inquiry: Ethnology and Canadian Realities*, ed. F. Manning. Ottawa: National Museums of Canada.

King. E. 1977. *Teaching about Multi-Ethnic Education in the Elementary School*. Denver: Center for Teaching International Relations, Denver University.

Lee, N., and L. Oldham (n.d.). *Hands on Heritage*. Los Angeles: Children's Book and Music Center.

Lee, Simi. 1972. *Multicultural Curriculum Materials: A Resource for Teachers Phase I: English and Social Studies*. San Mateo (California) Union High School District.

MacDonald, J. B. 1977. "Living Democratically in Schools: Cultural Pluralism." In *Multicultural Education: Commitments, Issues, and Applications*, ed. C. Grant. Washington, D.C.: Association for Supervision and Curriculum Development.

Masemann, V. 1978. "Ethnography of the Bilingual Classroom." *International Review of Education* 24: 295–307.

―――. 1979. "Bilingual Education in the United States." *Compare* 9: 171–178.

―――. 1981. "Comparative Perspectives on Multicultural Education." In *Education and Canadian Multiculturalism: Some Problems and Some Solutions*, ed. D. Dorotich. Saskatoon, Saskatchewan: Canadian Society for the Study of Education, Eighth Yearbook.

―――. 1983. "Cultural Reproduction in the Bilingual Classroom." In *The Sociogenesis of Language and Human Conduct*, ed. B. Bain. New York: Plenum.

McCarthy, C. 1988. "Rethinking Liberal and Radical Perspectives on Racial Inequality in Schooling: Making the Case for Nonsynchrony." *Harvard Educational Review* 58: 265–279.

Moodley, K. 1983. "Canadian Multiculturalism as Ideology." *Ethnic and Racial Studies* 6: 320–331.

————. 1986. "Canadian Multicultural Education: Promises and Practice." In *Multicultural Education in Western Societies*, ed. J. Banks and J. Lynch. New York: Praeger.

Novak, M. 1971. *The Rise of the Unmeltable Ethnics: The New Political Force of the Seventies*. New York: Macmillan.

Olneck, M. 1989a. "Americanization and the Education of Immigrants, 1900–1925: An Analysis of Symbolic Action." *American Journal of Education* 97: 398–423.

————. 1989b. "The Recurring Dream: Symbolism and Ideology in Intercultural and Multicultural Education." Revision of paper presented at the meetings of the American Educational Research Association, San Francisco, March 1989.

Omi, M., and H. Winant. 1986. *Racial Formation in the United States from the 1960s to the 1980s*. New York: Routledge and Kegan Paul.

Pasternak, M. G. 1979. *Helping Kids Learn Multi-cultural Concepts: A Handbook of Strategies*. Champaign, Ill.: Research Press Company.

Redford, D. 1977. *Ethnic Heritage Studies: Cultural Pluralism, Experimental Unit*. Louisville, Ky.: University of Louisville School of Education.

Rizvi, F. 1986. *Ethnicity, Class and Multicultural Education*. Victoria, Australia: Deakin University Press.

Seattle Public School District No. 1. 1975. *Rainbow Activities*. Seattle, Washington.

Seattle Public School District No. 1. 1979. *Rainbow ABC's: Curriculum Supplement*. Seattle, Washington.

Sleeter, C. 1989. "Multicultural Education as a Form of Resistance to Oppression." *Journal of Education* 171: 51-71.

Sleeter, C., and C. Grant. 1987. "An Analysis of Multicultural Education in the United States." *Harvard Educational Review* 57: 421–444.

Smith, G., and G. Otero. 1977. *Teaching about Ethnic Heritage*, vol. 1. Denver: Center for Teaching International Relations, Denver University.

Ternstrom, A. M. 1980. "E Pluribus Plura—Congress and Bilingual Education." *Public Interest* 60: 3–22.

Tiedt, P. L., and I. M. Tiedt. 1979. *Multicultural Teaching: A Handbook of Activities, Information, and Resources*. Boston: Allyn and Bacon.

United States Civil Rights Commission. 1972. *The Excluded Student*. Washington, D.C.: U.S. Government Printing Office.

Varenne, H. 1977. *Americans Together: Structured Diversity in a Midwestern Town*. New York: Teachers College Press.

CONTRIBUTORS

Michael W. Apple is John Bascom Professor of Curriculum and Instruction and Educational Policy Studies at the University of Wisconsin-Madison. Among his many books are *Ideology and Curriculum* (1979, second edition 1990), *Education and Power* (1985), *Teachers and Texts* (1988), and *The Politics of the Textbook* (1991).

Charles and Ronnie Blakeney have served as principal advisors to the White House Office of Domestic Policy. They founded and direct the Institute for Clinical-Developmental Psychology and Berkeley Academy (a residential treatment center for adolescent girls). Their research includes *Reforming Moral Misbehavior, Up From Dependency,* and *Stress and Moral Conflict.*

Dwight Boyd is Associate Professor of Philosophy of Education at the Ontario Institute for Studies in Education, Toronto. He also serves as the president of the Association for Moral Education and assistant editor of the *Journal of Moral Education.*

Ann Diller is Associate Professor in Philosophy of Education at the University of New Hampshire. She has published essays on education and ethics in *Curriculum Inquiry, Educational Theory* and the *Proceedings of the Philosophy of Education Society.*

Reverend Michael J. Himes is Associate Professor of Theology and director of the collegiate program in Theology at the University of Notre Dame.

Daniel K. Lapsley is Associate Professor at Brandon University. His research interests include adolescent and social development and moral psychology.

Walter Nicgorski teaches in the Program of Liberal Studies at the University of Notre Dame and is a member of the graduate faculty in the Department of Government and International Studies. He is an editor of *The Review of Politics*.

Michael Olneck is Professor of Educational Policy Studies and Sociology at the University of Wisconsin-Madison. His principal research interests include the sociology of education, social stratification, and ethnicity and cultural pluralism.

F. Clark Power is Associate Professor of Liberal Studies at the University of Notre Dame and a past president of the Association for Moral Education. He is principal author of *Lawrence Kohlberg's Approach to Moral Education*.

William J. Reese is Associate Professor of Education, History, and American Studies at Indiana University at Bloomington. He is editor of the *History of Education Quarterly*.